Phillip Stubbes, Frederick James Furnivall

Phillip Stubbes's Anatomy of Abuses in England in Shakspere's Youth

Part 2

Phillip Stubbes, Frederick James Furnivall

Phillip Stubbes's Anatomy of Abuses in England in Shakspere's Youth
Part 2

ISBN/EAN: 9783744710411

Printed in Europe, USA, Canada, Australia, Japan

Cover: Foto ©ninafisch / pixelio.de

More available books at **www.hansebooks.com**

PHILLIP STUBBES'S ANATOMY

OF THE

ABUSES IN ENGLAND

IN

SHAKSPERE'S YOUTH,

A.D. 1583.

PART II.

The Display of Corruptions Requiring Reformation.

EDITED BY

FREDERICK J. FURNIVALL.

PUBLISHT FOR
The New Shakspere Society
BY N. TRÜBNER & CO., 57, 59, LUDGATE HILL,
LONDON, E.C., 1882.

Series VI. No. 12.

BUNGAY: CLAY AND TAYLOR, THE CHAUCER PRESS.

TO

MY FRIEND AND HELPER

𝔗𝔢𝔢𝔫𝔞 (𝔐𝔞𝔯𝔶 𝔏𝔦𝔩𝔦𝔞𝔫) 𝔕𝔬𝔠𝔥𝔣𝔬𝔯𝔱-𝔖𝔪𝔦𝔱𝔥.

CONTENTS.

FORETALK, p. xi†.

Notes for Part II, p. xxix†; for Part I, p. xxxvi†.

The Display of Corruptions, p. 1—116.

PART I. THE TEMPORALTY.

The state of England, p. 2; its Iron Age, p. 3; the Pope and Jesuits, p. 5, 6. Queen Elizabeth, p. 7, and her Council, p. 8.

I. Abuses in the LAW: Delay, p. 9; rascally Lawyers, p. 12; bad Prisons, p. 12.
Will-do-all, or Money, Lord of the Law, p. 13. One law for the Rich, another for the Poor, p. 14. Lawyers' fees too high, p. 16. Princes are to be obeyd absolutely, p. 17.

II. Abuses in EDUCATION: in Schools, and Colleges, p. 19; every Parish to have a well-paid Schoolmaster, p. 21.

III. Abuses in TRADE: *Merchants* are too rich, p. 21, and export goods needed at home, p. 22. They uze false weights, and lie, p. 23.
Drapers' and *Clothmakers'* tricks, p. 24 (and p. 34).
Goldsmiths' rogueries, p. 25. *Vintners'* cheating, p. 25.
Butchers' tricks, p. 26. *Grasiers'* high prices, p. 26.
Commons enclozed, p. 27. Sheep eat up poor men, p. 28.
Woolsellers' dodges, p. 28.
Landlords' extortions, p. 29 (and p. 45). Great rise in Rents, p. 30.
Fines demanded, p. 31, on renewal of Leases, p. 32.
Landlords the cause of high prices, p. 33.

IV. Abuses in APPAREL and its makers:—
Tailors' abominations, p. 33. *Drapers'* cheating, p. 34.
Ruffs of awful size are worn; and Starching- and Trimming-Houses set up for these Devils Cartwheels, p. 35. Putting- and Setting-Sticks are uzed too, p. 36.
Tanners' and *Curriers'* rascalities in making bad leather, p. 36.
Shoemakers' tricks, p. 37; no good Shoes now, p. 38.

viii†   Contents.

Brokers' iniquities, in buying stolen Drapery, &c., p. 38; inciting servants to pilfer, p. 39, and then dodging the Law, p. 40.

V. Abuses in RELIEF OF THE POOR :—
Gentlemen keep the poor waiting for a few scraps, p. 41.
Strong, sturdy Beggars should be made to work, or be hangd, p. 42.
The old and sick poor—who now die like dogs in the fields, p. 43—should be relievd by their own Parish, helpt by a rate on richer Parishes, p. 42.
An Almshouse is wanted in every Parish, p. 43.

VI. Abuses in HUSBANDRY AND FARMING :—
Landlords are so grasping, p. 45. Corn is so dear, from hellish Ingraters buying it up, p. 45-6.
Husbandmen are up to all kinds of tricks, p. 47-8.

VII. Abuses among *Chandlers*, p. 49.
Of *Barbers*, and the beastly Ruffians who wear long hair, p. 50-1.

VIII. Abuses among *Doctors*, p. 52. Quacks and Women: need of Licenses, p. 53.
Apothecaries, p. 55.

IX. Abuses among *Astronomers and Astrologers*, p. 55; and *Prognosticators*, p. 56.
Absurdity of suppozing Men subject to Stars, p. 61-6.

PART II. THE SPIRITUALTY.

The Division of Congregations into Parishes, p. 68. The King of each country is Head of its Church, p. 69. Bishops are set over Dioceses, p. 71. All Ministers don't preach; some only read, 72.

Abuses of *wrong Preferment*, p. 73; *bad Pay*, p. 75; *Pluralism*, p. 75, or ignorant drunken *Substitutes*, p. 76-7; *Patronage* not being in each Church's hands, p. 79; *Evasion of the Law* by Patrons, p. 81; *Simony*, p. 81. Private Patronage should be abolisht, p. 82.

Ministers are entitled to Tithes, p. 83; but endowd ones should take no fees, p. 84. All Ministers should have fair Stipends, p. 86. Unbenefist ones may take pay for Preaching, p. 87; benefist ones may not, p. 88. Bishops should stop Vagrant Ministers, p. 89.

Every Church should appoint its own Minister, p. 90, 92. Bishops' Nominees should not be thrust on Churches, p. 91.

Unfit Ministers should resign, p. 93-5. Cowardly ones leaving flocks for fear of Disease are condemd, p. 95-8.

Ministers are to attend Death-beds, p. 98.

Contents.

Pastors are to be elected by each Church, with the Bishop's approval, p. 99. Eldership is not needed now, p. 100. Deacons' work is done by Churchwardens, p. 101.

Bishops are needful, p. 101. Their titles come from the Sovereign, p. 102, 104. Christians should tolerate them, p. 103. The Pope is the Devil's Lieutenant-General, p. 104. Bishops may take the titles their Prince gives them, p. 105-6, but they mustn't exercise temporal authority, p. 107.

Pastors' Dress; some abuse in it, p. 108. They may wear Surplices, &c., p. 109-110, and even Tippets and Forkt Caps, if their Prince orders em, p. 111. Garments are a matter of Indifference, p. 112. A Pastor who leavs his Flock on account of a Surplice, is no good Shepherd, p. 113.

Reformers should agree, and not quarrel about Trifles, p. 115.

This Second Part of Stubbes's *Anatomie* is partially described, after the First Part, in Sir E. S. Brydges's *Restituta*, i. 530-5, and quotations are given from the opening, the description of Q. Elizabeth (p. 7 below), the Ruff, Starching House and Poking-Stick bits (p. 35-6), and the scene in the Barber's Shop (p. 50-1). On p. 527 Haslewood says "that a limited impression of the whole work would materially assist the spirit of modern researches." A note on p. 530 states that "Copies of this edition [Part II] are attached to the third edition [1585] of the first part."

There is a copy of Stubbes's *Motive to good Workes*, 1593 (see Forewords to *Anatomie*, Part I, p. 67*), in Emmanuel College, Cambridge.—W. C. Hazlitt. *Bibliog. Collections and Notes*, 2nd Series, 1882. I hope we may be able to print it some day in our *Shakspere's England* Series.

Anthony Stapley, of Framfield, Sussex, grandfather of "Anne Stapley, 9 years olde, aº 1634," had for his 4th wife a "widow of Mr. Stubbes, but no issue." Harl. MS. 6164 (Visitation of Sussex, 1634), lf. 22, bk.

☞ The Committee of the *New Shakspere Society* give express notice that the Editor of any of the Society's Books is alone responsible for the opinions exprest in it.

FORETALK.

§ 1. *Stubbes still earnest, and finding fault only with real Evils*, p. xi†
§ 2. *Proofs of the Abuses he complains of in Education and Trade, from Elizabeth's and James I's Statutes, &c. ;— Colleges and Benefices*, 1588-9, p. xiii†
Clothiers, 1592-3, 1597-8, p. xiv† ; *Tanners and Shoemakers*, 1603-4, p. xv†
Brokers, 1603-4, p. xviii†

Regraters of Corn, and Failers to keep up Hospitality, 1596, p. xx†
§ 3. *Poor Law and other Reforms cald for by Stubbes, since wrought*, p. xxi†
§ 4. *Sum fresh news of Stubbes* p. xxiii† ; *none of his Family*, p. xxv†
A few Notes from Latimer, &c. p. xxix†
Corrections and Notes for Part I. p. xxxiii†

§ 1. IN the Forewords to my edition of the First Part of Stubbes's *Anatomie* for the New Shakspere Society in 1877-9, I said that I meant to reprint this Second Part, and I gave a list of the subjects treated in the first Division of it, that describing the Corruptions of the Temporalty. Of Stubbes's dealing with the Spiritualty, I gave only a mention at the foot of p. 35. Now pages viii-ix of the Contents above sufficiently sketch it.

Readers must not, as I warnd them before, expect to find in this Part II as much amuzement and interest as they found in Part I[1]. The only lively bit in the book is the scene in the Barber's shop, p. 50-1 below, the humour of which I commend to those who look on Stubbes as "a mere bitter narrow-sould Puritan." But the Men and Women who are in ernest themselvs now, will find Stubbes in like ernest in this Second Part, as in his First, dealing with real abuses in the Life of his time, demanding that Justice be dealt to the Poor as

---

[1] The pages against Ruffs, those Cartwheels of the Devil, is as fierce as anything in Part I. See too the beastly Ruffians who wear long hair, p. 35-6, p. 50.

xii† § 1. *Stubbes's Fault-finding, & liberal Church-views.*

fairly as to the Rich; that endowments be kept for the Poor who dezerve them, and not jobd in favour of the monied folk who abuze them; that Tradesmen shall deal honestly with their Customers,— Drapers and Clothiers not cheating, Butchers not selling diseazd meat;—that rich men's Pleasures and Profit shall not, by Parks and Sheep, eat up poor men's Homes and Lives; that Landlords shall not rack their Tenants to their ruin; that strong and able Beggars shall be made to work, or be hung, while an Almshouse shall be set in every Parish for the sick and aged Poor; that Doctors shall tend the Poor as well as the Rich, and that a Parish-Doctor shall be provided for the Poor; that the evils of Forestalling shall be checkt, Astrologers punisht,[1] and that in every act of dealing, Right shall be done through the land.

As to the Spiritualty and Church matters, the view that Stubbes was a mere narrow Puritan utterly breaks down. He comes out as a preacher of implicit obedience to the Sovereign even when he orders what is wrong (p. 17-18); he accepts Bishops, 'My Lord Bishop' too (p. 104-5), Surplices, Forkt Caps, and other externals which the Puritans held as signs of the Whore of Rome (p. 109— 112); and his advice about all the trifles of garments about which men then, and since have, made such a needless fuss, is (p. 116):—

"And seeing we do all agree togither, and iump in one truth
"having al one God our father, one Lord Jesus Christ our Sauiour,
"one holy Spirit of adoption, one price of redemption, one faith,
"one hope, one baptisme, and one and the same inheritance in the
"kingdome of heauen, Let vs therefore agree togither in these ex-
"ternall shadowes, ceremonies and rites. For is it not a shame to
"agree about the marrow, and to striue about the bone? to contend
"about the karnell, and to vary about the shell? to agree in the
"truth, and to brabble for the shadow?"

This is surely as much a proof of his good sense, as are his demands that every Congregation shall have the Patronage of its own living (p. 79), and nominate its own Pastor—presenting two

---

[1] The 5 Eliz. ch. 15, A.D. 1562-3. "An Act agaynst fonde and phantastical Prophecyes" only applies to folk who put them forth "to thintent therby to make anye Rebellion, Insurrection, Dissention, losse of Lief or other Disturbance within this Realme and other the Quenes Dominions."

§ 2. *Stubbes right as to corrupt Presentations.* xiii†

or three to the Bishop that he may pick the best (pp. 90-2, 100), that the abuses of private Patronage shall be stopt (p. 80-2), Pluralism (p. 75-6) and Simony abolisht, and that every Church shall have power to alter its form of external government from time to time (p. 101).

On the whole then, I claim that this Part II of the *Anatomie* more than bears out the favourable opinion of Phillip Stubbes that I utterd in my Forewords to Part I.

§ 2. In proof that Stubbes was not inventing the Abuses of which he complaind, I've thought it right to make some extracts from the Statutes and a Proclamation of Queen Elizabeth, and the Statutes of James I, 1. on the corrupt Presentations to Scholarships and Benefices; 2. on the tricks of Clothiers; 3. the bad work of Tanners and Shoemakers; 4. the thefts and evils (which we still know so well) arising from the wrongly-named 'Brokers'—our Pawnbrokers and Marine-Store Dealers;—and 5. from the practice of Regrating. As of old, I quote mainly the words of the Statutes. Any one who finds em too long and tedious, will skip em.

(I.) A.D. 1588-9, 31 Eliz. chap. VI. "An acte against Abuses in Election of Scollers and presentacions to Benefices."

"Whereas by the intent of the Founders of Colledges, Churches Collegiat, Churches Cathedrall, Scoles, Hospitals, Halles, and other like Societies within this Realme, and by the Statu*tes* and good Orders of the same, the Elecc*i*ons, p*r*esentac*i*ons and No*mi*nac*i*ons of Fellowes, Schollers, Officers and other P*er*sons to have roome or place in the same, are to be had and made of the fittest and most meete p*er*sons beinge capable of the same Elecc*i*ons, p*r*esentac*i*ons, and Nomi*n*ac*i*ons, freelye wi*t*hout anye Rewa*r*de, Guyfte, or thinge given or taken for the same; And for true p*er*formaunce whereof, some Ellectors, Presentors and Nomynators in the same, have or should take a Corporall Oathe to make their Elecc*i*ons, P*r*esentac*i*ons and No*mi*nac*i*ons accordinglye; Yet notwithstandinge it is sene and found by experience that the saide Elecc*i*ons, P*r*esentacions and Nomi*n*ac*i*ons *be many tymes wrought and brought to passe with Monye, Guyft*es *and Reward*es, whereby the fyttest p*er*sons to be p*r*esented, elected or no*mi*nated, wanting Money or Friend*es*, are sildome or not at all p*r*eferred, contrarie to the good meaninge of the saide Founders, and the saide good Statu*tes* and Ordynaunc*es* of the saide Colledges, Churches, Scholes, Halles, Hospitalls and Socyeties, and to the great prejudice of

xiv† § 2. *Stubbes justified in complaining of Clothiers.*

Learning and the Common Wealthe and Estate of the Realme: For Remedye whereof, Be it enacted "—that all Elections effected by Bribery of any kind shall be void, and that the Queen or other Presenter shall appoint fresh persons to the void Offices.

§ 2 enacts that any one bribing to procure the resignation of a Fellowship or Office, shall lose the place, and that the Resigner accepting the bribe shall forfeit double its value.

§ 4 declares Simoniacal Presentations to Benefices, Dignities, &c. void; and that the Presentations shall devolve to the Crown, both Briber and Bribee paying a fine of double the amount of the Bribe.

§ 5 fines any one corruptly instituting a man to a Benefice, double the yearly value of it; declares the Institution void, and empowers the Patron to present some one else.

(II.) As to Cloth, the 35 Eliz. c. 10, A.D. 1592-3, recites the Queen's Proclamation of the year before "for the Reformacion of thinsufficiencies growen in the Clothes called Devonshire Kersies or Dozens,"—cloths "of late marvailouslie discredited by the Invencions and newe Devises of the Weavers, Tuckers, and Artificers"— and "forbiddinge all other Deceiptes in Weaving, and all dymynishinge and unreasonable drawinge, stretchinge, and other Deceiptes in Tuckers," and then enacts that the Cloths shall be properly made, of good wool, and "without rackinge, stretching, streyning, or other Devise to increase the Lengh therof."

In 1597-8 "An Acte aginst the deceitfull stretching and taintering of Northerne Cloth," 39 Eliz. c. 20, is passt, because "the said Northern Clothes and Karsies doe yeerely and daylie growe worse and worse, and are made more light and muche more stretched and strayned ... which great Enormities your faythfull Subjectes doe chieflye impute to the great number of Tenters and other Engins daylie used and practized in the said Counties for the stretchinge and strayninge of the said Clothes and Karsies." So the Act forbids this stretching, and puts a penalty of £20 on any one who

"shall have use or occupie any Tenter, of what sorte or kynde soever, or any manner of Wrinche, Rope, or other Engins to stretch or strayne any Clothes, Kersies, Dozens, Penystones, Rugges, Frises, Cottons, Kighley Whites, Plaine Grayes, or any other Clothes"

made within the said Counties. (By the next-quoted Statute this Act is extended to all English Cloths.)

§ 2. *Stubbes's complaints of Clothiers and Tanners.* xv†

The abuse stretching over other Cloth Districts, and adulteration also prevailing, in 1601 "An Acte for the true workinge and making of Wollen Clothe" was past, saying that the former Acts "for the true makinge and workinge of Wollen Clothe" had been

"frustrated and deluded by strayninge, stretchinge, wante of weighte, Flocks, Sollace, Chalke, Flower, deceitfull things, subtill sleightes and untruethes,[1] soe as the same Clothes beinge put in Water are founde to shrincke rewey, pursey, squallie, cocklinge, baudy, lighte, and notablie faultie, to the great dislike of forraine Princes, and to the hynderance and losse of the buyer and wearer."

It is therefore enacted that

"no persone or persons shall put any Haire, Flocks, Thrummes or Yarne made of Lambes Wooll, or other deceivable thinge or things into or upon any broade Woollen Clothe, Half Clothe, Kersey, Frize, Dozen, Pennystone, or Cotton, Taunton Clothe, Bridgewater, Dunston Cotton ... or other Clothe ... upon paine to forfeit every suche Cloth. ... And that no persone ... shall ... have use or occupye ... any Tenter, Instrumente, Engine, or other Device ... with any lower Barre, Pynne, Ringe, or other Engine or Device ... wherebie ... any rough and unwroughte Woollen Broad Clothe, Halfe Clothe, Kersey, Cotton, Dozen, Pennystone, Frize, Rugge ... shall or may be stretched or strayned in breadthe," under a penalty of £20.

(III.) The Statute 1 James I. chapter 22 (A.D. 1603-4), not only confirms Stubbes's complaints about Leather-sellers, but also names another fault of theirs:—

§ x. "Much dammage hath redounded to the Common Wealthe by reason that divers Tanners for theire private lucre have used to convert to Sole Leather suche Hides as are altogether insufficient for that use, which Hides they doe raise in the workemanshippe by divers Mixtures, therebie making the same to seeme verie stronge and substantiall Leather, whereas the same doeth in the wearinge proove hollowe, deceitfull, and altogether unprofitable for the Common wealth,"—and enacts that all such raizd and converted Hides shall be forfeited.

[1] Compare in A.D. 1592-3, the 35 Eliz. ch. 8. "An Acte againste deceitfull making of Cordage": the makers of 'Cables, Halsers and other kinde of Cordage' made em of 'oulde, caste, and overworne' stuff, tarrd em, and sold em as new, whereby not only Ships of the Queen and her Subjects "but also the Lyves of diverse of her saide Subjectes have bene loste, perished and caste awaye."

xvi† § 3. *Stubbes's complaints against Tanners.*

About the not-enuf tand Leather with which Stubbes finds fault on p. 36, the Statute says (1 Jac. 1, c. 22,[1] A.D. 1603-4. Record Statutes, vol. iv. Pt. 2, p. 1041):

§ xii. ". . . if any person or persons usinge, or which shall use, the Misterie or Facultie of Tanninge, shall at any tyme or tymes hereafter offer or put to sale any kinde of Leather which shalbe insufficientlie or not throughlie tanned, or which shall not then have beene, after the tanninge thereof, well and thorowlie dried, so that the same by the Triers of Leather lawfullie appointed according to this present Acte for the tyme beinge shalbe founde to be insufficientlie or not throughlie tanned, or not throughlie dried, as aforesaide, that then all and everie suche person and persons so offendinge shall forfeite and loose so much of his or theire said Leather as shalbe soe founde insufficientlie and not throughlie tanned, or not throughlie dryed as aforesaide . . ."

Then, as to what Stubbes says of the Tanners taking " vp their hides before they bee halfe tanned," the Statute goes on in § xiii:

"And whereas divers Tanners, for greedines of gaine, doe overmuch hasten the tanning of their Leather, and for that purpose doe use divers craftie and subtile Practises, sometimes layinge theire Leather in theire Fattes set in theire old Tanhils, where it may be tanned in the hott Woozes, takinge unkinde heate in the same Hill, and sometimes by putting of hot Woozes into their Tanne Fats where the same Hides or Leather lie, by which and other like Fraudulent Practises they make theire Leather to seeme bothe faire and well, and sufficientlie tanned within a very short space.[2] For Reformation whereof, be it enacted by the authoritie aforesaide, That after the saide Feaste of St. Bartholomew next comminge, no person or persons shall sett their Fattes in Tanhils or other Places where the Woozes or Leather that shall be put to tanne in the same, shall or may take any unkinde heates, or shall put any Leather into any hotte or warme Woozes, or shall tanne any Hide, Calve Skinne or Sheep Skinne, with any hote or warme Woozes whatsoever, upon paine that everie person so offendinge shall forfeite for everie such Offence, Tenne Poundes; And shall also, for everie such Offence, stand upon the Pillorie three severall Markett Dayes in the Market Towne next to the Place where the saide Offence shall be committed."

[1] Compare its clauses with those of 5 Eliz. ch. 8, from which some are, more or less, taken.

[2] The right time is enacted by § ix: "Nor shall suffer the Hides for utter Sole Leather to lye in the Woozes any lesse tyme then Twelve Moneths at the leaste, nor the Hides for upper Leathers in the like Woozes any lesse time than Nyne Monethes at the leaste. . ."

§ 3. *Stubbes's complaints against Shoemakers.*

The Shoemakers, and their selling Horse hide for Ox-hide, &c. (p. 37, Stubbes), are dealt with in § XXIII. (p. 1043).

And forasmuch as Leather well tanned and curried, may, by the Negligence, Deceite, or evill Workmanshippe of the Cordwainer or Shoemaker, be used deceitfullie, to the hurte of the Occupier or Wearer thereof: Be it further enacted by the authoritie aforesaide, That no person or persons which, after the saide Feast of St. Bartholomew next comminge, shall occupie the Misterie or Occupation of a Cordwainer or Shoemaker, shall make or cause to be made any Bootes, Shoes, Buskins, Startups, Slippers, or Pantofles, or any parte of them, of Englishe Leather, wet curried (other then Deere Skinnes, Calve Skinnes, or Goate Skinnes, made or dressed, or to be made or dressed like unto Spanish Leather) but of Leather well and truelie tanned and curried, in manner and forme aforesaid, or of Leather well and truelie tanned onelie, and well and substantiallie sewed with good Threed well twisted and made, and sufficientlie waxed with waxe well rosoned, and the stitches harde drawen with Hand Leathers, as hathe bene accustomed, without mixinge or minglinge Overleathers, that is to say, parte of the Overleathers beinge of Neates Leather, and parte of Calves Leather, nor shall put into anie parte of anie Shooes, Bootes, Buskins, Startups, Slippers, or Pantofles, any Leather made of a Sheepe Skinne, Bull Hide or Horse Hide, nor into the upper Leather of any Shooes, Startups, Slippers, or Pantofles, or into the neither [nether] parte of any Bootes (the inner parte of the Shooe onlie excepted) any parte of any Hide from which the Sole Leather is cutte, called the Wombes, Neckes, Shancke, Flancke, Powle, or Cheeke, nor shall put into the utter Sole any other Leather then the beste of the Oxe or Steere Hide, nor into the inner Sole any other Leather than the Wombes, Necke, Poll, or Cheeke, nor in the Treswels of the double soled Shooes, other then the Flancks of any the Hides aforesaide: nor shall make or put to sale in any yeere, betwene the laste of September and the twentieth of Aprill, any Shooes, Bootes, Buskins, Startups, Slippers or Pantofles, meete for any person to weare exceedinge the age of foure yeeres, wherein shall be any drie English Leather (other than Calve Skinnes or Goate Skinnes made or dressed, or to be made or dressed like unto Spanishe Leather, or any parte thereof); nor shall shew, to the intent to put to sale, any Shooes, Bootes, Buskins, Startups, Slippers or Pantofles upon the Sunday; upon paine of forfeiture for everie paire of Shooes, Bootes, Buskins, Startups, Slippers and Pantofles made, solde, shewed or put to sale contrary to the true meaninge of this Acte, three shillinges and fourepence, and the juste and full value of the same."

(IV.) Against the evil of miscald 'Brokers'—really our Pawnbrokers and Marine-Store Dealers—buying stolen goods, and thus

§ 3. *Stubbes's complaints against Brokers.*

inciting folk to pilfer, which Stubbes condemns on p. 38-40, an Act was past twenty years later:—

1 James I, chap. 21 (A.D. 1603-4; p. 1038). "An Acte againste Brokers." This Act recites that "of large and ancient tyme by divers hundred yeeres .. certaine Freemen of the Citie" of London had been appointed "to be Brokers within the saide Citie and Liberties of the same, and have taken theire Corporall Oaths before the saide Mayor and Aldermen from tyme to tyme .. to use and demeane themselves uprightlie and faithfullie betweene Merchant Englishe and Merchant Strangers and Tradesmen, in the contrivinge, makinge, and concludinge, Bargaines and Contractes to be made betweene them concerning their Wares and Merchandizes to be bought and solde and contracted for within the Citie of London, and Moneys to be taken up by Exchange betweene such Merchant and Merchantes and Tradesmen, and these kinde of persons so presented, allowed, and sworne to be Brokers as aforesaide, have had and borne the name of Brokers, and bene knowen, called, and taken for Brokers, and dealinge in Brokerage or Brokerie, who never of any ancient tyme used to buy and sell Garmentes, Houshold stuffe, or to take Pawnes and Billes of Sale of Garmentes and Apparell, and all thinges that come to hand for Money, laide out and lent upon Usurie, or to keepe open Shoppes, and to make open Shewes, and open Trade, as now of late yeeres hathe [bene] and is used by a number of Citizens assuminge unto themselves the name of Brokers and Brokerage, as though the same were an honeste and a lawfull Trade, Misterie, or Occupation, tearminge and naminge themselves Brokers, whereas in trueth they are not, abusinge the true and honeste ancient name and trade of Broker or Brokerage: And forasmuch as many Citizens Freemen of the Citie, beinge Men of Manuall Occupation, and Handicraftesmen and others inhabiting and remayninge **neere** the Citie and Suburbes of the same, have **lefte** and given over, and daylie **doe leave and give over, their** handie and manuell Occupations, **and have and daylie doe set up a Trade of buyinge and selling, and taking to pawne of all kinde of** worne Apparell, whether it be **olde or little the worse for wearinge**, Houshold Stuffe and Goods **of what kind soever the same be of, findinge** therebie that the **same is a more idle and easier kinde of Trade of** livinge, and that there riseth **and groweth** [p. 1039] **to them a more** readie, more greate, **more** profitable and speedier Advantage and Gaine then by theire former manuall Labours and Trades did or **coulde** bringe them: And Forasmuch as the said kinde of **counterfeit Brokers,** and Pawnetakers upon Usurie, or otherwise for readie Money, **are** growne of late **to** many Hundreds within the Citie of London, and other places next adjoyninge to the Citie and Liberties of the same, and are like to **increase** to farre greater Multitudes, being Friperers, and **no** Brokers, nor exercisinge of any honest and

§ 2. *Stubbes's complaints against Brokers.*

lawfull Trade, and within the memorie of many yet livinge, such kinde of persons Tradesmen were verie fewe and of small number: And forasmuch as there are not any Garmentes, Apparell, Housholde Stuffe or other Goods of any kinde, whatsoever the same be of, either beinge stollen or robbed from any, or badlie or unlawfullie purloyned or come by, but these kinde of upstarte Brokers, under colour and pretence they be Freemen of the saide Citie of London, or inhabitinge in Westminster, where they pretende to have the like overt Market, as the Citie of London, and therebie presuminge to be lawfull for them to use and set up the same idle and needlesse Trades, being the verie meanes to uphold, maintaine, and embolden all kind of lewde and bad persons to robbe and steale, and unlawfullie to get and come by true Mens Goods, knowinge and findinge that no sooner the same Goods can be stollen or unlawfullie come by, but that they shall and may presentlie utter, vent, sell and pawne the same to such kinde of new upstart Brokers for readie Money: For Remedie whereof, and for the avoidinge of the saide Mischiefes and Inconveniences, and for repressinge and abolishinge of the sayd idle and needlesse Trades, and upstart Brokers, and for the avoidinge of Theftes, Robberies and Felonies, and bad People, and for the repressinge of such kinde of Nourishers and Ayders of Theeves and bad People, and for the defence of honest and true Mens properties and Interestes in theire Goods: Be it enacted ... That no Sale, Exchange, Pawne or Morgage of any Jewell, Plate, Apparell, Houshold Stuffe, or other Goods ... that shall be wrongfullie or unjustlie purloyned, taken, robbed or stollen from any person or persons or Bodies Politicke, and which at any tyme hereafter shall be sold, uttered, delivered, exchanged, pawned, or done awaye within the Citie of London or Liberties thereof, or within the Citie of Westminster in the Countie of Middlesex, or within Southwarke in the Countie of Surrey, or within two miles of the saide Citie of London, to any Broker or Brokers, or Pawne takers, by any way or meanes whatsoever, directlie or indirectlie, shall worke or make any change or alteration of the propertie or interest, of and from any person or persons or Bodie Politicke from whome the same Jewels, Plate, Apparell, Houshold Stuffe or Goods were or shalbe wrongfullie purloined, taken, robbed or stollen: Any Lawe, Usage of Custome to the contrarie notwithstandinge."

§ 2 enacts that Brokers and Pawntakers who refuse to produce Goods to the owner from whom they've been stolen, shall forfeit Double the Value of them.

§ 3, that the Act shall not affect those folk 'using and exercising the ancient Trade of Brokers betweene Merchant and Merchant.'

(V.) The evil of, and continued struggle of folk and lawmakers

xx† § 2. *Queen Elizabeth against Regraters.*

against Regrating or Ingrating,—that is, buying-up all the get-at-able Corn or other produce, and then selling it out at a large profit—are so well known that confirmation of Stubbes's complaints is hardly needed; but as the Dearth of 1594-6 has appeard before in our *Stafford*, p. xiv, and elsewhere with regard to the suppozed date of *Midsummer Night's Dream* and otherwise, I give here short extracts from Elizabeth's Proclamation of 1596 relating to Regraters, and the duty of continuing Hospitality:—

"BY THE QUEENE.

The Queenes Maiesties Proclamation, 1. *For obseruation of former Orders against Ingrossers, & Regraters of Corne,* 2. *And to see the Markets furnished with Corne.* 3. *And also against the carying of Corne out of the Realme.* 4. *And a prohibition to men of hospitalitie from remoouing from their habitation in the time of dearth.* 5. *And finally a strait commandement to all Officers hauing charge of Forts to reside thereon personally, and no inhabitant to depart from the Sea coast.*

THE Queenes Maiestie hauing had of late time consideration of great dearth growen in sundry parts of her Realme,[1] iudging that the Rich owners of Corne would keepe their store from common Markets, thereby to increase the prices thereof, and so the multitude of her poore people hauing no graine growing of their owne, to susteine great lacke, caused speciall orders to be made and published to all parts of her Realme, in what sort the Iustices of peace peace in euery quarter should stay all Ingrossers, Forestallers, and Regraters of Corne, and to direct all Owners and Farmers hauing Corne to furnish the Markets ratably and weekly with such quantities as vsually they had done before time, or reasonably might and ought to doe: By which orders, many other things were prescribed to be obserued for the staying of the dearth, and reliefe of the people: Yet neuerthelesse, her Maiestie is informed, that in some parts of her Realme the dearth doth not diminish, but rather increase for lacke of due execution of the sayd orders, and specially by the couetousnes of the Owners, forbearing to furnish the Markets, as reasonably they might do, and by secretly selling

---

[1] On July 31, 1596, in consequence of the scarcity of Corn, the Queen issued her Proclamation from Greenwich, forbidding Starch to be made of home-grown Corn, or even from Bran by the holders of the Patent for the manufacture of it from Bran.

In 1598 (May *A*o. 40) she granted the sole right to import Starch to John Packington for 8 years.

§ 2. *The Queen on Hospitality.*   § 3 *Poor Relief.*

out of their houses to a kinde of people that commonly are called Badgers, at prices vnreasonable, who like wise do sell and regrate the same out of the Markets at very high and excessiue prices. For remedy whereof, her Maiestie chargeth all officers to whom the obseruation of the sayd orders hath bene directed, presently as they haue any naturall care of their Christian brethren & Countreymen, being in need, to cause all and euery part of the sayd orders from point to point to be executed, and the offenders against the same to be seuerely punished, to the terrour of others. . .

Finally her Maiestie is particularly informed of some intentions of sundry persons, of abilitie to keepe hospitalitie in their Countreys, to leaue their said hospitalities, and to come to the Citie of London, and other Cities and townes corporate, thereby leauing the reliefe of theire poore neighbours, as well for foode, as for good rule, and with couetous minds to liue in London, and about the Citie priuately, and so also in other Townes corporate, without charge of company; for withstanding whereof, her Maiestie chargeth all maner of persons, that shall haue any such intention during this time of dearth, not to breake up their housholds, nor to come to the said Citie, or other towns corporate : and all others that haue of late time broken vp their housholds, to returne to their houses againe without delay. And whilest her Maiestie had thus determined, for reliefe of her people, to stay all good householders in their Countreys, there is charitable sort to helpe hospitalitie, her Maiestie hath had an instant occasion giuen her to extend her commandement euen for the necessary defence of her Realme . . .

The obseruation of all which, her Maiesties commandement, is to be performed vpon paine of her Maiesties heauie indignation.

Giuen at her Maiesties Mannour of Richmond the second day of Nouember 1596, in the eight and thirtieth yeere of her Maiesties reigne.

God saue the Queene."

§ 3. On the subject of the Relief of the Poor, and Stubbes's reazonable demands on it, I refer the reader to Sir George Nicholls's *History of the English Poor Law* (1854), i. 161—239. Among these reazonable demands I shoud not now include hanging a man who *can* work and won't; but before Stubbes's time, in 1547, the 1st of Edward VI, chapter 3, enacted that every idle person who ran away from work set him shoud be branded with the letter V, and be adjudgd a slave for 2 years to any person who should demand him ; then, if he ran away again, he should be branded in the cheek with the letter S, and adjudgd a slave for life; and lastly, if he ran away a third time, he was to suffer death as a felon. This act was repeald in 1549-50, by the 3 and 4 Edw. VI, ch. 16; but in 1572-3, measures almost as harsh were re-enacted: beggars and vagabonds were to be grievously whipt, and burnt thro the gristle of the right ear with a hot iron of the compass of an inch about, unless any honest person would take them into service for a year. If he would, and the beggar ran away, then he was to be whipt, and burnt thro the ear; for a second offence to be treated as a felon, unless some honest person would take him into his service for 2 years, and he continued in it; while for a third offence he was adjudgd to suffer death, and loss of land and goods as a felon, without allowance of benefit of clergy or sanctuary. Stubbes was then, in 1583, only asking that the actual law shoud be allowd to take its course, when he wisht that sturdy Beggars who woudn't work, shoud be hangd.

The same Act of 1572-3 orderd 'abiding places' to be provided for the aged and infirm poor, appointed Overseers to raise and apply taxes for their benefit, and sanctioned a rate on richer neighbours in aid of poor parishes who couldn't support their own poor. This legislation was developt by 18 Eliz. ch. 3, A.D. 1575-6, which enacted that a competent stock of wool, hemp, flax, iron, or other stuff should be got, by taxation, to set the poor on work, and if they wouldn't work, they were to be sent to 'houses of correction' and made to work.

After Stubbes wrote in 1583, came the 39 Eliz. chaps. 3 and 4, in 1597-8; 3 for the Relief of the Poor, and 4 for the Punishment of Rogues, Vagabonds and Sturdy Beggars. Chap. 3 makes the appointment of Overseers in every parish compulsory, empowers them to tax inhabitants—and to levy a rate in aid on richer parishes —in order to get material to support the idle poor at work, and provide for the sick and aged, and the care and apprenticing of children. This Act establishes the mutual responsibility of parents and children to maintain one another.

It also, by § 5 (vol. iv, Pt. 2, Record Com. Statutes, p. 897), empowers the Churchwardens and Overseers ' to erect, buylde, and sett upp in fit and convenyent Places of Habitacíon . . . at the

§ 3. *Stubbes's Poor-Law Requirements fulfild.* xxiii†

gen*er*all Chardges of the Parishe . . . convenyent Howses of Dwellinge for the sayde ympotent Poore ; and allso to place Inmates or more Famylies than one in one Cottage or Howse.'

Chap. 4 provides for the whipping of sturdy Beggars who won't work, and their committal to gaol, their banishment beyond seas, or their death, in case they won't give up their roguish kind of life.

'We are now arrived,' says Sir Geo. Nichols, i. 192, 'at the important period when by *The 43rd Elizabeth, cap.* 2 (A.D. 1601), the principle of a compulsory assessment for relief of the poor was fully and finally established as an essential portion of our domestic policy.' This Act, ' the great turning-point of our Poor-Law Legislation, is still the foundation and text-book of English Poor Law ' (i. 194). It carries out more effectually, and extends, the provisions of the prior Acts, and again sanctions the Rate in Aid. In 1610 the 7th of James I, chapter 4, provides for the building of Houses of Correction in every county ; but not till 1624 does the 21 James I—' An Act for the erecting of Hospitals and Workinghouses for the Poor '—carry out what I take to be Stubbes's demand for an Almshouse in every parish ; while not till 1834 does the Poor Law Amendment Act provide for the Poor the proper Medical Relief which Stubbes cald for in 1583.

As to Education, Harrison (see my Part I. p. 77), Latimer before him (*Sermons*, Parker Soc. edn. i. 186, 290, 291, 349), and many others, but utterd the same complaints about the jobbing of Scholarships, Fellowships, &c. that Stubbes makes, page 19 ; and not yet has the jobbing of the nominations of Bluecoat Boys to Christ's Hospital been done away with.

The hardship to the poor of wholesale enclosure of Commons— another complaint of Stubbes's—has been long admitted, and is now partially stopt by the Law. That Stubbes was right in calling for proper examination and licensing of Doctors, the keeping out of tag, rag, and quacks (p. 53), no one will deny. And that he took a reasonable and moderate view of the religious topics disputed in his day, I think every one will admit. His Part II, then, supports the character that I drew of him from his Part I.

xxiv† § 4. *Stubbes's possible 2nd Marriage, and Bond.*

§ 4. Of Phillip Stubbes himself I have some fresh tidings; of his family, none.

1. He may have married again in 1593, when he wrote his *Motiue to good Workes*. I have a melancholy interest in printing the late Col. Chester's letter to me on the point:—

124, *Southwark Park Road, London, S.E.*
18 *Nov.* '79.

"MY DEAR MR. FURNIVALL,

Did I ever send you the following Marriage from the Registers of St. Olave, Southwark?

1593, April 3, Philip Stubbes and Elenor Powell—by License.

It has this moment met my eye in one of my volumes that has recently been indexed.

It would have been only 3 years after the death of your Author's wife Katharine Emmes.[1]

Or, were there 'two Richmonds in the field'?

A search for the License would, I fear, be hopeless, as those for that date issued from the Faculty and Vicar General's Offices are not in existence, and one from the Bp. of London would not have availed in Southwark.

Sincerely yours
JOS. L. CHESTER.

"The Powell Wills of the period might reveal the Connection.

The marrying *by license*, at that period, indicates that they were certainly not of the lower orders."

2. Our Phillip Stubbes may be the man of that name at Benefield in Northampton, who in July 1586 executed a Bond of which Mr. Henry Stubbes of Danby, Ballyshannon, got hold in 1879. He writes on 13 Nov. 1879:—

---

[1] Katharine Stubbes is alluded to in George Powell's '*Very Good Wife*, a Comedy. London. S. Briscoe, 1693,' p. 21, Act III. sc. i.

"*Well*. Death, fight now, or you'll die infamous, was your Mother a Whore?

Squeez. Comparatively she might be in respect of some Holy Women, as the late Lady *Ramsey*, Mrs. *Katherine Stubbs*, and such, ha, ha, is that a Cause!"

§ 4. *Stubbes's possible Bond. Other Stubbeses.*

'I have now very little doubt that I have in my possession the Autograph of the Author of the "Anatomie," and it may besides furnish a clue to his family, and perhaps bring to light some particulars of his life hitherto unknown. The following is the reason of my forming this opinion: The Bond relates to a "messuage or tenement" in Congleton, Cheshire, which Phil. S. is granting to Will. S. to hold for ever, and the former binds himself to leave the latter in undisturbed possession. The Bond itself is in Latin, the Conditions in English—Now, coupling this with what the Author of the *"Anatomie"* says of knowing a man "for a dozen or sixteene yeares togither" in Congleton (Part I. p. 136), whose death he relates as a warning to swearers, makes, I think, a very good case to show that they were one and the same person; and the house referred to in the Bond was in all probability where the Puritan spent a good many yeares of his life. He is described in the Bond as "Philippus Stubbes de Benefeild al[ias] Beningfeilde in Com. Northt. generosus," and the other as "Will*el*mus Stubbes de Ratcliffe in Com. Midd. generosus"—

'I conjecture Phil. in the course of his rambles had settled for a time at Benefeild, as he did afterwards at Burton-on-Trent. It is not stated whether Willm. was any relative, but it seems probable he was; perhaps brother. I enclose two extracts from the Chancery Proceedings relating to Willm., but I am not certain that the second extract refers to the same person. These I got the other day. I have made no searches at Congleton, Chester, or Benefeild.'

'CHANCERY PROCEEDINGS.

1 Nov. 1584. Bill filed by Robt. Wright, Citizen and Goldsmith of Lond. against William Stubbs of Ratcliff, Co. Middx., Gent.

23 Nov. 1598. Bill filed by William Stubbes of Radcliff, Co. Middx., Ropemaker (who about 4 yeares now last past inhabited and dwelt at Boston, Co. Linc., being unmarried and having a great family household by reason of his trade) against Thomas Strangrushe of the same town, Fuller.'

As to Phillip Stubbes's family, Prof. Stubbs felt sure that Phillip

§ 4. *Stubbes folk and Wills in Cheshire.*

came from Congleton, and that a gentle family of the name was still in that neighbourhood. So I wrote there, and found that no Stubbes was known but a sweep. Still, Mr. J. P. Earwaker says in his *East Cheshire*, ii. 362: "In 1654 I find it stated in a MS. at Capesthorne that "Nell, Nan, and Bess Stubbs, being mother and two daughters, were hanged [at Chester] for bewitching to death Mrs. Furnivall, wyfe to Mr. Anth. [a mistake for Ralph] Furnivall, daughter to Mr. J. Fellowes." Prof. Stubbs sent me this bit, and he finds that in 1595, William Stubbes of Congleton, gentleman, presented to the living of Gauseworth. The Congleton Records are, he says, full of Stubbeses; he has traced three generations of Congleton Jurors in the Town book—Ralph or Reynold, from 1540 onwards; John from 1565 or so; and then another Ralph at the beginning of James I's reign. He also found a Randall Stubbes in the first year of Elizabeth, who would do for our Phillip's father. He thinks the Astbury registers will most likely settle the matter. There is an account of some Stubbeses, he says, among the Rawlinson MSS. I paid for a search of the Chester Indexes, with the following result:

Chester Registry. List of Wills proved and Admons granted in the names of Stubbs and Stubbes from the earliest date of the Indexes, 1540 to 1630 both inclusive

1586 Will of Geffrey Stubbs of Ludlow
1591 Will of Willam Stubbs of Gawsworth, County of Chester
1595 Admon of Lawrence Stubbs of North Rode, Co. of Chester
1597 Will of Hugh Stubbs of North Rode, County of Chester
1603 Admon of Thomas Stubbs of Allostock in the County of Chester
1617 Will of George Stubbs of Lower Tabley, County of Chester
1617 Admon of John Stubbs of Heaton, County of Chester
1621 Will of Nicholas Stubbs of North Rode, County of Chester
1622 Will of Thomas Stubbs of Hulse
1622 Will of Thomas Stubbs of North Rode, County of Chester
1623 Will of George Stubbs of Knutsford, County of Chester
1624 Will of John Stubbs of Merton
1630 Will of Ann Stubbs of North Rode, County of Chester

None of these look likely.

4. *Stubbeses in Lincolnshire, Essex, &c.*

Mr. Walter Rye felt sure that he'd find some traces of Phillip Stubbes at Donnington in Lincolnshire (where there's a town of that name as well as in Leicestershire): see Forewords to Part I. p. 59*),—but diligent search showd none, tho' the Will of a Richard Stubbes of Donnington in 1622 is in the Lincoln Consistory Court.

It is clear that our Phillip was not the son of Ralph Stubbes of St. Mary le Wigford in the City of Lincoln, whose will is dated 4 April 1558, prov'd 29 July 1559, and of whose estate a *de bonis non* grant was issued on Jan. 29, 1562-3. Ralph's will was registered twice over, being in 36 Chaynay and 5 Chare (Somerset House). It mentions his children John, Henry, Justinian, and Elizabeth Stubbes, &c. &c., of whom Justinian may well be the M.A. of Gloucester Hall, Oxford, mentiond by Wood, *Ath. Ox.*, in the note on p. 53* of my Forewords to Part I. In the Chancery Proceedings temp. Eliz., S. s. 25, no. 31, Ralph Stubbes's executors claim £11 6s. 8d. of one Edmund, and in S. s. 23, £4 17s. 11½d. of Thos. Burton's executor.

The Essex Stubbeses yield no result either. There was a Philip Stubbes of Little Clacton, Essex, Will dated 19 June 1551, to whose estate the first Letters of Administration were granted on Sept. 25, 1555, and the second Letters on Oct. 31, 1561. He had an only son John, and a daughter Margaret. This John Stubbs of Cocks, Little Clacton, Essex, and Cotton Hall, Suffolk, made his will dated in 1587, but his son Phillip was not then of age. The Will was prov'd in the Commissary Court of Essex and Hertfordshire on Sept. 10, 1596. The right of Administration to this Philip Stubbs, then late of Clacton Parva deceasd, was renounced by Elizabeth, his Relict, in March 1626; and in May 1627, Administration was granted to Edward Luckin of Tiltey, one of Philip Stubbes's Creditors.

In the Chancery Proceedings of the time of Elizabeth are notes of other Stubbeses:

> Richard Stubbe, and Anne his wife, Norfolk. G. g. 4, no. 59.
> John Stubbs of Norfolk. C. c. 14, no. 57.
> Richard Stubbs of Norfolk and Shropshire in vol. 3.

xxviii†   § 4. *Divers Stubbeses in divers Parts.*

John Stubbs of Rutland, with sons William and Thomas, and a grandson Henry, 21 Eliz. 1579.
Wm. Stubbs of Radcliffe, Ropemaker, 23 Nov. 1598.—S. s. 5.
Alexander Stubbes of Codsall, Staffordshire yeoman. S. s. 6.
Richard Stubbs of Southwark, yeoman. S. s. 13.
Christopher Stubbs of Berkshire and Hampshire.
Edward Stubbs of Norfolk.
William Stubbs of Devonshire.

The name Stubbes occurs in a book dated 1626. John Gee. *New Shreds of the Old Snare:*—p. 121, " Factors employed for the conueying ouer of the said Women to the Nunneries. ...
Master Peeters
Stubbes."

Then Mr. Ellacombe hoped that he'd hit on traces, in his parish, Bitton, Glo'stershire, of our Stubbes, and he sent me up his Register; but the only Stubbes entries in it show that the Rev. Henry Stubbes or Stubbe, when doing duty at Bitton—not being Vicar of it, had a daughter and a son baptized there:

"Mary daught*er* of Henry Stubbs, Cl*ericus*, was baptised February xith 1643."
"John the sonne of Mr. Henrie Stubbs, was babt. October xxvii." 1647.

There is no entry of the burial of any Stubbes from 1594 to 1643 (and a few years later).

Whether our Phillip Stubbes had anything to do with any of the folk above-named, I must leave to some future searcher to decide.

I have not tried to get up many Notes for this 2nd Part. Those to Part I. cost so much, that a second set, even were one possible, must not be indulged in. The text is reprinted from the copy of *The Display of Corruptions* in the Grenville Library, British Museum.

What have Books like the present one to do with Shakspere? They help us to realize the England of his day, and the social evils that he must have seen.

3, *St. George's Square, N.W.*
July 18, 1882.

NOTES FOR PART II.

p. xxvii† Wills of John and Phillip Stubbes of Essex, and Ralph Stubbes of Lincoln :—

Jn. Stubbes, 1587.

(In Room 32) Will of John *Stubbes* of Cocks, Little Clacton, Essex (and Cotton Hall, Suffolk), dated 1587, gives Cocks and appurtenances, and lease of Cotton Hall to his son Phillip (under age) when he attains 21. If he dies under 21, then to testator's wife Agnes for life, and then over. Provision for boy Phillip's maintenance, &c. Prov'd in Com. *Court* of Essex and Herts, 10 Septr. 1596. (Phillip livd. Admōn to him ab. 1622.—Grigson.)

19 *June*, 1551.

(P. C. C. Bucke, quire 25) *Will of Phillip Stubbes* of Little Clacton, Essex—most lands to wife Johane for life, part to son John on attg. 21—if he doesn't, then to daughter Margret. If she dies under 18, then her share of personalty to son John. Evidently, only son John, and daughter Margret. No son Phillip.

25 Septr. 1555, authority to administer Ph. Stubbes's goods, granted to Rd. Blaxton, Ed. Assheman, and Edwd Shorte, the exōr Jn. Hockett having died.

31 Octr. 1561, Commission to Rd. Godfrey and Alice his wife to administer the goods not administerd.

Ralph Stubbes, Alderman of *Lincoln*, *April* 4, 1558 (of the parish of St. Mary's, Wygford, in the suburbs of the City of Lincoln). Will proved, *July* 29, 1559 :—

Gives all his property, less legacies and special bequests, to his 4 children, *John, Henry, Justynyan*, and *Elizabeth*. If any die without issue—they're evidently under age—his share is to go to the survivors.

Gives Christabell *Bartram* his sister, to her marriage, 20£; and if she die or she be maryed, then 16£ to go to his 4 chil*d*ren, and 4£ 'to my thre bretherne, *Henry* Stubbes, *Iohn* Stubbes and *Thomas* Stubbes'.

Gives to his 'father *Bartrame* xij li. to bye the rest of the said house whiche he shulde purchase. And I wille . . that John *Bartrame* shalhaue the said house' in fee . . (As to children's bringing-up) 'I will that my mother in lawe [Margarete Smythe] shall haue the kepinge and bringyng vppe of my children durynge her lif, and after her death I will that John Stubbes and

xxx† Notes on p. xxviii†. *Two Henry Stubbeses.*

Justynyan Stubbes, with theire part*es* and portions shalbe in the Rule, ordre, and kepinge of Mr. John Hutchynson, and Henrye Stubbes . . of Thomas *Dauson* my brother-in-lawe' (Elizth. not given to any one). Residue to 4 chi*ld*ren Exōrs. 4 chi*ld*ren, and "Margarete Smythe my mother in lawe."

p. xxviii† *Henry Stubbes.* See Ant. Wood's *Ath. Oxon.* ed. Bliss, 1817; 1255 :—

HENRY STUBBE, son of a father of both his names of Bitton in Glocestershire,[1] was born in that county, became a student in Magdalen hall in the latter end of 1623, aged eighteen years; admitted bachelor of arts the 26th of January 1627, & master of arts the 8th of July 1630, took holy orders, and became a curate or vicar, sided with the puritans in the beinning of the rebellion, took the covenant, preached seditiously—took the engagement, and as a minister of the city of Wells was constituted one of the commissioners for the ejecting of such whom they then (1654) called scandalous, ignorant, and insufficient ministers and schoolmasters. After his majesty's restoration, he lost what he had for want of conformity, retired to London, and lived there. He hath, among several things pertaining to divinity, written

Great Treaty of Peace, Exhortation of making Peace with God. Lond. 1676-77, oct.

Dissuasive from Conformity to the World. Lond. 1675, in oct.

God's Severity against Man's Iniquity. Printed with the *Dissuasive.*

God's Gracious Presence, the Saint's great Privilege—a farewel Sermon to a Congregation in London, on 2 Thes. 3, 16. Printed also with the *Dissuasive.*

Conscience the best Friend upon Earth : or the happy Effects of keeping a good Conscience, very useful for this Age. London 1678, 8vo. ; 1685 in twelves, and other things which I have not yet seen; among which is his *Answer to the Friendly Debate*, an. 1669 in octavo. When he died, I know not ; sure I am that after his death, which was in London, his books were exposed to sale by way of auction the 29th of Nov. 1680.

[See a very amiable character of this writer in Calamy, who adds

1. *A Funeral Sermon for a Lady in Gloucestershire.*
2. *A Voice from Heaven ; with his last Prayer.*

Granger, who mentions a small head of Stubbe, gives us the title of a third book omitted by Wood :

3. *Two Epistles to the professing Parents of baptized Children*, written a little before his death.

Calamy says that Stubbe was of Wadham college, which I cannot believe. He was certainly matriculated of Magdalen hall, April 16 [18, Col. Chester], 1624. See *Reg. Matric. Univ. Oxon.* PP. fol. 299, b.] He died on July 7, 1678, aged 73, and was buried in Bunhill Fields.—(Col. Chester.)

Of this Henry Stubbes, Richard Baxter says in his *Reliquiæ Baxterianæ*, Part III. (written in 1670) p. 189 [After his *Answer to Mr. Dodwell and Dr. Sherlock*, &c.], § 66. In a short time I was called on, with a grieved heart,

---

[1] He was born, says Calamy [wrongly], at Upton in this county, **upon an** estate that was given to his grandfather by king James I, with whom **he came** from Scotland. *Ejected Ministers*, ii. 319.

Notes on p. xxviii†.   *Two Henry Stubbeses.* xxxi†

to Preach and Publish many Funeral Sermons, on the Death of many Excellent Saints.

Mr. *Stubbes* went first, that Humble, Holy, Serious Preacher, long a blessing to Gloucestershire and Somersetshire, and other parts, and lastly to London. I had great reason to lament my particular Loss, of so holy a friend, who oft told me, That for very many years he never went to God in solemn Prayer, without a particular remembrance of me: but of him before.—*Reliquiæ Baxterianæ*, 1696.

Part III. p. 95, § 205 (written 1670). But because there are some few who by Preaching more openly than the rest, and to greater Numbers, are under more Men's displeasure and censure, I shall say of them truly but what I know . . .

11. Old Mr. *Stubbs*, who joineth with him [Mr. *Turner*], is one of a Thousand, sometimes Minister at Wells, and last at *Dursley* in *Gloucestershire*, an ancient grave Divine, wholly given up to the Service of God, who hath gone about from place to place Preaching with unwearied Labour since he was silenced, and with great Success, being a plain, moving, fervent Preacher, for the work of converting impenitent sinners to God: And yet being settled in peaceable Principles by aged Experience, he every where expresseth [= presses out, excludes] the Spirit of Censoriousness, and unjust Separations, and Preacheth up the ancient zeal and sincerity with a Spirit suitable thereunto. *Reliq. Baxt.* 1696.

Ant. Wood gives an account of another Henry Stubbes, whose father was a clergyman at Partercy in Lincolnshire, where he was born on Feb. 28, 163½. He was at Oxford, and ultimately turnd Doctor. He was drownd on July 12, 1676, and buried in the Abbey Church at Bath. Him, Baxter mentions in the following passage of his *Reliq. Baxterianæ*, 1696: *Life*, Part I. (written 1664), p. 75-6, "being writing against the Papists, coming to vindicate our Religion against them, when they imparte to us the Blood of the King, I fully proved that the Protestants, and particularly the Presbyterians, abhorred it, and suffered greatly for opposing it; and that it was the Act of *Cromwell's* Army and the Sectaries, among which I named the *Vanists* as one sort. . . . Hereupon, Sir Henry *Vane* being exceedingly provoked, threatened me to many, and spake against me in the House, and one *Stubbs* (that had been whipt in the Convocation House at *Oxford*) wrote for him a bitter Book against me, who from a *Vanist* afterwards turned a Conformist; since that, he turned Physician, and was drowned in a small Puddle or Brook as he was riding near the Bath."

Chaucer and Stubbes. In a short poem 'The | Laurel, | and the | Olive': | Inscrib'd to | George Bubb, Esq; | By Geo. Stubbes, M.A. | Fellow of Exeter-College in Oxon. | London, | Printed for Egbert Sanger at the Post-Office at the | Middle Temple-Gate in Fleetstreet . M.DCC.X. are some lines 'To the Author' ending thus:

> So when revolving Years have run their Race,
> Bright the same Fires in different Bosoms blaze;
> Known by his glorious Scars, and deathless Lines,
> Again the *Hero*, and the *Poet* shines.
> In gentler *Harrison*, soft *Waller* sighs,
> And *Mira* wounds with *Sacharissa's* Eyes.

xxxii† Notes on pp. 6—9. *Jesuits. Latimer's Sermon.*

> *Achilles* lives, and *Homer* still delights,
> Whilst *Addison* records, and *Churchill* fights.
> This happy Age, each Worthy shall renew,
> And all dissolv'd in pleasing Wonder, view
> In Ann—*Philippa, Chaucer* shine in you.

p. 6. *Papal Plots, Jesuits,* &c. Stubbes may allude specially to Campion's conspiracy two years before, of which Stowe—or Antony Munday—gives the following account in his *Annales* (ed. 1605, p. 1169), and a longer one in his additions to Holinshed's (or Reginald Wolfe's) Chronicle:—

[1581]. "On the 20. of Nouember, Edmond Campion, *Jesuit*, Ralfe Sher-
Ant. Monday. wine, Lucas Kerbie, Edward Rishton, Thomas Coteham, Henrie
Campion Orton, Robert Iohnson & Iames Bosgraue, were brought to the
and others high bar at Westminster, where they were seuerally, & al
arraigned. together indicted vpon high treason, for that, contrary both to loue & duty, they forsooke their natiue country, to liue beyond the seas under the Popes obedience, as at Rome, Rheimes, and diuers other places, where (*the Pope hauing with other princes practised the death and depriuation of our most gracious princesse, and vtter subuersion of her state and kingdome,* to aduance his most abhominable religion), these men, hauing vowed their allegiance to the Pope, to obey him in all causes whatsoeuer, being there, gaue their consent, to aide him in this most traiterous determination. And for this intent & purpose, they were sent ouer to seduce the harts of her maiesties louing subiects, & to conspire and practise her graces death, as much as in them lay, against a great day set & appointed, when the generall hauocke should be made, those onely reserued that ioyned with them. This laid to their charge, they boldly denied; but by a iurie they were approoued guilty, and had iudgement to be hanged, bowelled & quartered.

The first of December, Edmond Campion, *Jesuit,* Ralfe Sherwine and
Campion Alexander Brian, seminarie priests, were drawne from the Tower of
and others London to Tiborne, and there hanged, bowelled & quartered.
executed. Looke more in my continuation of Reine Woolfes Chronicle."

p. 9, *as that blessed martyr of God, Maister* Latimer *hath said in a sermon made before King* Edward *the sixt.* This is 'The seconde Sermon of Master Hughe Latemer, whych he preached before the Kynges maiestie, wythin hys graces Palayce at Westminster yᵉ .xv. day of Marche M.CC[C]CC. xlix.' *Sign.* E. 1. "I must desyre my Lorde protectours grace to heare me in thys matter, that your grace would heare poor mens sutes your selfe. Putte it to none other to heare, let them not be delayed. The saying is nowe, that mony is harde euery wher: if he be ryche, he shall soone haue an ende of his matter. Other ar fayn to go home with weping teares, for ani help they can obtain at ani Iudges hand. Heere mens suets your selfe, I requyre you in godes behalfe, & put it not to the hering of these veluet cotes, these vp skippes. Nowe a man can skarse knowo them from an auncyent Knyght of the countrye.

"I can not go to my boke, for pore folkes come vnto me, desirynge me that I wyll speake that theyr matters maye be heard. . . . I am no soner in the garden

Notes on pp. 9—24. *Angel. Clothiers' Tricks.* xxxiii†

and haue red a whyle, but . . some one or other . . . desireth me that I wyll speake that hys matter myght be heard, & that [*Sign.* E. ii.] he hathe layne thys longe at great costes and charges, and can not once haue hys matter come to the hearing . . . [E. ii. back]. I beseche your grace that ye wyll loke to these matters.

"Heare them your selfe! Vieue your Iudges! And heare pore mens causes. And you proude Iudges, herken what God sayeth in hys holy boke. *Audite illos, ita parum ut magnum.* Heare theym, sayeth he, the small as well as the greate, the pore as well as the ryche. Regarde no person, feare no man—Why? *Quia domini iudicium est.* The iudgment is Goddes.

"Marcke thys sayinge, thou proude Iudge! The deuyl will [E. iii.] brynge thys sentence at the daye of Dombe. Hel wyl be ful of these Iudges, if they repente not and amende.

"They are worsse then the wicked Iudge that Christe speaketh of, that neyther feared God nor the worlde. There was a certain wyddowe that was a suter to a Iudge, & she met hym in euery corner of the streete, cryinge: 'I praye you heare me, I beseche you heare me, I aske nothyng but ryght.' When the Iudge saw hyr so importunate, 'though I fear neyther God, sayth he, nor the worlde, yet bycause of hyr importunatenes I wyll graunte hyr requeste.'

"But our Iudges are worsse then thys Iudge was. For [*sign.* E. iii. back] they wyll neyther heare men for Gods sake, nor feare of the worlde, nor importunatenes, nor any thynge else. Yea, some of them wyll commaund them to ward, if thei be importunat."

p. 12, *an angell, (for that is called a counsellers fee).* The well-known lawyer's 'six and eightpence.' Miss Rochfort Smith sends me the following Epigram, 594, from *Wits Recreations*:—

"Upon Anne's marriage with a Lawyer.

Anne is an angel: what if so she be?
What is an angel but a lawyer's fee?"

p. 19. *Colleges, &c, abused and peruerted.* See my Harrison's *Description of England*, 1577-87, p. 77. On Education in Early England, see my Forewords to the *Babees Book*, or *Meals and Manners*: Early English Text Society.

p. 24, *stretching and thicking Cloth.* "I here saye, there is a certayne connyng come vp in myxyng of wares.

Cloth makers are become Poticaryes, yea and amonge the Gospellers.

"Howe saye you, were it not wonder to here that clothe makers should become poticaries.

"Yea, and as I heare saye, in such a place, where as they haue professed the Gospell, and the word of God most earnestly of a long tyme. So how busie the Deuell is to sclaunder the word of god. Thus the pore gospel goeth to wracke. Yf his clothe be xviii. yerdes longe, he wyl set hym on a racke,

A pretti kind of multiplyinge. and streach hym tyll the senewes shrinke agayne, whyles he hath brought hym to xxvii. yardes. When they haue brought hym to that perfection, they haue a prety feate [*sign.* E. iiii.] to thycke him againe. He

Flocke powder. makes me a pouder for it, an playes the poticary: thei cal it floke

Notes on pp. 24—33. *Commons. Tailors.*

pouder: they do so incorporate it to the cloth, that it is wonderfull to consider: truely a goodly inuention."

p. 24, *Dark Shops.* p. 49, *False Weights.* p. 22, *Merchants.* p. 47, *Farmers.* p. 29, *Griping Landlords.* These Shop-keepers that can blind mens eyes, with dym and obscure lights, and deceiue their eares with false & flattering words, be they not Vsurers?

These Tradesmen that can buy by one weight, and selle by another, be they not Vsurers?

These Marchants that doe robbe the Realme, by carrying away of Corne, Lead, Tinne, Hydes, Leather, and such other like, to the impouerishing of the common wealth, bee they not Vsurers?

These *Farmers* that doe hurde vppe their Corne, Butter, & Cheese, but of purpose to make a dearth, or that if they thinke it to rayne but one houre to much, or that a drought doe last but two dayes longer then they thinke good, will therfore the next market day hoyse vp the prises of all manner [p. 46] of victuall, be not these Vsurers?

The *Land-Lordes* that doe sette out their liuings at those high rates, that their *Tenants* that were wont to keepe good Hospitalitie, are not nowe able to giue a peece of Bread to the *Poore*, be they not Vsurers? 1614. Barnabee Rych. *The Honestie of this Age.* p. 45-6.

p. 27, *the commons ... are inclosed, made seuerall.* Compare Shakspere's phrase, in *Loues Labor's Lost*, II. i. 223, Qo. 1 :—

    Bo. So you graunt pasture for me.
    Lady.   Not so, gentle Beast,
My lippes are no Common, though seuerall they be.

Thomas Greene's Diary says, on 1615, Sept. 1. "Mr. Shakspeare told Mr. J. Greene that he was not able to beare the enclosing of Welcombe" Common. Leop. Shaksp. Introd., p. cix. See p. 45* and 116 in Stubbes, Part I.

p. 28. *Enclosures of Commons,* &c. See Harrison, Part I., p. 306-7, and Latimer's 7th Sermon before Edw. VI, Serm. 14, Parker Soc., p. 248.

p. 28, *rich men's game eating up poor men's corn, grass*, &c. This goes on still, as every one in a game-preserving county knows. I heard Joseph Arch once say how his garden was cleard by Lord Warwick's rabbits, and how he in return took his own compensation in game.

p. 33, *Tailors.* "now it were a hard matter for me to distinguish betweene men, who were good and who were bad, but if I might giue my verdict to say who were the wisest men nowe in this age, I would say they were *Taylers*: would you heare my reason? because I doe see the wisedome of women to be still ouer-reached by *Taylers*, that can euery day induce them to as many new-fangled fashions, as they please to inuent : and the wisedome of men againe, are as much ouer-reached by women, that canne intice their husbandes to surrender and giue way to all their newe-fangled follies : they are *Taylers* then that canne ouer-rule the wisest women, and they be women that can besot the wisest men : so that if Ma. Maiors conclusion be good, that because *Iacke*, his youngest sonne, ouer-ruled his mother, and *Iackes* mother agayne ouerruled M. Maior himselfe, and M. Maior by office ouerruled the Towne, *Ergo*, the whole Towne was ouerruled by *Iacke*, Ma. Maiors sonne : by the same consequence, I may likewise conclude, that *Taylers* are the wisest men : the reason is alreadie rendered, they doe make vs all *Fooles*, both men and women, and doe mocke the whole worlde with their newe inuentions: but are they women alone that are thus seduced by *Taylers?* doe but looke amongst our gallants in this age, and tell me, if you shall not finde men amongst them to be as vaine, as nice, and as gaudie in their attyres, as shee that amongst women is accounted the most foolish . . . . .

"The holy scriptures haue denounced a curse no lesse grieuous to the *Idolemaker*, then to the *Idole* it selfe ; now (vnder the correction of *Diuinitie*) I would but demaund, what are these *Puppet*-making *Taylers*, that are euery day inuenting of newe fashions, and what are these, that they doe call *Attyre-makers*, the first inuenters of these monstrous Periwygs, and the finders out of many other like immodest Attyres: what are these, and all the rest of these *Fashion* Mongers, the inuenters of vanities, that are euery day whetting their wits to finde out those *Gaudes*, that are not onely offensiue vnto God, but many wayes preiudiciall to the whole Common wealth : if you will not acknowledge these to be *Idolemakers*, yet you cannot deny them to be the *Deuils enginers*, vngodly instruments, to decke and orniſie such men and women, as may well be reputed to be but *Idolles*, for they haue eyes, but they see not into the wayes of their own salvation, & they haue eares, but they cannot heare the Iudgements of God, denounced against them for their pride and vanitie." 1614. Barnabee Rych. *The Honestie of this Age*, p. 23.

p. 35. *Ruffes.* See Part I, p. 52, 240-2.

p. 41, 42. *The Poor, and Beggars.* See my Harrison, Part I, p. 213, &c.

p. 51, *long hair.* In 1614, Barnabee Rych asks : "And from whence commeth this wearing, & this imbrodering of long lockes, this curiositie that is vsed amongst men, in freziling and curling of their hayre, this gentlewoman-like starcht bands, so be-edged, and be-laced, fitter for *Mayd Marion* in a *Moris dance*, then for him that hath either that spirit or courage, that should be in a gentleman ?"—*The Honestie of this Age*, p. 35. "There are certaine new inuented professions that within these fourtie or fiftie years, were not so much as heard of," says Rich, p. 24, "& yet have become flourishing, namely, 'Attyre-makers,' Coach-makers & Coachmen, Body-makers, and Tobacco-dealers. The 3 most gainful trades are," he says, p. 28, "the first is to keepe an *Ale house*, the 2. a *Tobacco House*, and the third to keepe a *Brothell House.*"

p. 57. *A marvellous strange coniunction.* This alludes to R. Harvey's notorious tract addrest to his brother the author Gabriel Harvey, "An Astrological Discourse upon the great and notable Conjunction of the two superiour Planets, Saturne and Jupiter, which shall happen the 28 day of April, 1583," 18 mo. *black letter. H. Bynneman*, 1583. The years 1588 and 1593 were to be "dangerous years" too. See my note in *N. Sh. Soc. Trans.*, 1875-6, p. 151-4.

p. 82. *Such a dish of apples as Master Latimer talketh of, with thirty angels in every apple.* This is in "The fifte Sermon of Mayster Hughe Latimer, whyche xxxvi†   Notes for Part I, pp. 60*—236.

he prached before the kynges Maiestye wythin hys Graces Palaice at Westminster the fyft daye of Aprill" [1549]. *Sign.* R. iii. "Ther was a patron in England (when it was) that had a benefyce fallen into hys hande, and a good brother of mine came vnto hym, and brought hym xxx. Apples in a dysh, and gaue them hys man to carrye them to hys mayster. It is like he gaue one to his man for his laboure to make vp the game, and so ther was .xxxi.

<small>The merye tale of the patrone that sold a benefyce for a deyntye dyshe of Apples.</small>

"This man commeth to his mayster, and presented hym wyth the dyshe of Apples, sayinge: 'Syr, suche a man hathe sente you a [*R. iii. back*] dyshe of frute, and desyreth you to be good vnto hym for suche a benefyce.' 'Tushe, tushe,' quod he, 'thys is no apple matter. I wyll none of hys apples. I haue as good as these (or as he hath any) in myne owne orcharde.' The man came to the preest agayne, and toulde hym what hys mayster sayed. 'Then,' quod the priest, 'desyre hym yet to proue one of them for my sake, he shal find them much better then they loke for.' He cut one of them, and founde ten peces of golde in it [£10 = 30 Angels]. 'Mary,' quod he, 'thys is a good apple. The pryest standyng not farre of, herynge what the Gentle man sayed, cryed out and answered, 'they are all one apples, I warrante you, Syr, they grewe all on one tree and haue all one taste.' 'Well, he is a good fellowe [*sign.* R. iiii.], let hym haue it,' quod the patrone, &c. Get you a grafte of thys tre, and I warrante you it shall stand you in better steade then all Sayncte Paules learnynge. Well, let patrons take hede, for they shall aunswere for all the soules that perysshe throughe theyr defaute." See too the Third Sermon, p. 145-6, Parker Soc., on the bribe-taking Judge flayd alive by Cambyses; the pudding-story, p. 140.

<small>A graft of gold to get a benefyce wythal is worth a great deale of learnynge.</small>

NOTES FOR PART I.

p. 60*, note 2. The woodcut is at the back of the Dedication, p. 2*.

p. 86*. See too the *Homily* against Idleness.

p. 89*. Dice, wine, and women, wonne, drunke, & spent all,
And now he liues a vassall at each call.

1600. *Quips vpon Questions*, sign. E. 2, back, 'On a ruind Gallant.'

p. 95*. The cut of Irish Costumes is from the Additional MS. 28,330 in the British Museum: a Dutch 'Short Description of England, Scotland & Ireland,' 1574.

p. 97*. There is no ornamental border round the original 1584 Title-page.

p. 231. *Velure*, &c. See note p. 363-4, Dekker's Works, 1874, vol. iii.

p. 232. Nash's *Anatomie of Abuses* was enterd in the Stationers' Registers in advance, on Sept. 19, 1588.

p. 236. *Farrefetched and deare bought*. "we vse to say by manner of

Notes for Part I, pp. 248—375. *Football, &c.* xxxvii†

Prouerbe, 'things farrefet and deare bought are good for Ladies.'" 1589. Puttenham, p. 193, ed. Arber.

p. 248. Andrew Boorde's cut is also alluded to in the Homily against Excess of Apparel; and by Dekker, p. 77* above.

p. 271, 273. *Women's face-painting.*

> "Whers the Deuill? . . .
>   He's got into a boxe of Women's paint. . . .
>   Where pride is, thers the Diuell too."
>   1600. *Quips vpon Questions*, sign. F. 2.

p. 280. See the Homily against Whoredom and Adultery.

p. 284. See the Homily against Gluttony and Drunkenness.

p. 293. *Prisons.* See too in 1618, Geffrey Mynshul's *Essayes and Characters of a Prison and Prisoners.*

p. 296. *Sunday Sports*, &c. See Humphrey Roberts's, 'An earnest Complaint of diuers vain, wicked and abused Exercises practised on the Sabath day,' 1572. Hazlitt's *Collections and Notes*, p. 360-1.

p. 307, at foot: *beaten with a Brewers washing bittle*, drunk.

> "these people
> Are all brainde with a Brewers washing beetle."
>   1600. *Quips vpon Questions*, sign. F. 2, back.

p. 318. *Deaths at Football.* Coroner's inquest on one Gibbs kild in a game. "The Coroner, in summing up, advocated a return to the rules practised in football twenty years ago, for, *as now played, it was only worthy of a set of costermongers.*" See also the notice of the Mayor of Southampton prohibiting football under Association or Rugby rules, on the town's public lands.—*Echo*, Dec. 11, 1880. On Saturday . . . Mr. Joseph Hunter at Sheffield had his arm and three ribs broken; at Mexborough a young man named William Howitt had his arm and leg dislocated.—*Daily News*, Dec. 13, 1880.

p. 349. Insert *Abandon*, v. t. banish, 125. *Ames ace & the dice*, 37*. *Deuse ace*, 272; a man's genitals.

p. 352, col. 2. Insert *Breasts :* see Bare, and Naked.

p. 356, col. 2. *Disgesture*, digestion. "Glut with gazing, surfet with seeing and rellish with reading [my book]:—It may be there are some preseruatiues, not poyson, though harsh in *disgesture.* 1600. *Quips vpon Questions*, sign. A. iij.

p. 362, col. 1. Insert *Honeymoon*, p. 376, n. 1.

p. 371, col. 2, to 'Spanish &c.' add 'boots, 242.'

p. 375, col. 1. Insert *Venetians* 250. '*Grecques;* f. Gregs, Gallogaskins, wide venitians.' 1611. Cotgrave; and *Venetian hose*, 56.

THE Second part

of the Anatomie of Abuses, containing The display of Corruptions, with a perfect description of such imperfections, blemishes, and abuses, as now reigning in euerie degree, require reformation for feare of Gods vengeance to be powred vpon the people and countrie, without speedie repentance and conuersion vnto God: made dialogwise by Phillip Stubbes.

Except your righteousnes exceed the righteousnes of the Scribes and Pharises, you cannot enter into the kingdome of heauen.

LONDON.

Printed by R. W. for William Wright, and are to be sold at his shop ioining to S. Mildreds Church in the Poultrie, being the middle shop in the rowe.

THE DISPLAY OF

corruptions, requiring refor-

mation for feare of Gods iudge-

ments to be powred vpon the people

and country without spee-

die amendement.

The speakers, THEODORVS and AMPHILOGVS.[1]

OD bleſſe you my friend, and well ouertaken.
Amphilogus. You are hartilie welcome, good ſir, with all my hart.
Theod. How farre purpoſe you to trauell this way by the grace of God?

Amphil. As far as *Nodnol* if God permit.
Theod. What place is that, I pray you, and where is it ſcituate? <small>Stubbes is going to London.</small>
Amphil. It is a famous citie and the chiefeſt place in *Dnalgne*: haue you not heard of it?
Theod. No truely. For I am a ſtranger, and newly come into theſe countries, onely to ſee faſhions, and to learne the ſtate and condi²tion of thoſe things whereof I am ignorant.
Amphil. What country man are you, I pray you, if I may be ſo bold as to aſke?
Theod. I am of the country and nation of the *Idumeans,* a cruell, fierce, and ſeruile kind of people.
Amphil. I haue beene in thoſe countries my ſelfe ere now, and therefore it is maruell that you knowe me not. <small>He says he's been in Idumea.</small>
Theod. Me thinke I ſhould knowe you, but yet I cannot call your name to remembrance.
Amphil. My name is *Amphilogus,* ſomtime of your acquaintance, though now you haue (through tract of time, which is *Omnium*

---

[1] *Amphilogus* is Stubbes. The side notes are all mine. Stubbes put notes to his First Part only.

[2] B 1, back. The headline all thro, is 'The Display of Corruptions.'

2 II. 1. *England the wickedest Country under the Sun.*

rerum edax, A deuourer of al things) forgot the same. But notwithstanding that you haue forgot me, yet I remember you very well: is not your name Maister *Theodorus*?

Theod. Yes truly, my name is *Theodorus*; I neither can, nor yet will, euer denie the same.

Amphil. What make you in these countries, if I may aske you without offence?

Theod. Truly I came hither to see the country, people, and nation, to learne the toong, and to see (as I told you) the state generally of all things.

Amphil. You are most hartily welcome, and I, hauing beene a traueler, borne in these countries, and knowing the state thereof in euerie respect, to congratulate your comming, will impart vnto you the substance and effect therof in as few words as I can.

Theod. I praie you then giue me leaue (vnder correction) to aske you such necessary questions, as are incident to my purpose, and which may serue for my better instruction in all the foresaide premisses?

Amphil. Go to then, aske on in the name of God, and I will addresse myself to satisfie your reasonable requests in anything I can.

Theod. What be the inhabiters of this countrie? Be they a vertuous, godlie, and religious kinde of people, or otherwise cleane contrarie?

Amphil. Surely they are, as all other countries and nations be for the most part, inclined to sinne, and wickednes, drinking vp iniquitie as it were water; but yet I am perswaded that, albeit all flesh hath corrupted his way before the face of GOD, yet is there not any nation or countrey vnder the sunne, that for pride, whoredome, droonkennes, gluttonie, and all kinde of oppression, iniurie and mischiefe, may compare with this one country of *Dnalgne*, God be mercifull vnto it, and hasten his kingdome, that all wickednes may be done away.

Theod. Then, as in all other countries where euer I haue trauelled, so in this also is verified the old adage, namely, that the first age of the world was called *Aurea ætas*, the golden age, for that men liued godlie and in the feare of God; the second age was called *Argentea ætas*, the siluer age, for that men began somewhat to decline, and fall from their former holinesse, and integritie of life, to sinne and wicked-

Sidenotes:
Stubbes will describe the state of England. [¹ Sig. B 2]

No nation is so proud, drunken, and so full of mischief, as England is. [² Sig. B 2, back]

1. The Golden Age.
2. The Silver.

II. 1. *After Pride cometh Destruction.*

nes: the thirde and laſt age, which is this that we are fallen into, is and may juſtlie be called *Ferrea* or *Plumbea ætas*, the yron or leaden age, in as much as now men are fallen from all godlineſſe whatſoeuer, and are as it were wedded to iniquitie, committing ſinne without any remorſe, and running into all kinde of abhomination and impietie, without reſtraint. All which things dulie in the good hart of a faithful chriſtian conſidered & weied, may eaſily perſuade a wiſe man to think their deſtruction to be at hand, except they repent.

Amphil. You ſay verie well. Therefore I would wiſh them to take heed to themſelues, and to leaue their wickednes before the Lords wrath be gon out againſt them; for let them be [1] ſure, that when the meaſure of their wickedneſſe is full, then will the Lord cut them off from the face of the earth, if they repent not, and truely turne to the Lord. The wiſe man ſaith, that a little before deſtruction come, the hart of man ſhall ſwell into pride, and wickednes. Our ſauiour Chriſt ſaith, when men flatter themſelues, and 'ſaie "peace, peace, al things are well, we neede not to feare anything," then, euen then, ſhall ſudden deſtruction fall vpon them, as ſorrow commeth vpon a woman trauelling with childe, and they ſhall not eſcape, bicauſe they would not knowe the Lord, nor the day of his viſitation.' Which thing we ſee to be true through all the hiſtories of the ſacred Bible; for when the Sodomits and Gomorreans had filled vp the meaſures of their iniquitie, and ſaciate themſelues in ſinne, then came there fire and brimſtone raining from heauen vpon them and their citie, and conſumed them all, from the vpper face of the earth. When all the worlde in the daies of Noah, was giuen ouer to ſinne, and wickednes, immediatelie came the floud of Gods vengeance, and deſtroied them all, eight perſons—to wit, Noah, his wife, his three ſonnes and their wiues,—who ſerued the Lord in true ſimplicity of hart, onelie excepted. The Hieroſoltinitanes [2] when their ſinne was ripe, were they not confounded, and put to the edge of the ſworde? When Pharao the king of Egypt his ſinne was ripe, did not the Lord harden his hart to purſue the Iſraelits, and ſo drowned him and all his retinue in the read ſea? Herod and Nabuchadnezer ſwelling in ſinne, and riſing vp againſt the maieſtie of God in the malice of their harts, was not the one ſtroken dead in a moment, and eaten vp with worms, the other depoſed from his kingdome, and conſtrained to eate

[1 Sig. B 3] But God 'll cut the ſinners off.
Deſtruction'll follow Pride,
as it did with Sodom and Gomorrah,
in Noah's days,
[2 Sig. B 3, back]
with Pharaoh,
Herod and Nebuchadnezzar.

grasse with the beasts of the earth; with the like examples, which, for the auoiding of prolixitie, I omit. By all which it appeareth, that when destruction is neerest, then are the people the securest, and the most indurate and frozen in the dregs of their sinne; and being so, the sequele is either confusion in this life, or perdition in the world to come, or both. And therefore I beseech the Lord, that both this country, and all others, may repent, & amende euerie one their wicked waies, to the glorie of God and their owne saluation.

Theod. Is this country fruitfull, and plenty of all things, or barren, and emptie?

Amphil. There is no nation or country in the world, that for store, and abundance of all things, may compare with the same; for [1] of all things there is such plentie (God haue the praise thereof) as they may seeme to haue neede of no other nation, but all others of them. In so much as if they were wise people (as they be wise inough, if they would vse their wisedome well) to keepe their owne substance within themselues, and not to transport it ouer to other countries (as many couetous wretches for their owne priuate gaine doe) they might liue richly and in abundance of all things, whilest other countries should languish and want. But hereof more shall be spoken hereafter.

Theod. I pray you how is this country adiacent vpon other countries?

Amphil. It lieth inuironed with the occean sea rounde about; vpon the one side eastwarde, it bordereth vpon the confines of France: vpon the other side westward, vpon Irelande; towards the septentrionall or north part, vpon Scotland; and vpon the south side it respecteth Germanie. And is inhabited with three sundrie sortes of people, Englishmen, Cornishmen, and welchmen, all which, if not in lawes and constitutions, yet in language, doe differ one from another. But as they doe differ in toong and speech, so are they subiect (and that *Patrio iure*, By iustice and law) [2] to one Prince, and gouernour onely to whom they owe their allegeance.

Theod. Is the country quiet, peaceable, and at vnitie within it selfe, or otherwise troubled with mutenies, wars, and ciuill dissentions?

Amphil. The whole lande (God be praised therefore, and preserue hir noble Grace by whom it is gouerned and maintained!) is,

II. 1. *Plots of the Pope against England.* 5

and hath beene, at peace and vnitie, not onely within it selfe, but also abroad, for this foure or fiue and twenty yeeres. During all which time there hath beene neither wars, inuasions, insurrections, nor any effusion of blood to speake of, except of a sort of arch-traitours, who haue receiued but the same reward they deserued, and the same that I pray God all traitours with their complices may receiue hereafter, if they practise the same which they haue done. The like continuance of peace was neuer heard of, not this hundred yeeres before, as this country hath inioied since hir maiesties reigne: the Lord preserue hir grace, and roiall Maiestie for euer!

England has been at peace for 25 years.

Theod. Are the other countries, lands, and nations about them (for as I gather by your former intimations, this country is scituate as it were in the centrie, or midst of [1]others) their friends, and well-willers, or their enimies?

[¹ Sig. B 5]

Amphil. It is an old saieng and true: *Ex incertis, & ambiguis rebus optimum tenere sapientis est:* Of things vncerteine, a christian man ought to iudge and hope the best. They hope wel that all are their friends and welwillers: but it is thought (and I feare me too true) that they are so far from being their friends (*Nisi verbo tenus,* From mouth outward onely) that they haue vowed and sworne their destruction, if they could as easily atchiue it, as they secretly intend it. Which thing to be true, some of their late practises haue (yet to their owne confusion, Gods name be praised) proued true. For how manie times hath that man of sinne, that sonne of the diuell, that *Italian* Antichrist of *Rome,* interdicted, excommunicated, suspended, and accursed with booke, bell and candle, both the Prince, the Nobilitie, the Commons, and whole Realme? How often hath he sent foorth his roring buls against hir Maiestie, excommunicating (as I haue said) hir Grace, and discharging hir Highnesse liege people and naturall subiects, from their allegeance to hir Grace? How often hath he with his adherents conspired and intended the death and ouerthrowe of hir Maiestie and Nobilitie, by con[2]iuration, necromancy, exorcismes, art magike, witchcraft, and all kind of diuelrie besides, wherein the most part of them are skilfuller than in diuinity? And when these deuises would not take place, nor effect as they wished, then attempted they by other waies and meanes to ouerthrowe the estate, the Prince, nobles, people and country: sometime by secret irruption, sometime

But it has lip-friends who hate it.

That son of the Devil, the Pope,

has conspired the Queen's death,
[² Sig. B 5, back]

and tried to overthrow the land.

by open inuasion, insurrection, and rebellion, sometime by open treason, sometime by secret conspiracie, and sometimes by one meanes, sometimes by another. And now of late attempted they the ouerthrowe and subuersion of hir Maiestie, people, country, and all by sending into the realme a sort of cutthrotes, false traitors, and bloudthirstie Papists, who vnder the pretence of religious men (in whom for the most part there is as much religion as is in a dog) should not onely lurke in corners like howlets that abhorre the light, creepe into noble mens bosoms, thereby to withdrawe hir Maiesties subiects from their allegeance, but also moue them to rebellion, and to take sword in hand against Prince, country, yea, and against God himselfe (if it were possible) and to dispense with them that shall thus mischieuouslye behaue themselues. And forsooth these goodlie fellowes, the diuels agents, that must worke these feates, are called (in the [1]diuels name) by the name of Iesuites, seminarie preests, and catholikes, vsurping to themselues a name neuer heard of till of late daies, being indeed a name verie blasphemously deriued from the name of Iesus, and improperly alluded and attributed to themselues. But what will it preuaile them to be like vnto Iesus in name onely, or how can they, nay, how dare they, arrogate that name vnto themselues, whereas their doctrine, religion, life and whole profession, togither with their corrupt liues and conuersations are directly contrarie to the doctrine, religion, life, and profession of Christ Iesus? There is nothing in the world more contradictorie one to another, than all their proceedings in generall are to Christ Iesus and his lawes, and yet will they, vnder the pretence of a bare and naked name, promise to themselues such excellencie, such integritie, and perfection, as GOD cannot require more, yea, such as doth merite *Ex opere operato*, Eternall felicitie in the heauens. And thus they deceiue themselues, and delude the world also with their trash: but of them inough.

Theod. Surely that country had neede to take heed to it selfe, to feare, and stand in awe, [2]hauing so manie enimies on euerie side. And aboue all things next vnto the seruing of God, to keepe themselues aloofe, and in any case not to trust them, what faire weather soeuer the make them. The sweeter the *Syren* singeth, the dangerouser is it to lend hir our eares: the Cocatrice neuer meaneth so much crueltie, as when he fawneth vpon thee and weepeth: then take heed, for he

Side notes:
The Pope has sent here bloodthirsty Papists
to stir up rebellions.
[1 Sig. B 6] These Devil's agents are call'd Jesuits,
but their every deed and word is directly contrary to Christ's.
They delude the world with their trash.
[2 Sig. B 6, back

meaneth to sucke thy bloud. The stiller the water standeth, the more perilous it is. Let them remember it is an old and true saieng: *Sub melle iacet venenum*, Vnder honey lieth hid poison. *Sub placidis herbis latitat coluber*, vnder the pleasantest grasse, lurketh the venemoust adder. Take heed of those fellowes that haue *Mel in ore, verba lactis*, sweet words and plausible speeches: for they haue *Fel in corde*, and *Fraudem factis*, Gall in their harts, & deceit in their deeds. So falleth it out with these ambidexters, these hollowe harted friends, where they intend destruction, then will they couer it with the cloke or garment of amity & friendship; therefore are they not to be trusted. These Jesuits are ambidexters, hollow-hearted friends,

Amphil. You say the truth. For I am thus perswaded, that he who is false to God (as all [1] Papists with their complices and adherents are) can neuer be true and faithfull, neither to prince nor country. Therefore God grant they may be taken heed of betimes. [¹ Sig. B 7]
never true to prince or country

Theod. Considering that this country of *Dnalgne* is enuied abroad with so many enimies, and infested within by so many seditious Papists, and hollowe harted people, it is great maruell, that it can stand without great wars, and troubles. Belike it hath a wise politike prince, and good gouernors, either else it were vnpossible to preserue the same in such peace and tranquillitie, and that so long togither. I pray you therefore by what prince is the same gouerned, and after what maner?

Amphil. The whole realme or country of *Dnalgne* is ruled and gouerned by a noble Queene, a chaste Maide, and pure Virgin, who for all respects may compare with any vnder the sunne. In so much as I doubt not to call hir sacred breast the promptuarie, the receptacle, or storehouse of all true virtue and godlines. For if you speake of wisdome, knowledge and vnderstanding, hir Grace is singular, yea, able at the first blush to discearne truth from falsehood, and falsehood from truth, in any matter, how ambiguous or obscure soeuer: so as it may iustly be called into question whether [2] *Salomon* himselfe had greater light of wisedome instilled into his sacred breast, than hir Maiestie hath into hir highnes roiall minde. If you speake of learning and knowledge in the toongs, whether it be in the Latine, Greeke, French, Dutch, Italian, Spanish, or any other vsuall toong, it may be doubted whether Christendome hath hir peere, or not. If you speake England is gouerned by a noble Queen,

virtuous and godly, wise and vnderstanding,

[² Sig. B 7, back]

learned in the tongues.

8 II. 1. *The Queen's Council, and the Magistrates.*

modest, gentle, affable,

merciful,

religious, just,

more divine than earthly.

The Lord preserve her!
[¹ Sig. B 8]

of fobrietie, modeftie, manfuetude and gentleneffe, it is woonderfull in hir Highneffe; yea, fo affable, fo lowly and humble is hir Grace, as fhe will not difdaine to talke familiarlie to the meaneft or pooreft of hir Graces fubjects vpon fpeciall occafions. If you fpeake of mercie, and compaffion to euery one that hath offended, I ftande in fufpence whether hir like were euer borne. If you fpeake of religion, of zeale and feruencie to the truth, or if you fpeake of the vpright execution or adminiftration of iuftice, all the world can beare witnes, that herein (as in all godlineffe elfe) hir Highnes is inferior to none that liueth at this day. So that hir Grace feemeth rather a diuine creature, than an earthly creature, a veffel of grace, mercie and compaffion, whereinto the Lord hath powred euen the full meafures of his fuperabundant grace, and heauenlie influence. The Lord increafe the fame in hir ¹Highnes roiall breaft, and preferue hir Grace, to the end of the world, to the glorie of God, the comfort of hir Maiefties fubiects, and confufion of all hir enimies whatfoeuer.

Theod. What is hir Maiefties Councell? It fhould feeme that they muft needes be excellent men, hauing fuch a vertuous Ladie and Phenix Queene to rule ouer them?

The Queen's Council are wise and experienst men,

Amphil. The Councell are Honorable and noble perfonages indeed, of great grauitie, wifedome, and pollicie, of fingular experience, modeftie and difcretion, for zeale to religion famous, for dexteritie in giuing counfell renoumed, for the adminiftration of iuftice incomparable, finally, for all honorable and noble exploits inferior to none, or rather excelling all. So as their worthie deedes, through the golden trumpe of fame are blowne ouer all the worlde. The whole regiment

who make the laws, which are carried out by Magistrates.

of the Realme confifteth in the execution of good lawes, fanctions, ftatutes, and conftitutions enacted and fet foorth by hir royall Maieftie and hir moft honorable Councel, and committed by the fame to inferior officers, and maieftrates to be put in practife, by whofe diligent execution thereof, iuftice is maintained, vertue erected, iniurie repreffed, and finne feuerely punifhed, to the great glorie of God, and

[² Sig. B 8, back] ²common tranquilitie of the Realme in euery condition.

Theod. Is the lande diuided into fhires, counties, precincts, and feuerall exempt liberties, to the ende iuftice may the better be maintained? And hath euery county, fhire, and precinct, good lawes in the fame for the deciding and appeafing of controuerfies that happen

II. 1. *Of Shires; the Law, and the Abuses in it.*

in the same, so that they neede not to seeke further for redresse than in their owne shire?

Amphil. The whole land indeede is diuided (as you say,), into shires, counties, and seuerall precincts, (which are in number, as I take it, 40). In euerie which shire or countie, be courts, lawe daies, and leets, as they call them, euery moneth, or every quarter of a yeere, wherin any controuersie (lightlie) may be heard and determined, so that none needs (except vpon some speciall occasions) to seeke to other courts for deciding of any controuersie. But as there be good lawes, if they were executed dulie, so are there corruptions and abuses not a few crept into them. For sometimes you shall haue a matter hang in sute after it is commenced a quarter of a yeere, halfe a yeare, yea, a twelue month, two or three yeeres togither, yea, seauen or eight yeeres now and then, if either friends or money can [1] be made. This deferring of iustice is as damnable before God, as the sentence of false iudgement is, as that blessed martyr of God, Maister *Latimer*, hath said in a sermon made before King *Edward* the sixt. Besides this deferring and delaieng of poore mens causes, I will not say how iudgement is perverted in the end. I reed them take heed to it that be the authors thereof. Therefore the reformed churches beyond the seas are worthie of commendations; for there the Iudges sit in the open gates, streets, and high waies, that euery man that will, may speake vnto them, and complaine if he haue occasion. And so farre from delaieng, or putting of [2] poore mens causes be they, as they will not suffer any matter, how weighty soeuer, to hang in sute aboue one day, or two, or at the most three daies, which happeneth verie seldome. But if the lawes within euery particular countie or shire were dulie administred without parcialite, and truly executed with all expedition, as they ought, and not so lingred as they be, then needed not the poore people to run 100, 200, yea 300, or 400 miles (as commonly they doe) to seeke iustice, when they might haue it neerer home: through the want whereof, besides that their sutes are like to hang in ballance peraduenture seuen yeeres, [3] they, hauing spent al, in the end fall to extreme beggerie; which inconuenience might easilie be remoued, if all matters and causes whatsoeuer were heard at home in their owne shire or countie with expedition. And to say the truth, what fooles

England is divided into shires and precincts, in each of which Law-Courts are held monthly or quarterly.

But abuses have crept in: causes are delayd, and that's as bad as false judgment, as Latimer said.

[1 Sig. C 1]

Also poor folk have to go 100 miles off to get justice,

[2 Sig. C 1, back] *and perhaps wait for 7 years.*

[2] off.

II. 1. *Englishmen are very fond of going to law.*

are they (yea, woorthie to be inaugurated fooles with the laurell crowne of triple follie) that, whilst they might haue iustice at home in their owne country, and all matters of controuersie decided amongst their neighbors and friends at home, will yet go to lawe two or three hundred miles distant from them, and spend all that they haue to inrich a sort of greedie lawiers, when at the last a sort of ignorant men of their neighbors must make an end of it, whether they will or not. This, me thinke, if euerie good man would perpend in himselfe, he would neither go to lawe himself, nor yet giue occasion to others to doe the like.

Theod. I gather by your speeches that these people are very contentious and quarellous, either else they would neuer be so desirous of revenge, nor yet prosecute the lawe so seuerely for euery trifle.

Amphil. They are very contentious indeed. Insomuch as, if one giue neuer so small occasion to another, sute must straight be commenced; and to lawe go they, as round as a ball, till [1]either both, or at least the one, become a begger all daies of his life after.

Theod. But on the other side, if they shuld not go to lawe, then shuld they sustaine great wrong, and be iniuried on euery side.

Amphil. Indeed the lawe was made for the administration of equitie and iustice, for the appeasing of controuersies & debates, and for to giue to every man (*Quod suum est*) That which is his owne, but being now peruerted and abused to cleane contrarie ends (for now commonly the law is ended as a man is fr[e]inded) is it not better to suffer a little wrong with patience, referring the reuenge to him who saith : *Mihi vindictam, & ego retribuam.* 'Vengeance is mine, and I wil reward,' than for a trifle to go to lawe, and spende all that euer he hath, and yet come by no remedie neither? Our sauiour Christ biddeth vs, if any man will go to law with vs for our cote, to giue him our cloke also, and if any man will giue thee a blowe on the one cheeke, turne to him the other, whereby is ment, that if any man will iniurie vs, and doe vs wrong, we should not resist nor trouble our selues, but suffer awhile, and with patience refer the due reuenge thereof to the Lord.

Amphil. Why ? Is it not lawful then for one Christian [2] man, to go to lawe with another ?

Amphil. The Apostle saith 'many things are lawfull which are not

[Margin notes:]
They spend their all, too, on greedy lawyers.

Englishmen are very contentious, and fond of going to law.
[1 Sig. C 2]

The Law was made to do right and to still strife, but it's now perverted to contrary ends.

Christ teaches us to suffer wrong patiently, and let God revenge it.

[2 Sig. C 2, back]

expedient,' and therefore, though it be after a sort lawfull, yet for euery trifle it is not lawfull, but for matters of importance it is. And yet not neither, if the matter might otherwise, by neighbors at home, be determined.

Theod. Yet some doubt whether it be lawfull or no for one Christian man to go to lawe with another for any worldly matter, bringing in the apostle Paule rebuking the Corinthians for going to lawe one with another.

Amphil. The apostle in that place reprehendeth them not for going to law for reasonable causes, but for that they, being christians, went to lawe vnder heathen iudges, which tended to the great discredite and infamie of the Gospell. But certeine it is, though some anabaptists *Quibus veritas odio est*, and certeine other heritikes haue taught the contrarie, yet it is certeine, that one christian man may go to lawe with an other for causes reasonable. For it being true, as it cannot be denied, that there is a certeine singularitie, interest, and proprietie in euery thing, and the lawe being not onely the meane to conserue the same propriety, but also to restore it againe, [1]being violate, is therefore lawfull, and may lawfully be attempted out, yet with this prouiso, that it is better, if the matter may otherwise be apeased at home, not to attempt lawe, than to attempt it. But if any schismatikes (as alas the worlde is too full of them) should altogether deny the vse of the lawe, as not christian, besides that the manifest word of God in euery place would easilie conuince them, the examples and practises of all ages, times, countries, and nations, from the first beginning of the world, togither with the example of our sauiour Christ himselfe, who submitted himselfe to the lawes then established, would quicklie ouerthrow their vaine imaginations. The lawe in it selfe, is the square, the leuell, and rule of equitie and iustice, and therefore who absolutely contendeth the same not to be christian, may well be accused of extreeme folly. But if the lawes be wicked and antichristian, then ought not good christians to sue vnto them, but rather to sustaine all kind of wrong whatsoeuer.

Theod. Then it seemeth by your reason, that if the lawe be so necessarie, as without the which Christian kingdomes could not stand, then are lawiers necessarie also for the execution thereof.

[2]*Amphil.* They are most necessarie. And in my iudgement a man

St. Paul rebukes the Corinthians, who were Christians, for going to law before Heathens.

But as it's Law's business to keep things straight, Christians may go to law.
[1 Sig. C 3]

Law is the square and level of Equity.

[2 Sig. C 3, b ck]

II. 1. *English Lawyers are Rogues.*

Lawyers are necessary, and can serve God; but English ones don't, they've such cheveril consciences.

Lawyers take bribes, and beggar the poor, and

turn Law topsy-turvy.

can serue God in no calling better than in it, if he be a man of a good conscience, but in *Dnalgne* the lawiers have such chauerell consciences, that they can serue the deuill better in no kind of calling than in that: for they handle poore mens matters coldly, they execute iustice parcially, & they receiue bribes greedily, so that iustice is peruerted, the poore beggared, and many a good man iniuried therby. They respect the persons, and not the causes; mony, not the poore; rewards, and not conscience. So that law is turned almost topsie turuie, and therefore happy is he that hath least to doe with them.

Theod. The lawiers must needes be verie rich if they haue such large consciences.

Amphil. Rich, quoth you? They are rich indeede toward the deuill and the world, but towards God and heauen, they are poore inough. It is no meruaile if they be rich and get much, when they will not speak two words vnder an angell (for that is called a counsellers fee.) But how they handle the poore mens causes for it, God and their owne consciences can tell; and one day, I feare me, they shall feele to their perpetuall paine, except they repent and amend.

Their fee is an Angel, 10s.

[? Sig. C 4]

¹ *Theod.* How be iudgments executed there vpon offenders, transgressours, and malefactors? with equitie, & expedition, or otherwise?

The abuses of our procedure and Prisons are frightful.

A man is clapt in irons, thrown into a dungeon, with only a little straw fit for a

dog; and there he lies, lice-bit, ill-fed, till he looks like a ghost, or dies.

Amphil. It greeueth me to relate thereof vnto you, the abuses therein are so inormous. For if a felone, homicide, a murtherer, or else what greeuous offender soeuer, that hath deserued a thousand deaths, if it were possible, happen to be taken and apprehended, he is straightway committed to prison, and clapt vp in as many cold yrons as he can beare, yea, throwne into dungeons and darke places vnder the ground, without either bed, clothes, or anything else to helpe himselfe withall, saue a little straw or litter bad inough for a dog to lie in. And in this miserie shall he lie, amongst frogs, toades, and other filthie vermine, till lice eate the flesh of² his bones. In the meane space hauing nothing to eate, but either bread and water or else some other modicum scarce able to suffice nature; and many times it hapneth, that for want of the same pittance they are macerate and shronke so low, as they either looke like ghosts, or else are famished out of hand. And this extreme miserie they lie in some

He stops there for 3 months, 3 years, perhaps his whole life.

time (perhaps) a quarter of a yeere, sometimes halfe a yeere, a

² off.

II. 1. *Reprieves & Pardons are bought in England.* 13

tweluemonth, yea, sometimes two or three yeeres, and perchance [1]all [1 Sig. C 4, back]
their life, though they have deserued death, by their flagitious facts
committed. Who seeth not that it were much better for them to die
at once, than to suffer this extreme miserie? Yea, the sufferance of
this extremitie is better vnto them, than the tast of present death
it selfe. And therefore in the cities reformed beyond seas, there is   The oversea Reformd Cities try
notable order for this: for as soone [as] any fellon or malefactor what- culprits at once,
soeuer that hath deserued death is taken, he is brought before the   and execute em.
magistrate, witnesse comes in, and giues euidence against him, and
being found gilty, and conuict by iustice, is presently, without any
further imprisonment, repriuation or delay, condemned, and being
condemned, is led presently to the place of execution, and so committed to the sword.

Theod. What is the cause why they are kept so long before they
go to execution in *Dnalgne*.

Amphil. Sometimes it commeth to passe by reason of (will doe   *Will-do-all* or
all) otherwise called mony, and sometimes by freends, or both, for   money.
                                                                      In England the
certeine it is, the one will not worke without the other. Hereby it   delay's due to
commeth to passe, that great abuses are committed. For if any man   Will-Do-All,
                                                                      money.
that hath freends and mony (as mony alwaies bringeth freendes with
him) chance to haue [2]committed neuer so heinous, or flagicious a   [2 Sig. C 5]
deed, whether robbed, stollen, slaine, killed or murthered, or what- If a felon or
                                                                      murderer has
soeuer it be, then letters walke, freends bestir them, and mony carrieth friends and
                                                                      money, he's safe
all away: yea, and though the lawe condemne him, iustice conuicteth   to get reprievd
him, and good conscience executeth him, yet must he needes be   or pardond.
repriued, and in the meane time his pardon, by false suggestion forsooth,
must be purchased, either for friendship or mony.

Theod. That is a great abuse, that he whom the lawe of God and
of man doth condemne, should be pardoned. Can man pardon or
remit him whom God doth condemne? Or shall man be more
mercifull in euill, then the author of mercie himselfe? it is God that
condemneth, who is he that can saue? Therefore those that ought
to die by the lawe of God, are not to be saued by the lawe of man.
The lawe of God commandeth that the murtherer, the adulterer, the
exorcist, magician and witch, and the like, should die the death. Is
it now in the power or strength of man to pardon him his life?

Amphil. Although it be wilfull and purposed murther, yet is the

14 II. 1. *One law for the Rich, another for the Poor.*

The crime is set down to chance medley, accident.
[¹ Sig. C 5, back]

prince borne in hande that it was plaine chance medley (as they call it) meere casuall, and fortunate, and therefore ¹may easily be dispensed withall. Indeede, the wisedome of God ordeined, that if any man chanced to kill an other against his will, he should flie to certeine cities of refuge, and so be saued, but if it were proued that he killed him wittingly, willingly, & prepensedly, then he should without al exception be put to death. And herein is great abuse, that two hauing committed one and the same fault, the one shall be pardoned and the other executed. If it be so that both haue committed offence worthy of death, let both die for it; if not, why should either die? Experience prooueth this true, for if a Gentleman commit a greeuous offence, and a poore man commit the like, the poore shal

If a Gentleman and a Poor Man commit the same offence, the Gentleman gets pardond, and the Poor Man hung.

be sure of his *Sursum collum*? But the other shall be pardoned. So Diogenes, seeing a sort of poore men going to hanging, fell into a great laughter. And being demanded wherefore he laughed, he answered at the vanitie and follie of this blind word. For, saith he, I see great theeues lead little theeues to hanging. And to say the

Yet isn't a grasping landlord or lawyer, a bigger thief than the poor man who steals from hunger?

truth, before God, is not he a greater theefe that robbeth a man of his good name for euer, that taketh a mans house ouer his head, before his yeeres be expired, that wresteth from a man his goods, his lands and liuings whervpon he, his wife, children and familie should

[² Sig. C 6]

²liue, than he that stealeth a sheepe, a cow, or an oxe, for necessities sake onely, hauing not otherwise to releeue his neede? And is not he a great theefe that taketh great summes of mony of the poore (vnder the names of fees), and doth little or nothing for them? Though this be not theft before the world, nor punishable by penall lawes, yet before God it is plaine theft, and punishable with eternall torments in hel. Let them take heede to it.

Theod. Cannot the prince then pardon any malefactor?

Amphil. Some are of opinion that the prince, by his power imperiall and prorogatiue, may pardon and remit the penaltie of any law, either diuine or humane, but I am of opinion that if Gods lawe

No prince should pardon him whom God's law condemns.

condemne him, no prince ought to saue him, but to execute iudgement and iustice without respect of persons to all indifferently. But in causes wherein Gods lawe doth not condemne him, the prince may pardon the offender, if there appeere likelyhoode of amendment in him. And yet let the prince be sure of this, to answere at the day of

II. 1. Magistrates and Officers favour the rich. 15

iudgement before the tribunall feate of GOD, for all the offences that the partie pardoned fhall commit any time of his life after. For if the prince had cutte him off when the [1]lawe had paffed on him, that euill had not been committed. To this purpofe I remember I haue heard a certeine pretie apothegue vttered by a iefter to a king. The king had pardoned one of his fubiectes that had committed murther, who, being pardoned, committed the like offence againe, and by meanes was pardoned the fecond time alfo, and yet filling up the meafure of his iniquitie, killed the third, and being brought before the king, the king being very forie, afked why he had killed three men, to whom his iefter ftanding by replied, faieng: "No (O king) he killed but the firft, and thou haft killed the other two: for if thou hadft hanged him vp at the firft, the other two had not beene killed, therefore thou haft killed them, and fhalt anfwere for their bloud." Which thing being heard, the king hanged him vp ftraightway, as he very well deferued: yet notwithftanding, I grant that a prince by his power regall and prerogatiue imperial may pardon offenders, but not fuch as Gods lawes and good confcience doe condemne, as I faid before. The power of a prince is comprehended *In Rebus licitis in Deo*, but not *in Rebus illicitis contra Deum*: In things lawfull in God, not in things vnlawfull contrarie to God. No power or principalitie vpon the earth [1]whatfoeuer may difpenfe with the lawe of God, but what it fetteth downe muft ftand inuiolable. Therefore if it be afked me wherein a prince may pardon any malefactor, I anfwer, for the breach or violation of any humane lawe, ordinance, conftitution, ftatute, or fanction, but not againft Gods word and lawe in any condition.

[1 Sig. C 6, back]

How a king was shewn by his jester that, by pardoning a murderer, he had killd 2 men.

[1 Sig. C 7]

A prince can only pardon breaches of man's law, not God's.

Theod. How is iuftice miniftered there, fincerely and truely, fo as the poore haue no caufe iuftly to complaine, or otherwife?

Amphil. If any haue caufe to complaine (as alas too many haue) it is for want of due execution of the lawes, not for lacke of good lawes. For, God be praifed, there be many good lawes, but indeed now and then through the negligence of the officers they are coldly executed. But if the lawes there in force were without parcialitie dulie executed, there fhuld be no iuft occafion for any to complaine. And truly to fpeake my confcience there is great parcialitie in the magiftrates and officers, nay, great corruption. For if a rich

There's great partiality in English magistrates and officers.

The rich man is favoured against the poor.

[¹ Sig. C 7, back]

Judges should go by justice, not by bribes.

Lawyers rob their poor clients by taking big fees,

and fees from 3 people when they can only do one's work.

The fees for warrants, &c. are too high.

[² Sig. C 8]

The marrow's suckt out of poor men's bones.

Bailiffs take bribes to let defendants get away.

All officials should act with a single eye to God's glory.

man and a poore man chance to haue to doe before them, the matter I warrant you fhall quickly be ended, and, my life for yours, fhall go vpon the rich mans fide, notwithftanding the poore mans right be apparent to all the world. But ¹if two poore men of equall eftate go to lawe togither, then their fute fhall hang three or foure yeeres, peraduenture feuen yeeres, a dozen, yea twentie yeeres, before it be ended, till either the one or both be made beggers. For reformation whereof, I would wifh iudges and officers to refpect the caufe, not the perfons, the matter, not the gaine? and not to regard either letter or any thing elfe, which might be fent them to peruert true iudgement. And iuftice being miniftred, then to read ouer their commendatorie letters in Gods name, remembring what the wife man faith : 'Gifts blinde the eies of the wife, and peruert iudgement.' The lawiers I would wifh to take leffe fees of their clients. For is not this a plaine theft before God, to take ten, twentie, or fortie fhillings of one poore man at one time, and fo much of a great fort at once, and yet to fpeake neuer a word for the moft part of it? And notwithftanding that they can be prefent but at one barre at once, yet will they take diuers fees of fundry clients to fpeake for them at three or foure places in one day. The other officers who grant foorth the warrants, the *Subpœnas*, the *Scire facias*, and diuers other writs, and thofe who keepe the feales of the fame, I would wifh to take leffe fees alfo. For is not ²this too vnreafonable, to take a crowne, or ten fhillings for writing fix or feuen lines, or little more. And then the keeper of the feale, for a little waxe, he muft haue as much as the other. And thus they fucke out (as it were) euen the very marrowe out of poore mens bones. The fhirifs, bailifs, and other officers alfo, I would wifh, for fees, for bribes, for friendfhip and rewards, not to returne a *Tarde venit*, or a *Non eft inuentus*, when they haue either fent the partie word to auoid couertly, or elfe, looking through their fingers, fee him, & will not fee him, forcing herby the poore plaintife to lofe not only his great & importable charges in the lawe, but alfo peraduenture his whole right of that which he fueth for. Thus let euery officer by what kind of name or title foeuer he be called, or in what kind of calling foeuer he be placed, doe all things with fingle eie, and good confcience, that God may be glorified, the common peace maintained, iuftice fupported, and their owne confciences dif-

II. 1. *No Subject may take Arms against his Prince.* 17

charged againſt the great daye of the Lorde, when all fleſh ſhall be conuented before the tribunall ſeate of G O D all naked as euer they were borne, to render accounts of all their dooings, whether they bee good or badde, and to receiue a rewarde according to their deeds. [1] By all which it appeareth, that if any for want of iuſtice have cauſe to complaine, it is thorow the corruption of iniquitie, auarice, and ambition of greedy and inſaciable cormorants, who, for deſire of gaine, make hauocke of all things, yea, make ſhipwracke of bodies and ſoules to the deuill for euer, vnleſſe they repent.

[1] Sig. C. 8, back?

Theod. How farre are princes lawes to be obeied, in all things indifferently without exception?

Princes are to be obeyd in all things not contrary to God's law.

Amphil. In all things not contrarie to the lawe of God and good conſcience, which, if they be againſt God and true godlineſſe, then muſt we ſay with the apoſtles, *Melius eſt deo obedire, quam hominibus,* It is better to obey God than man.

Theod. If the prince than doe ſet foorth a lawe contrarie to the lawe of God, and do conſtraine vs to doe that, that Gods word commandeth vs we ſhall not doe. In this or like caſe, may ſubiects lawfully take armes, and riſe againſt their prince?

Amphil. No, at no hand, vnleſt they will purchaſe to themſelues eternall damnation, and the wrath of God for euer. For it is not lawfull for the ſubiects to riſe up in armes againſt their liege prince for any occaſion what[2]ſoeuer. For proofe whereof we read that our ſauiour Chriſt was, not onely obedient to the maigiſtrates, and ſuperior powers in all things, but alſo taught his apoſtles, diſciples, and in them all people and nations of the world, the very ſame doctrine. And therefore the apoſtle faith, *Omnis anima poteſtatibus ſuperioribus ſubdita ſit:* Let euery ſoule ſubmit himſelfe to the higher powers, for there is no power but of God. And he that reſiſteth this power, reſiſteth the ordinance of God, and purchaſeth to himſelfe eternall damnation. Peter alſo giueth the like charge, that obedience in all godlines be giuen to the ſuperior powers, and that praiers and interceſſions be made for kings and rulers, and giueth the reaſon why, namely, that we may lead *Vitam pacificam,* A peaceable life vnder them.

But their subjects musta'n't in any case take arms against them.

[2] Sig. D. 1]

If subjects do, they resist God's ordinance.

Theod. Why? How than? If we ſhall not reſiſt them, then we do obey them in any thing either good or bad.

II. 1. Even Tyrants must be obeyd.

Amphil. No, not so neither. In all things not contrarie to Gods word we must obey them, on paine of damnation. But in things contrarie to the word and truth of God, we are thus to doe. We must depose and lay foorth ourselues, both bodie, and goods, life, and time, (our [1] conscience onely excepted, in the true obedience whereof we are to serue our God) euen all that we haue of nature, and committing the same into the hands of the prince, submit our selues, and lay downe our necks vpon the blocke, choosing rather to die than to doe any thing contrarie to the lawe of God and good conscience. And this is that, that the apostles ment when they saide: It is better to obey God than man. Not that obedience to man in all godlinesse is forbid, but that obedience to God is to be preferred before the obedience to man.

Theod. What if the prince be a tyrant, a wicked prince, and an vngodly, is he notwithstanding to be obeied?

Amphil. Yea, truely in the same order as I haue shewed before. For whether the prince be wicked, or godlye, hee is sent of GOD, bicause the Apostle saith: There is no power but of GOD. If the prince be a godlye prince, then is hee sent as a great blessing from GOD, and if hee be a tyrant, then is he raised of GOD for a scourge to the people for their sinnes. And therefore whether the prince be the one, or the other, he is to be obeied as before.

Theod. And bee kings and rulers to [2] bee beloued, and praied for of their subiects.

Amphil. That is without all doubt. For hee that hateth his prince in his hart, is a contemner of Gods ordinance, a traitour vnto GOD, and to his countreye: yea, hee is to loue his prince as well as himselfe, and better, if better can bee, and to praye for him as for himselfe. For that an infinite number doe rest and depend vppon his Maiestie, which doe not so vppon himselfe. So that the miscarrieng of him, were the destruction (peraduenture) of manye thousands.

Theod. This being so, then hath *Dnalgne* great cause to praye for their prince, by whose woorthye indeuour, and wise gouernement, the state of that realme is so peaceably maintained.

Amphil. They haue great cause indeede not onely to loue hir Maiestie, but also to praye for hir Grace, and whosoeuer will not doe so, I beseech the LORDE in the bowels of his mercie, to stoppe their

---

Sidenotes:

If princes order things against God's law, subjects must lay down goods and life, and

[1 Sig. D. 1, back]

put their necks on the block, rather than disobey God.

Even if the prince is ungodly, he's sent by God,

and is to be obeyd.
[2 Sig. D. 2]

Every one is to love his prince as himself.

May every Englishman who won't love and pray for Queen Elizabeth, die straight off!

breath, and to take them awaye quicklye from the face of the earth. For by hir Highneſſe wiſe gouernement, the realme is in peace, Gods word flouriſheth, and aboundance [1] of al things floweth in the ſame, the Lord God be praiſed therefore, and preſerue hir noble Grace long to reigne amongſt vs. Amen.

[1 Sig. D. 2, back]

Theod. Let vs proceed a little further: I pray you how is the youth of that country brought vp, in learning or otherwiſe?

As to Education,

Amphil. The youth truely is well brought vp, both in good letters, nurture, and maners for the moſt part. For the better performance whereof, they haue excellent good ſchooles, both in cities, townes, and countries, wherein abundance of children are learnedly brought vp. But yet notwithſtanding, ſome parents are much to be blamed in the education of their children, for the moſt keepe their ſonnes to ſchoole but for a time, till they can write and read, and well if all that too, and very ſeldome or neuer doe they keepe them ſo long at their bookes, as vntill they atteine to any perfect knowledge indeed. So that by this means learning doth, and is like, greatly to decay. And if one aſke them, why they keepe not their children to ſchoole till they prooue learned, they will anſwer, "Bicauſe I ſee learning and learned men are little eſteemed, and ne thinke the beſt of them can hardly live by the ſame. And therefore I will ſet him to an occupation, which will be alwaies ſure." As herein they ſay [2] true, for I cannot but lament the ſmall preferment now adaies that learning getteth in the world amongſt men, & the ſmal account that is made of the ſame. This is the cauſe why learning doth, and will in time, greatly decay. For who is he, that hauing ſpent all his ſubſtance vpon learning, yea, his bodie, ſtrength, and all, and yet can hardly liue thereby, and maintaine himſelfe withall, that will couet after learning, which is both ſo chargeable, and painfull to be come by?

we've good schools, and plenty of children at 'em,

but the boys stay only till they can read and write;

then they're put to business, because they can't live by Learning, which gets small preferment now-adays.

[2 Sig. D. 3]

Theod. Be there not Vniuerſities, colledges, and free ſchooles, where youth may bee brought vp in learning *Gratis* without any charges to their parents?

The free Colleges and Schools are abused and perverted

Amphil. There are ſuch places indeed. But alas they are abuſed & peruerted to other ends than was intended by them at the firſt. For whereas thoſe places had great liuings, rents, reuenues & poſſeſſions giuen to them, it was to this onely end and purpoſe, that thoſe poore children whoſe parents were not able otherwiſe to main-

II. 1. *Free Schools and Colleges are jobd.*

from poor children to rich ones.
[¹ Sig. D. 3, back]

Unless a father can bribe the Master,

his son 'll not get into College or School.

The places are jobd, not given to the needy.

taine them at learning, fhould be brought vp vpon the charges of the houfe, and not thofe whofe parents are able to maintaine them of themfelues. But now we fee the contrarie is true, and whereas they were giuen to maintaine none but the poore only, now ¹ they maintaine none but the rich onely. For except one be able to giue the regent or prouoft of the houfe, a peece of mony, ten pound, twentie pound, fortie pound, yea, a hundred pound, a yoke of fatte oxen, or a couple of fine geldings, or the like, though he be neuer fo toward a youth, nor haue neuer fo much need of maintenance, yet he comes not there, I warant him. If he cannot preuaile this way, Let him get him letters commendatory from fome of reputation, and perchance he may fpeed, in hope of benefite to infue. So that the places in the vniuerfities and free fchooles, feeme rather to be folde for mony and frienfhip, than giuen *gratis* to them that haue neede, as they ought to be.

Theod. Are there not many inferior fcholes in the country befides, both for the inftruction and catechifing of youth?

In poor schools, Schoolmasters are so badly paid that pupils snort in palpable ignorance all their days.

Amphil. There are fo, almoft in euery parifh. But alas, fuch fmall pittance is allowed the fchoolmaifters, as they can neither buy the libraries, nor which is leffe, hardly maintaine themfelues; which thing altogither difuadeth them from their bookes, and is occafion why many a one fnorteth in palpable ignorance all daies of their life.

Theod. Would you haue any man without exception, to take vppon him the office of a ² fchoolmaifter, and to teach the youth?

[² Sig. D. 4]

Every Schoolmaster should be examind for character and knowledge,

Amphil. No, at no hand. Firft I would wifh that euery one that is a fchoolmafter, how learned or vnlearned foeuer, fhould be examined, as wel for his religion, and his fufficiencie in knowledge, as alfo for his integritie of life, & being found found in them all, to be alowed & admitted to teach. For if euerie one that wold, fhould take vpon him to teach without further triall, then might there great inconuenience follow. For papifts and other fchifmatikes, apoftataes, or elfe whatfoeuer, might thruft in themfelues, & fo corrupt the youth. Ignorant & vnlearned would take vpon them high learning & fo delude their fchoolers. And if his life fhould not be anfwerable to his profeffion, then fhould he peruert his auditorie alfo. Therefore in my iudgement is there great choife to be made of

and then pay no fees to teach.

fchoolmaifters. Thus they being tried, let them be admitted *gratis.*

by authoritie. But now there is great abuses herein, for being found sufficient in all respects, yet must he be constrained to take a license, whether he will or not, and must pay xxvi. or xx. shillings for it, & yet will this serue him no longer than he tarieth in that dioces, & comming into another he must pay as much there for ye like licenfe also, whereas peraduenture he shall scarcely get [1] so much cleere in three or foure yeeres in that dioces, they haue such fat pasture. But if they would needes haue them to haue licenses, (which I grant to be very good,) I would wish they might haue them *gratis*, without mony, for if it be lawfull for them to teach for mony, it is also lawfull without. And if they be not woorthie it is pittie that mony should make them woorthie; and againe, if they be woorthie, it is pittie that without mony they cannot be so accepted.

Theod. What way were best to be taken for the good education of youth?

Amphil. It were good (if it might be brought to passe) that in euery parish throughout the Realme, there were an indifferent able man appointed for the instruction of youth in good letters, hauing a reasonable stipend alowed him of the same parish for his paines, But now they teach and take paines for little or nothing, which vtterly discourageth them, and maketh manie a cold schooler in *Dnalgne*, as experience daily teacheth.

Theod. Be there men of all kinde of trades, occupations, and artes, as there be in other countries.

Amphil. Yea, truely: there are men of all sciences, trades, mysteries, faculties, occupa[2]tions, and artes whatsoeuer, and that as cunning as any be vnder the sunne. Yea, so expert they be, as if they would let a thing alone when it is well, they were the brauest workmen in the world. But as they seeke to excell and surpasse al other nations, in finenes of workmanship, so now and than they reape the fruits of their vaine curiosity, to their owne detriment, hinderance, and decay.

Theod. How liue the marchant men amongst them? are they rich and wealthy, or but poore?

Amphil. How should they be poore, gaining as they do, more then halfe in halfe in euerie thing they buy or sell? And which is more, sometimes they gaine double and triple; if I said quadruple, I lied not.

[Side notes:]
Now he must pay 26s. or 30s. for a license for every diocese he teaches in.

[1 Sig. D. 4, back]

Licenses should be given to fit men gratis.

Every Parish ought to have its Schoolmaster with a good stipend.

As to Tradesmen,

English Artisans are as clever as any under the sun.

[2 Sig. D. 5]

The Merchants are rich, making from 100 to 400 per cent.

II. 1. *Merchants export goods wanted at home.*

Theod. I pray you how can that be so?

Amphil. I will tell you. They haue mony to lay foorth vpon euerie thing, to buy them at the first and best hand, yea, to ingrosse, and to store themselues with abundance of al things. And then will they keepe these marchandize till they waxe verie scarse, (and no maruaile, for they buy vp all things) and so consequently deere. And then will they sell them at their owne prices, or else (being able to beare the mony) they will keepe them still. By this [1] meanes they get the deuill and all; besides these, they haue a hundred slights in their budgets to rake in gaine withall.

Theod. I pray you, what be those?

Amphil. They will go into the countries, and buy vp all the wooll, corne, leather, butter, cheese, bacon, or else what marchandize soeuer they knowe will be vendible, and these they transport ouer seas, whereby they gaine infinit summes of mony.

Theod. That is woonderful that they are so permitted: are there no lawes, nor prohibitions to the contrarie, that no wooll, corne or leather, shoulde be transported ouer seas?

Amphil. There are good lawes, and great restraints to the contrary, in so much as they be apparent traitors to God, their prince and country, that carrie any of the foresaid things ouer without speciall licence thereto. Yet notwithstanding, either by hooke or crooke, by night or day, by direct or indirect meanes, either knowne or vnknowne, they wil conveigh them ouer, though their owne country want the same. But to auoide all dangers, they purchase a licence & a dispensation for mony, bearing the prince in hand that they do it for some good cause, when indeed the cause is their owne [2] priuate gaine. And for the speedier obtaining of their desires, they demand license for the cariage ouer but of so much and so much, when in truth they conuey ouer, vnder the colour of this their licence, ten times, twenty times, yea, a hundred times, fiue hundred times, yea, a thousande times as much more. And thus they delude their prince, impouerish their country, and inrich themselues, feeding, clothing and inriching our enimies with our owne treasure. Hereby it commeth to passe that all things are deerer, and scarser, than otherwise they would be if restraynt were had, and I warrant them many a blacke curse haue they of the poore commons for their doing.

Marginal notes:

They buy up the whole stock of an article, hold it till it gets dear, and then sell it at their own price.

[1 Sig. D. 5, back]

Merchants also buy up English goods and export them.

Traitors to God and their country they are, dodging the laws by buying the Queen's license,

[2 Sig. D. 6]

and then exporting 500 times as much as they've leave to. They thus make things dear; and

many a black curse do they get from the poor for it!

II. 1. Merchants' false weights & lies.

Theod. Would you not haue licenses granted for the transporting ouer of such things for no cause?

Amphil. Yes. But first I would haue our owne people serued, that they wante not in any case. For it is very vnmeete to feede forren nations, and our owne country famish at home. But if it were so, that *Dualgne* flowed in abundance and plentie of all things, whatsoeuer are necessarie for the vse and sustentation of man in this life, and other nations (prouided that they bee our freendes [1] and of christian religion) wanted the same then would I wishe that some of our superfluitie might be erogate to them, to the supplie of their necessities, but not otherwise. And this standeth both with the lawes of God, charitie, and good conscience.

We ought to feed our own folk first.

Then we may export our surplus to friendly lands.

[1 Sig. D. 6, back.

Theod. These are marueilous sleights to get mony withall. But I pray you, haue they no more?

Amphil. They want none, I warrant you; for rather than to faile, they haue their false weights, their counterfet ballances, their adulterate measures, and what not, to deceiue the poore people withall, and to rake in mony. But the Wise man telleth them, that false ballances, counterfet weightes, and vntrue measures, are abomination to the Lord. And the Apostle telleth them, that God is the iust reuenger of all those that deceiue their brethren in bargaining. And yet shall you haue them, in the sale of their wares, to sweare, to teare, and protest, that 'before God, before Iesus Christ, as God shall saue my soule, as God shall iudge me, as the Lord liueth, as God receiue me, as God helpe me, by God and by the world, by my faith and troth, by Iesus Christ,' and infinite the like othes, that such a thing cost them so much, & so much, and it is woorth [2] this much and that much, when in truth they sweare as false, as the liuing Lord is true, as their owne consciences can beare them witnesse, and I feare me will condemne them at the day of the Lord, if they repent not. For if a thinge cost them ten shillings, they will not blush to aske twentie shillings for it. If it cost them twentie shillings, they will not shame to aske forty shillings for it, and so of all others, doubling, tripling, and quadrupling the price thereof, without either feare of God, or regard of good conscience.

Merchants use false weights and measures too.

And they swear by all that's holy that their wares cost so much, and are worth so much, lying loudly.

[2 Sig. D. 7]

They'll not blush to ask 20s. for what cost 'em 10s. I having no fear of God.

Theod. What say you of the Drapers and cloth sellers? liue they in the same order that the other doe?

II. 1. Drapers and Clothmakers' dodges.

Amphil. Of Drapers I haue little to say, sauing that I thinke them cater cosins, or cosin germans to merchants. For after they haue bought their cloth, they cause it to be tentered, racked, and so drawne out, as it shall be both broader and longer than it was when they bought it almost by halfe in halfe, or at lest by a good large sise Now the cloth being thus stretched forth in euery vaine, how is it possible either to endure or hold out; but when a shower of raine taketh it, then it falleth and shrinketh in, that it is shame to see it. Then haue they their shops and places where they [1] sell their cloth commonly very darke and obscure, of purpose to deceiue the buiers. But *Caueat empto* (as the old saieng is) Let the buiers take heed. For *Technas machinant, & retia tendant pedibus*, as the saieng is: 'They meane deceit, and lay snares to intrap the feet of the simple.' And yet notwithstanding, they will be sure to make price of their racked cloth, double and triple more than it cost them. And will not sticke to sweare, and take on (as the other their confraters before) that it cost them so much, and that they doe you no wrong. God giue them grace to haue an eie to their consciences, and to content themselues with reasonable gaines.

Theod. I thinke there is great fault to bee found in the first makers of the cloth, for the naughtinesse thereof, as well as in the Drapers, is there not?

Amphil. No doubt of that. For some put in naughty wooll, and cause it to be spun & drawne into a very small thred, and then compounding with the Fuller to thicke it very much, and with the Clothier also to sheare it very lowe, and with some liquide matter to lay downe the wooll so close, as you can hardly see any wale, and then selleth it as though it were a very fine cloth indeed. Other some mixe good [2] wooll and naughty wooll togither, and vsing it as before, they will sell it for principall good cloth, when it is no thing lesse. And then for their further aduantage, euery vaine, euery ioint, and euery thred must be so tentered and racked, as I warrant it for euer being good after. Now, it being thus tentered at his hands, and after at the Drapers handes, I pray you how should this cloth be ought, or endure long?

Theod. Be there Goldsmithes there any store also, as in some other countries there be?

Side notes:

And the Drapers are as bad.

They rack and stretch their cloth, so that it won't keep out rain.

[1 Sig. D. 7, back] They have dark shops, to take buyers in.

They charge 100 per cent. profit, and swear the goods cost em all the money.

The Clothmakers are a bad lot too.

They use bad wool; get the Fuller to thicken it, and the Clothier to shear it low; then they sell it for fine cloth.

[Sig. D. 8]

They stretch it too.

Our Goldsmiths

II. 1. Tricks of Goldsmiths and Vintners.

Amphil. There are inow, and more than a good meanie. They are (for the moſt part) very rich and wealthye, or elſe they turne the faireſt ſide outwards, as many doe in *Dnalgne*. They haue their ſhops and ſtalles fraught and bedecked with chaines, rings, golde, ſiluer, and what not woonderfull richly. They will make you any monſter or antike whatſoeuer, of golde, ſiluer, or what you will. They haue ſtore of all kinde of plate whatſoeuer. But what? Is there no deceit in all theſe goodlye ſhewes? Yes, too many. If you will buy a chaine of golde, a ring, or any kinde of plate, beſides that you ſhall paye almoſt halfe in halfe more than it is woorth (for they will perſuade[1] [2] you the workmanſhip of it comes to ſo much, the faſhion to ſo much, and I cannot tell what:) you ſhall alſo perhaps haue that golde which is naught, or elſe at leaſt mixt with other droſſie rubbage, and refuſe mettall, which in compariſon is good for nothing. And ſometimes, or for the moſt part, you ſhal haue tinne, lead, and the like, mixt with ſiluer. And againe, in ſome things ſome will not ſticke to ſell you ſiluer gilt for gold, and well if no worſe too now and then. But this happeneth very ſeldome, by reaſon of good orders, and conſtitutions made for the puniſhment of them that offend in this kind of deceit, and therfore they ſeldome dare offend therein, though now and then they chance to ſtumble in the darke.

Theod. Haue you good wines in *Dnalgne?*

Amphil. Indeede there are excellent wines as any be in the world, yet not made within the Realme, but comming from beyond ſeas: which when the vintners have once got into their clouches, and placed in their ſellers, I warrant you they make of one hogſhead almoſt two, or at leſt, one and a halfe, by mixing & blenting one with another, & infuſing other liquor into them. So that it is almoſt vnpoſſible, to get a cup of pure wine of it ſelfe at the tauerne. But harſhe, rough, ſtipticke, and hard [3] wine, neither pleaſant to the mouth, nor wholſome to the bodie. And notwithſtanding that they gaine (welneare) one hogſhead in another, yet ſhall their meaſures, their gallons, pints, and quarts be ſo ſpare, and their prices ſo hie, that it is woonderful to ſee. And if a poore ſimple man go to drinke a pint of wine for the ſtrengthening of his bodie, and for neceſſities ſake onely, he ſhall be ſure to haue that wine brought him, that is too bad, though his monie (I am ſure) is as good as the rich mans. But

are very rich, and have ſhops and ſtalls loaded with gold and ſilver ornaments.

[1 uſade *orig.*]
[2 Sig. D 8, back]
Goldſmiths mix gold with baſe alloy; and ſome ſell ſilver-gilt for gold.

Vintners mix bad wine with good;

[3 Sig. E 1]

give ſhort meaſure, and palm off bad wine on poor men.

if a man of countenance come to drinke for pleasure & nicenesse, he shall haue of the best wine in the seller, though his mony be no beter than the poore mans. With infinite the like abuses, which I omit.

Theod. Haue you anything to say of Butchers, and those that kill and sel meate to eate?

Amphil. Nothing but this: that they are not behind in their abuses, fallacies, and deceits. For whereas they pay a certeine price for a fat beefe, they are so impudent that they thinke their market is naught, except they may gaine halfe in halfe, or the best quarter at the least. And to the end their meate may be more saleable to the eie, the fairer, and the fatter, they will kill their beasts, and suffer the bloud to remaine within them still, for this cause that [1] it may incorporate it selfe in the flesh, and so thereby the flesh may not onely be the weightier (for in some places they buy all by waight) but also may seeme both fresher, fairer, newer, tenderer, and yonger. And, which is more commonly, they vse to blowe and puffe it vp with winde, to the end it may seeme bigger, fatter, and fairer to the eie. Or if the meate it selfe be leane, and naught, then will they take the fat of other meate, and pin vpon the same very artificially, and all to delude the eies of the beholders. And though it be neuer so old meate, tough, and stale, yet will they sweare, protest, and take on woonderfully, that it is very new, fresh and tender. So that no more in them than in others, there is little conscience at all. There be some of them also now and then that will not sticke to sell meate which hath died (perchance) in a ditch, if it be worth the eating (which is most lamentable), and yet wil beare the world in hand that it is excellent meate, that it died kindly, and so foorth. So that hereby infinite diseases are caught, and manie times present death insueth to the eaters thereof.

Theod. Is meate deere or good cheape there for [2] the most part?

Amphil. It is commonly deere, seldom good [3]cheape, and the reason is, bicause a sort of insaciable cormorants, greedie grasiers I meane, who, hauing raked togither infinite pasture, feed all themselues, and will not sell for anie reasonable gaine, and then must the Butchers needes sell deere, when as they buie deere.

Sidenotes:

Butchers are impudent enough to try and make 100 per cent profit!

Butchers let the blood soak into their meat.

[1 Sig. E 1, back]

They puff lean meat up with air, and pin fat on it.

Some 'll also sell meat that has died in a ditch.

[2 for for, orig.]

[3 Sig. E 2]

Meat is dear. Greedy grasiers keep up the price of beasts.

II. 1. Evils of enclosing Commons & making Parks. 27

Theod. Why? would you haue no grasiers? then how coulde there bee anie meate fatted?

Amphil. Yes I would haue grasiers. But I would not haue a few rich cobs to get into their clowches almost whole countries, so as the poore can haue no releefe by them. For by this meanes pastures and groundes are not onely excessiuely deere, but also not to be got of any poore men for monie, whereby it commeth to passe, that the poore are impouerished, and the rich onlie benefited. Yea, so greatly are the poore hereby inthralled, that they can hardly get a peece of ground to keepe so much as a poore cow or two vpon for the maintenance of themselues, and their poore families. This is a great abuse: for by this meanes rich men eate vp poore men, as beasts eate vp grasse.   *[margin: A few rich cobs get whole counties into their hands, and stop poor folk keeping a cow. Rich men eat up poor ones as beasts do grass.]*

Theod. Doe the gentlemen and others, take in commons & inclosures (as your words seeme to implie) for their better feeding?

[1] *Amphil.* Yea, almost all indifferently. For whereas before was any commons, heathes, moores, plaines, or free places of feeding for the poore and others, euen all in generall, now you shall haue all seuerall, inclosed, and appropriate to a few greedy gentlemen, who will neuer haue inough, till their mouths be full of clay, and their bodie full of grauell. Commons and moores which were woont to be the onely staie of the poore, & wheruppon eche might keepe cattle, both neate and sheepe, according to his estate, are now taken from them, wherby manie are constrained either to famish, or else to beg their breade from doore to doore. So that in proces of time, if these inclosures be suffered to continue, the state of the whole Realme will mightily decay, a few shall be inriched, & many a thousand poore people, both men, women, and children, in citie and country, vtterlie beggered. Oh it was a goodlie matter, when the poore man might turne out a cow, or two, & certeine numbers of sheepe to the commons, and haue them kept well vpon the same, both winter & sommer, freely without costing them ought; whereas now they are inclosed, made seueral, and imploied to the priuate commoditie of a few ambicious gentlemen, so as the poore man cannot keepe so much as a pig or a goose vpon [2] the same.   *[margin: [¹ Sig. E 2, back] The gentry enclose the poor folk's commons, and make em starve. A good time it was when a poor man could keep a cow on the common! Now he can't keep a goose. [² Sig. E 3]]*

Theod. It is great pittie that such oppression of the poore should be borne withall or suffered in any of what degree soeuer.

II. 1. Sheep turn-out Men. Wool-sellers' Tricks.

Amphil. It is so. But what than? You shall haue some that, not for the benefit of grasing and feeding onely, will take in commons, and inclosures, but also some that for vaineglorie, worldly pompe, promotion & foolish pleasure, will not sticke to pull downe whole townes, subuert whole parishes, and turning foorth all a begging, rather than to faile, make them parkes, chases, warrants, and I cannot tell what of the same. And when they haue thus done, their bucks, their does, their stags, harts, hinds, conies and the like, not onely not fead *intra gyrum suum*, Within their circuit, but eate vp and deuoure all the poore mens fields, corne, grasse and all. So that it is hard if any poore mans corne scape their fangs within a dozen myles compasse, which is a pitifull and a lamentable case.

Theod. Would you not haue parkes, and chases for game?

Amphil. I disalow them not. But I would not hane them to be made of the poore mens liuings, nor yet to stand to the preiudice of the whole country adioining. Therefore if they [1] will haue parkes and chases, First let them see that they be of their owne proper lande, and then that they be no annoiance to the country about, and then let them haue them, in the name of God.

Theod. Be there any grasiers of sheepe there also?

Amphil. Two [2] manie, if it pleased God. For nowe euerie meane gentleman, if he can pretend (though neuer so little) title to any common, heath, moore or pasture, he will haue it, *quo iure, quaue iniuria*, Either by hooke or crooke. And wheras before time there hath bin a whole parish or towne maintained vpon the same, now is there no bodie there dwelling, but a sheepeheard and a dogge lolling vnder a bush. Thus are whole parishes and townes made praies to rich grasiers. Yea, you shall haue some grasiers to keepe fiue hundred, a thousand, fiue thousand, ten thousand, twentie thousand sheepe of his owne at one time: now iudge you what infinite commodities ariseth hereof. Besides that, when they sell their wooll (as though they gayned not inough otherwise), it is a worlde to see what subtilties, (I will not saie what falsities), they vse in the sale thereof. As first to intermixt and blente the good and naughtie wooll [3] togither, to winde it vppe cloosely that it shall not be seene within. And which is more, becaufe they sell all by waight, they will not sticke to vse sinister meanes to make it pease well in waight. Some lay it, after it

---

Sidenotes:

Then vain rich men pull down villages to make parks and warrens;

and their conies eat up poor men's corn.

Parks must not be made out of poor men's livelihoods.

[¹ Sig. E 3, back]

[² read Too]

Commons are inclosd; and instead of a village you've only a shepherd and a dog.

Some grasiers keep from 500 to 20,000 (?) sheep.

[³ Sig. E 4] They cheat in selling their wool, mixing bad with good;

II. 1. *Landlords rach Tenants.   Incoming Fines.*

is clipped from the sheepes backe, in a moyst seller, vnderneath the grounde, to the ende that the moysture, humiditie and wette of the seller may instill into it, and so may pease the more. Otherfome will cast wette salt into it, which in time will liquifie, and cause it to be the waightier. With manie other the like wicked sleights and legerdimeanes, whereof, for that I would rather giue them a taste in hope of amendment, then a plaine description for feare of displeasing them, at this time I will omit to speake any more till further occasion be offered.

wetting it, putting salt into it, &c.

Theod. Is the lande there possessed in common, or else is their propertie in all things, and so consequently landlords?

Amphil. There is not onelie a propertie in lands there, but also in all things else, and so landlords inow more than be good ones iwis.

Landlords

Theod. Doe they let out their lands, their farmes, and tenements, so as the poore tenants may liue well vpon them?

[1]Amphil. Oh no. Nothing lesse. But rather the contrarie is most true. For when a gentleman or other hath a farme or a lease to let: first he causeth a surueior to make strict inquirie what may be made of it, and how much it is woorth by yeere; which being found out, and signified to the owner, he racketh it, straineth it, and as it were so setteth it on the tenter hookes, stretching euery vaine, and ioint thereof, as no poore man can liue of it. And yet if he might haue it freely for this racked rent too, it were somewhat well. But (out alas, and fie for shame) that cannot be. For though he pay neuer so great an annuall rent, yet must he pay at his entrance a fine, or (as they call it) an income of ten pound, twenty pound, forty pound, threescore pound, an hundred pound, whereas in truth the purchase thereof is hardly woorth so much. So that hereby the poore man, if hee haue scraped any little thing togither, is forced to disburse it at the first dash, before he enter the doores of his poore farme, wherein, what through the excessiue fine, and the vnreasonable rent, he is scarse able to buy his dog alofe, liuing like a begger, or little better, all his life after. The time hath beene, and not long since, when men feared God & loued their brethren, that one might haue had a house, with pasture [2]lieng to it, yea good farmes, leases and liuings for little or nothing. Or (as some hold) for a Gods penie, as they called it. But howsoeuer it be, certeine it is, that that farme or

[¹ Sig. E 4, back]

get their farms valued, and not only rack the rent higher,

but make the tenant pay a fine as an Incoming,

so that he's hardly enough left to buy his dog a loaf.

[² Sig. E 5]

II. 1. Landlords should not grind their Tenants.

Rents have risen twentyfold of late years.

leafe, which one might haue had then for ten fhillings, is now woorth ten pound. For twentie fhillings, now is woorth twentie or threefcore pound. For fortie fhillings, is now woorth fortie pound, or a hundred pound and more.

Theod. Then I perceiue, they let not out their land after the old rent : doe they?

Amphil. No. You may be fure of that, they loue nothing worfe. They cannot at any hand brooke or digeft them that would counfel them to that.

Theod. Why? Haue not landlords authoritie, and may they not make as much of their owne lands as they can? They count that good policie, and I haue heard them fay: Is it not lawfull for me to liue vpon mine owne, and to get as much for it as I can?

Landlords should think that they've only the use of the land; and so they ought to give the poor a chance of living by it.
[¹ Sig. E 5, back]

Amphil. They muft firft confider that the earth is the Lords (as the Pfalmograph faith : *Domini eft terra, & plenitudo eius*, The earth is the Lords, and the fulneffe thereof) and all that dwelleth therein. And therefore being the Lords in propertie, it is theirs but in vfe onely. And yet not fo. But that they ¹ought to lay it foorth to the fupport of the poore, that all may liue iointly togither, & maintaine ye ftate of the common wealth to Gods glorie. For other wife, if a few rich cobs fhuld haue al, & the poore none, it fhuld come to paffe, that the ftate of the common wealth would foone decay, & come to confufion. They ought alfo to confider how they came by their lands, whether by right or wrong. If by right, then are they bound by Gods lawe, and good confcience, to let forth the fame fo as the poore may well liue vpon them. But if they poffes them wrongfully, then ought they to furrender their tytle, and giue it to the right heire :

No man ought to plunder his fellow-man,

but take them with that fault, & cut of their necks : No man ought to poole and pill his brother, nor yet to exact and extort of him more than right and reafon requireth, being fure that the fame meafure which he meafureth to others, fhal be meafured to him againe. Euery one muft fo deale with his owne, fo let it out, & fo liue, as others may liue by him, and not himfelf alone, for the earth is comon to al *Adams* children; & though fortune haue given more abundance to fome than to other fome, yet dame nature hath brought foorth al alike, & will receiue them againe into hir wombe alike alfo. And

but do to him as he'd be done by.

therefore ought euerie chriftian to doe to others, as they would wifh to

II. 1. *How Landlords pillage their poor tenants.* 31

be done to: which ¹lawe, if it were obserued well, would cut of all [¹ Sig. E 6]
oppression whatsoeuer.

Theod. I pray you, how came noble men and gentlemen by their lands at the first?

Amphil. Cicero saith that in the beginning, before the world was impeopled, men comming into huge & wast places inhabitable, either toke to themselues as much land as they would, or else wan it by yͤ sword, bought it by purchase, had it by gift, or else receiued it from their forefathers, by lineal discent, or hereditary possession. Which saieng of his must needes be true, both in the people of the former world & in vs also. Then seeing this is so, ought not euery good christian to set forth his lande, so as poore men may liue upon it as wel as himselfe: whosoeuer doth not this, eschewing al kind of exaction, polling, pilling & shauing of his poore tenants, he is no perfect member of Christ, nor doth not as he would be done by. Christian landlords are bound to let their land at moderate rents.

Theod. You talked before of fines, and incomes: what if a poore man be not able to paye them, what then?

Amphil. Then may he go sue yͤ goose, for house gets he none, yͤ deuill shal haue it before him, if he will giue him mony inough: no, if yͤ fine be not paid (thogh the rent be neuer so gret) he shall haue a fig, assone as a house. If yᵗ a poore man haue got neuer so litle a stock to liue vpon and to ²maintaine his occupation or trade withall, yet shall he be constrained to sell the same, yea, peraduenture all the goods and implements he hath, to pay this fine, so that during yͤ whole terme of his life, he shall hardly recouer the same againe. And then his lease being expired, out of doores goes he, for that he is not able to pay as great a fine or greater than before. Thus are many a one, with their wiues, children, and whole families, turned out a beging, and die, not a fewe of them, in extreeme miserie. [² Sig. E 6, back] Poor men haue to sell all their stock to pay Fines to Landlords; and at the end of their lease, out they go.

Theod. I thought one might haue had a farme or a lease for a reasonable rent yeerely, without any fine or income paieng.

Amphil. One would thinke so. For, paieng as much yeerely, as can be made of the thing it selfe: I wonder what deuill put it into their heads to receiue such fines and incomes, to vndoe the poore withall. The deuill himselfe, I thinke, will not be so straite laced, nor yet so nigard to his seruants, as they are to their poore tenants. For whereas they will not let out a farme or a lease for one and twentie yeeres The Devil himself is not so niggardly as some Landlords.

II. 1. *Landlords cheat by Renewal-Fines.*

[¹ Sig. E 7]

Some cheat their tenants out of the first year or two's rent when paid in advance.

Landlords force tenants to renew their Leases at heavy fines,

and make 'em forfeit their Leases too.

[² Sig. E 7, back]

Leases and Conveyances are also terribly long, and contain so many provisoes that a poor man can hardly keep em all.

without a great fine, the deuill will giue them his whole territorie and kingdome of hell, to their inheritance for euer, and that freely, paieng nothing for the same. And yet notwith¹ſtanding all this. There are ſome landlords, (nay lewdlords) that hauing racked their rents to the vttermoſt, exacted fines, & made all that euer they can of their farmes, will yet proceede further, and as men neuer content with inough, will haue their poore tenants to pay a yeere or two yeeres rent before hande, promiſing them (before they haue it) that they ſhall pay no more rent yeerelie, till the ſame be runne vp. But when they haue it, they pay their yeerely rent notwithſtanding, and neuer receiue any reſtitution for the other. And at euerie change forſooth they muſt take newe leaſes, and pay new fines, being borne in hand that their leaſes before are inſufficient, and of no effect. And ſometimes foure or fiue yeres, yea ten, twentie, fortie, or fiftie yeeres before their former leaſe be expired, ſhall they be conſtrained to renue their leaſes, and diſburſe great ſomes, or elſe haue their houſes taken ouer their heads. Beſides, as though theſe pollages and pillages were not ill enough, if their leaſes be not warely and circumſpectly made (all quirks and quiddities of the lawe obſerued), they will finde ſuch meanes (or elſe it ſhal go verie hard) that the poore man ſhall forfait his leaſe, before his leaſe be expired: which thing if it happen, out goes the poore man, ²come on it what will.

Theod. Are the inſtruments, the writings, & conueiances in that land ſo intricate, as they are hard to be kept, for ſo I gather by your words?

Amphil. Yea, truly. For whereas in times paſt when men dealt vprightly, and in the feare of God, ſixe or ſeuen lines was ſufficient for the aſſurance of any peece of land whatſoeuer, now 40. 60. 100. 200. 500. nay a whole ſkin of parchment, and ſometimes 2. or 3. ſkins will hardly ſerue. Wherin ſhalbe ſo many prouiſoes, particles, & clauſes, & ſo many obſeruances, that it is hard for a poore ignorant man to keep halfe of them: and if he fail in one of the left, you knowe what followeth. In former time a mans bare word was ſufficient, now no inſtrument, band, nor obligation can be ſure inough. Fy vpon vs! what ſhal become of vs? we are they of whom the prophet ſpeaketh, ſaieng: There is no faith, there is no truth nor righteouſnes left vpon the earth. God be mercifull vnto vs!

II. 1. *Landlords the cause of Dearness. Tailors.*

Theod. Seing that farms and leafes are fo deere, I am perfuaded that euerie thing elfe is deere alfo: is it not fo?

Amphil. Yea truly it cannot be chofen. And yet it is ftrange, that in abundance of althings there fhuld be dearth of all things, as there is.

Theod. Who is it long of, can you tell?

[1] *Amphil.* Truly of the landlords onlie in my fimple iudgment: for whenas they inhance the rents, & fet their fines on tenter as they do, how fhould the poore man do? Muft he not fel al his things a great deale the deerer? Elfe how fhuld he either faue himfelfe, pay his rent, or maintaine his familie: fo that thefe greedy landlords are the very caufers of al the derth in *Dnalgne;* for truly they are worfe than the caterpillers & locufts of Egypt, for they yet left fome thing vndeuoured, thefe nothing; they fpoiled but for a time, thefe for euer: thofe by commandement from God, thefe by commiffion from the diuel.

[1 Sig. E 8] *Landlords are the only caufe o. high prices.*

Landlords are worfe than the Locufts of Egypt.

Theod. How, I pray you, doe thefe iollie fellowes fpend thefe wicked gotten goods?

Amphil. I fhame to thinke, & I blufh to tell you how. For, for the moft part, they fpend it in dicing, carding, bowling, tennife plaieng, in rioting, feafting & banketing, in hauking, hunting, & other the like prophane exercifes. And not onlie vpon thefe things do they fpend their goods (or rather the goods of the poore) but alfo in pride their *Summum gaudium,* & vpon their danfing minions, that minf it ful gingerlie, God wot, tripping like gotes, that an egge would not brek vnder their feet. But herof inough, & more than perchance wil plefe their deinty humors.

They spend their ill-gotten gains in rioting, prophanities, and women.

Theod. Do they exceed in pride of apparel, or are they very temperate, & fober minded people?

As to Apparel,

[2] *Amphil.* They are not onely not inferior to any nation in the world in the exceffe of apparell, but are farre woorfer, if woorfer can be. For the taylers doe nothing elfe but inuent new fafhions, difguifed fhapes, and monftrous formes of apparell euery day. Yea furely I thinke they ftudie more in one day for the inuention of new toies, and ftrange deuifes in apparell, than they doe in feauen yeeres, yea, in all the daies of their life, for the knowledge of Gods word.

[2 Sig. E 8, back]

Tailors inve u new fafhions every day,

Theod. Me thinke then by your reafons it feemeth, that Tailors

II. 1. Tricks of Tailors. Cheating Drapers.

and are the causers of all the monstrous English dress.

are the causers of all that monstrous kind of attire worne in *Dnalgne*, and so consequently are guiltie of all the euill committed by the same.

Amphil. You say very truly. For *Mali alicuius author, ipsius mali, & malorum omnium, quae ex inde orientur, reus erit coram Deo,* The author of any euill, is not onely giltie before God of the euill committed, but also of all the enill which springeth of the same. Therefore I would wish them to beware, and not *Communicare alienis peccatis,* To be partakers of other mens sinnes, for be sure they shall finde inough of their owne to answer for. But so far are they from making conscience hereof, that they heape vp sinne vpon sinne.

[Sig. F 1]
Tailors ask one fourth too much cloth and more lace, for a coat.

For if a man ¹aske them how much cloth, veluet, or silke wil make a cote, a dublet, a cloke, a gowne, hosen, or the like, they must needs haue so much, as they may gaine the best quarter thereof to themselues. So play they with the lace also: for if tenne yards would serue, they must haue twentie; if twentie would serue, they must haue fortie; if fortie woulde serue, they must haue sixtie; if sixtie would serue, they must an hundred, and so forward. Besides that, it must be so drawne out, stretched, and pulled in in the sowing, as they

And they charge too high for making it.

get the best quarter of it that way too. Then must there as much go for the making, as halfe the garment is woorth. Besides this, they are in league, and in fee, with the Drapers and Clothsellers, that if a man come to them to desire them to helpe them to buy a peece of cloth,

They're in league with the Draper, to cheat their customers.

and to bring them where good is, they will straightway conduct them to their feer, and whatsoeuer price hee setteth of the cloth, they persuade the buier it is good, and that it is woorth the money, whereas indeed it is nothing so, nor so. And thus they betwixt them diuide the spoile, and he (the tailor) receiues his wages for his faithfull seruice done. If a man buy a garment of them made, hee shall haue

[² Sig. F 1, back]

it very faire to the eie (therfore it is true: *Omne quod gliscit non ²est aurum,* Euerie faire thing is not the best) but either it shall be lined with filthie baggage, and rotten geare, or else stretched & drawne out vpon the tenter, so as if they once come to wetting, they shrinke almost halfe in halfe, so as it is a shame to see them. Therefore I aduise euery one to see to his garments himselfe, and according to the old prouerbe: *Sit oculus ipsi coquus,* Let his eie be his best cooke, for feare lest he be serued of the same sauce, as manie haue beene to their great hinderance.

II. 1. Great Ruffs worn. Starching-Houses for Ruffs. 35

Theod. I haue heard it faide that they vfe great ruffes in *Dnalgne*: do they continue them ftill as they were woont to doe, or not? — As to *Ruffs*,

Amphil. There is no amendement in any thing that I can fee, neither in one thing nor in other, but euery day woorfer and woorfer, for they not only continue their great ruffes ftill, but alfo vfe them bigger than euer they did. And whereas before they were too bad, now they are paft al fhame & honeftie, yea moft abhominable and deteftable, and fuch as the diuell himfelfe would be afhamed to weare the like. And if it be true, as I heare fay, they haue their ftarching houfes made of purpofe, to that vfe and end only, the better to trimme and dreffe their ruffes to pleafe the diuels eies withall. — men wear bigger ones than ever, such as the Devil himself 'ud be ashamd to put on. They have Starching Houses for Ruffs,

Theod. Haue they ftarching houfes of purpofe made to ftarch in? Now truly that paffes [¹ Sig. F 2] of all that euer I heard. And do they nothing in thofe brothell houfes (ftarching houfes I fhuld fay) but onelie ftarch bands and ruffes?

Amphil. No, nothing elfe, for to that end only were they erected, & therefore now are confecrate to Belzebub and Cerberus, archdiuels of great ruffes.

Theod. Haue they not alfo houfes to fet their ruffes in, to trim them, and to trick them, as well as to ftarch them in? — and *Trimming Houses* too

Amphil. Yea, marry haue they, for either the fame ftarching houfes (I had almoft faid farting houfes) do ferue the turn, or elfe they haue their other chambers and fecret clofets to the fame vfe, wherein they tricke vp thefe cartwheeles of the diuels charet of pride, leading the direct way to the dungeon of hell. — for these Cartwheels of the Devil's chariot.

Amphil. What tooles and inftruments haue they to fet their ruffes withall. For I am perfuaded they cannot fet them artificially inough without fome kind of tooles?

Amphil. Very true: and doe you thinke that they want any thing that might fet forth their diuelrie to the world? In faith fir, no, then the diuell were to blame if he fhould ferue his clients fo, that maintaine his kingdome of pride with fuch diligence as they doe. And therefore I would you wift it, they haue their tooles and inftruments for the purpofe.

²*Theod.* Whereof be they made, I pray you, or howe? [² Sig. F 2, back]

Amphil. They be made of yron and fteele, and fome of braffe kept as bright as filuer, yea, and fome of filuer it felfe; and it is well, — They've metal Tools too,

D 2

36 II. 1. *Putters and Setting-Sticks. Bad Leather.*

like a Squirt or Squib,

calld Putters or Putting-Sticks. Setting-Sticks they have too, for their cursed Ruffs.

if in proceſſe of time they grow not to be gold. The faſhion whereafter they be made, I cannot reſemble to anything ſo well as to a ſquirt, or a ſquibbe, which little children vſed to ſquirt out water withall; and when they come to ſtarching, and ſetting of their ruffes then muſt this inſtrument be heated in the fire, the better to ſtiffen the ruffe. For you know heate will drie and ſtiffen any thing. And if you woulde know the name of this goodly toole, forſooth the deuill hath giuen it to name a putter, or elſe a putting ſticke, as I heare ſay. They haue alſo another inſtrument called a ſetting ſticke, either of wood or bone, and ſometimes of gold and ſiluer, made forked wiſe at both ends, and with this (*Si diis placet*) they ſet their ruffes. But bicauſe this curſed fruit is not yet grown to his full perfection of ripeneſſe, I will therefore at this time ſay no more of it, vntil I here more.

Theod. What is the leather in that country? excellent good, and wel tanned, or but indifferently? I haue heard ſome complaine of it.

[¹ Sig. F 3]

Some Leather is only half tand,

and won't keep out water.

[² Sig. F 3, back]

¹*Amphil.* There is of both ſorts, as of all things elſe; but as there is ſome naught (I can not denie) ſo is there otherſome as good as any is vnder the ſunne. And yet I muſt needes confeſſe, there is great abuſe in the tanners, makers, curriers, and dreſſers of the ſame: for you ſhall haue ſome leather ſcarcely halfe tanned, ſo that within two or three daies or a week wearing (eſpecially if it come in any weat) wil ſtraight-way become browne as a hare backe, and which is more, fleete and run abroad like a diſhclout, and which is moſt of all, will holde out no water, or very little. And the ſaieng is (*Erubeſco dicere*, I ſhame to ſpeake it) that to the ende they may ſaue lyme and barke, and make the ſpeedier returne of their mony, they will take vp their hides before they bee halfe tanned, and make ſale of them. And as herein they are faultie and much to be blamed, ſo in the ſurpriſing of their hides, they are worthie of reprehenſion. For that which they buy for ten ſhillings, they will hardly ſell for twentie ſhillings; that which they buy for twentie ſhillings they will not willingly ſell for fortie ſhillings. And thus by this meanes, they make ſhooes unreaſonable deere.

Theod. Then the fault is not in the ſhoomakers onely, that ſhooes be ſo deere?

²*Amphil.* There is fault inough in them alſo. For whereas the

others inhanfe the price of their hides exceffiuely, thefe felowes racke it very vnconcionably. And yet if the fhooes were good, though deere, it were fomwhat tollerable ; but when they fhall be both naught, and yet deere too, it is too bad, and abhominable. Now if you afke the fhoomakers in whom the fault doth confift, they will anfwere you ftrait, in the tanner. But this is certeine, that as there is a horrible fault in the tanner, fo there is more, or as much in the fhoomaker. For firft of all the fhoomaker liquoreth his leather, with waterifh liquor, kit- then ftuffe, and all kinde of baggage mingled togither. And as though that were not ill inough, they faie they vfe to put falt in the liquor, wherewithall they greafe the leather of purpofe, to the ende that the leather fhal neuer hold out water. And truelie it is verie likelie they doe fo, or fome fuch like thing, for furelie almoft none of their leather will holde out water, nor fcarfelie durt neither. Befides this, it is a worlde to fee how lowfely they fhall be fowed, with hotte alles, and burning threedes, euerie ftitch an inch or two from another, fo as with-in two or three daies you fhall haue them feamerent and all too betorne. And yet as though this were not [1] ill inoughe, they adde more. Sometimes they will fell you calues leather for cow leather, horfe hides for oxe hides, and truelie I thinke rotten fheepe fkins for good fubftantial & dureable ftuffe. And yet fhall a man pay for thefe as well as for better ftuffe. And to the ende they may feeme gaudie to the eie, they muft be ftitched finelie, pincked, cutte, karued, rafed, nickt, and I cannot tell what. And good reafon, for elfe would they neuer be fold. The inwarde foole of the fhooe commonlie fhall be no better than a cattes fkinne, the heeles of the fhooes fhall be little better. And if the fooles be naught (as they be indeede yet muft they be vnderlaied with other peeces of leather, to make them feeme thicke and excellent ftuffe, whereas indeede they are nothing leffe. And to make the fooles ftiffe, and harde, they muft be parched before the fire, and then they are moft excellent fooles, And fuch as will neuer be worne, no, I thinke not in halfe a coopple of daies, which is a woonderfull thing. Oh, farewell former worlde, for I haue hearde my Father faie, and I thinke it moft certeinely true, that a paire of fhooes in thofe daies woulde haue kept a man as drie as a feather, though he had gone in water all the daye thorowe, [2] yea, all the weeke thorow, to the very laft day, and would haue

Shoemakers liquor their leather, and falt it, so that it won't keep out water.

They sow with hot awls and rotten thread [1 Sig. F 4]

They sell you horse-hide for ox-hide, and use cat-skin for inside soles.

They parch the soles too.

Why, in my Father's days, a pair of shoes 'ud keep the wet out, and last a year. [2 Sig. F 4, back]

Of Brokery. Rascally Brokers of clothes, etc.

Margin: Now, they'll hardly last a month.

serued a man almoft a whole yeere togither, with a little repairing. But now fiue or fixe paire, halfe a fcore, yea, twentie paire of fhooes will fcarfely ferue fome a yeere, fuch excellent ftuffe are they made of. But let all fhooemakers, tanners, and the reft, take heed, for at the day of iudgement they fhal render accounts for this their doing. And here-of hitherto.

Theod. Be there any Brokers, or fuch kind of fellowes in your country?

Amphil. If it be a thing that is good, it is a doubt whether it be there, or no, but if it bee naught (as brokerie is) then paft peraduenture it is there.

Margin: Brokers are

Theod. What maner of fellowes are thofe Brokers, for truly their profeffion, and the vfe thereof, is vnknowne to me, saue onely that I haue heard of some of their dealings?

Amphil. Seeing that you are ignorant of this goodly myfterie, and high profeffion of brokerie, and alfo fo defirous to knowe the truth of them, I will in few words (as briefly as I can) declare vnto you the fubftance thereof. Thefe Brokers are iolly fellowes forfooth, and such as in the beginning of their occupation, haue either iuft nothing,

Margin: Jolly fellows

or elfe very little [1] at all, who, when they haue attempted, and affaied

Margin: [1 Sig. F 5] who, not being able to live by anything else,

by all kind of meanes and waies to liue, and cannot by any of them al either any thing thriue, or which is leffe, not fo much as maintaine their poore eftate withall, though but meanly, then fall they into

Margin: make friends with thieves, and buy everything these steal,

acquaintance with loofe, diffolute, and licentious perfons, either men or women, to whom all is fifh that comes to net, and who haue limed fingers, liuing vpon pilfering, and ftealing, and of thefe they buy for little or nothing, whatfoeuer they fhal haue filched from any. And thus by this meanes in proceffe of time, they feather their nefts well inough, and growe (many of them) to great fubftance and wealth.

Theod. Will they buy any thing whatfoeuer commeth to hand?

Amphil. Yea, all things indifferently without any exception. All is good fifh with them that comes to net. They will refufe nothing, whatfoeuer it be, nor whom-foeuer bringeth it, though they be neuer to fufpitious, no, although it be as cleere as the day, that it hath beene purloined by finifter meanes from fome one or other. And can you

Margin: for half its value:

blame them For why? They haue it for halfe it is woorth.

II. 1. *Dunghill Brokers bring men to the Gallows.* 39

Amphil. What wares be they (for the moſt part) which theſe Brokers doe buy and ſell?

[1]*Amphil.* I told you they wil refuſe nothing. But eſpecially they buy remnauts of ſilks, veluets, ſatins, damaſks, grograins, taffeties. laſe, either of ſilke, gold, ſiluer, or any thing elſe that is worth ought Otherſome buy cloakes, hoſen, dublets, hats, caps, coates, ſtockings, & the like. And theſe goodly marchandize, as they haue them good cheape, ſo they will ſel them againe to their no ſmall gaines. [Sig. F 5, back] drapers' and haberdaſhers' goods chiefly.

Theod. If this be true, that they will receiue all, and buy al that comes to hand, than it muſt needes be that this is a great prouocation to many wicked perſons, to filch & ſteale whattſoeuer they can lay their hands vpon, ſeing they may haue ſuch good vent for y^e ſame. Is it not?

Amphil. You ſay very true. And therefore I am perſwaded that this dunghill trade of brokerie newly ſprong vp, & coined in the deuils minting houſe, the ſhoppe of all miſchiefe, hath made many a theefe more than euer would haue bin, & hath brought many a one to a ſhamefull end at Tiburne, & elſe where. Yea, I haue hard priſoners (and not any almoſt but they ſing the ſame ſong) when they haue gone to execution, declaime & crie out againſt brokers. For, ſaid they, 'if brokers had not bin, we had not come to this ſhamefull death; if they would not haue receiued our ſtollen goods, we woulde neuer [2] haue ſtollen them; and if we had not ſtollen them, we had not bin hanged.' This dunghill Brokery's made many thieves, and brought many a man to the Gallows. [2 Sig. F 6]

Theod. Then it ſeemeth by your reaſons, that brokers are in effect acceſſary to the goods felionouſlie ſtolen, & are worthie of the ſame puniſhment *that* the others that ſtale them are worthy of? Brokers ought to be hung with Thieves.

Amphil. They are ſo, if before they buy them they know preciſely that they are ſtolen, & yet notwithſtanding will not onely willingly buy them, but alſo rather animate, than diſanimate them to perſeuere in their wickednes, as this their greedy buieng of their wares doth argue *that* they doe. This maketh many a tailer to aſke more cloth, more ſilk, veluet, & lace, than he nedeth, & all to the ende the broker may haue his ſhare; for, be they neuer ſo litle ſcraps or ſhreds or ſhort ends of lace, or ſmal peces of veluet, ſatan, ſilk or ye like, the broker will giue mony for the*m*, with a wet finger. This maketh many ſeruants to pilfer, filch, & purloin from their maſters, Brokers' willingness to buy. makes Tailors cheat, and servants pilfer.

some a yard or two of veluet, satin, taffety, lace, silk, & what not, some hats, cots, cloks, & the like, & some one thing, some another: this hindereth the merchant man, is discomodious to yᵉ tailer, & beneficial vnto none, but to themselues: & therfore, as they be the seminaries of wickednes, so I besech God, they may be supplanted, except they amend, which I hardly looke for at their hands.

Brokers are seed-beds of villainy.

[¹ Sig. F 6, back]

¹ *Theod.* What woulde you haue them to do, that they may exercise their trade, with good conscience, both before God, and the world?

Amphil. I would wish them to doe thus, which, if they would doe, they might vse their trade in the feare of G O D, both with good conscience before the Lord, with honestie before the world, and finallie to the lesse detriment of the common wealth. First, let them be sure, that the goods which they buy be truely and justly come by of the sellers thereof. And to the end, that herein they may not be decciued, Let them examine the matter strictly, where they had it, whose it is, vpon what occasion they would sel it. And in conclusion not to buy it, vntill they haue gone themselues to the right owners of the goodes, and if they find all things well, that they may with good conscience buy it, let them giue reason for it, else not. And if euerie brooker would deale thus, their would not so many false knaues bring them such lauish of stollen goods, as they do, neither should their trade grow, as it doth, into hatred and contempt.

To deal honestly, Brokers should buy only goods honestly come by,

and should find out the owners themselves.

[² Sig. F 7]

Theod. You saide before (except I be deceiued) that if they know before they buy any wares, that the same is stollen, if they than buy them, they are accessary to the same goods so ² feloniously stollen, & so are worthie of the same punishment, that the principals are woorthie of. I pray you, what punishment is inflicted vpon accessaries in *Dnalgne*.

Amphil. Accessaries are punishable by the lawes of *Dnalgne* with the same punishment that the principals are to be punished withall (for so the lawe standeth); but in the execution thereof, we see the cleane contrarie practised. For when as a theefe, or a fellon stealeth any thing, hee bringeth it to his receiuer, who, though he knowe it to be stolen, yet with alacritie admitteth it into his custodie, and reteineth it, hereby making himselfe accessorie, and guiltie of the felonie committed. And yet notwithstanding when execution is to be done for the same, the principall is (peraduenture) hanged vp, the other that

Brokers get out of the claws of Justice.

II. 1. *Little kindness to the Poor.* 41

is the accefforie is not once fpoken of, nor none can faie 'blacke is his eie.' But howfoeuer it be, I cannot be otherwife perfuaded, but that the receiuers and acceffories are a great deale more woorthie of death (by the penall lawes) than he who ftealeth the thing it felfe, whatfoeuer it be. Bicaufe if they had [not] any to receiue their ftolen goods, they would not fteale at all. And therefore are the receiuers (in my fimple opinion) rather the authors, and the principals (efpecially if ¹they know before they receiue it, that it is ftolen) then they that commit the fact, and being the authors of the euill comitted, they are to be punifhed rather than the perpetrators of the fact it felfe. But for want of due punifhment to be executed as well vppon the one as vppon the other, we fee greeuous crimes, and flagicious facts without all remorfe, or feare of God, daily committed. Good lawes there are, both for the reprefling of thefe, and al other enormities whatfoeuer, but the want of the due execution thereof, is the caufe why all wickednes and mifchiefe dooth reigne and rage euerie where as it doth: God amend it, if it be his good pleafure! And thus much briefly of the noble fcience of brokerie.

Theod. What hofpitalitie is there kept, or reliefe for the poore?

Amphil. Very fmal. For as for the poore tenants and commons, they are not able to maintaine any hofpitalitie, or to giue any thing to the poore, their rents are fo raifed, & their fines fo inhanfed, and yet notwithftanding they minifter (I am perfuaded) more releefe to the poore than the rich & wealthie doe: more poore are fed at their dores than at the rich: more clothed at their hands than at the rich, & more lodged and harboured in their poore houfes, than in the ²rich. But yet can I not denie but that the gentlemen, & others, keepe fumptuous houfes, lufty ports, and great hofpitalitie, but fo as the pore hath the left part thereof, or rather iuft nothing at all. If the poore come to their houfes, their gates be fhut againft them, where they, ftanding³ froft and fnow, haile, wind or raine whatfoeuer, are forced to tary two houres, 3. 4. yea fometimes halfe a day, and then fhal they haue but the refufe, and the very fcraps neither. And well if they haue anything too; in fteed whereof they are fometimes fent to prifon, clapt in irons, manicled, ftocked, and what not. This is the almes that moft men giue.

Marginalia:
But Receivers deserve hanging more than the Thieves they tempt.
[¹ Sig. F 7, back]
Against these, and like evils, we have good Laws, but they're not put in force.
As to *Hofpitality*, the poor can't afford it,
tho in fact they help other poor more than the rich do.
[² Sig. F 8]
Gentlemen keep grand houses, but make poor folk stand for hours in the cold for a few scraps.

³ ?=suffering, putting up with; or is 'in' left out?

II. 1. *Sturdy Beggers should be hung.*

Of Beggers

we have two kinds, the Strong, who won't work;

[¹ Sig. F 8, back]

Drones, who ought to be put in prison till they do *work;)*

and the old, sick, and diseasd.

The Sturdy Beggars who can work, and won't,

I'd just hang.

[² Sig. G 1]

The aged and sick ones I'd have kept in their own parish, and rate richer parishes for em.

Theod. Then it seemeth that the poore are simplie prouided for?

Amphil. They are so indeed, God amend it. And yet I am not so full of foolish pittie that I would haue all kind of beggers indifferently without any exception to be fed and nourished vpon the sweat of other mens browes.

Theod. Doe you make a difference of beggers then? Are there two sorts of them?

Amphil. Yea, there are two sorts. One sort is of stout, strong, lustie, couragious, and valiant beggers, which are able to worke, and will not. These at no hand are not to be relieued (for *qui non operatur non manducet,* ¹saith the apostle, He that will not worke, let him not eat) but are to be compelled to worke, and not to liue vpon other mens labours. For he that releeueth these, maintaineth them in their idlenesse, and taketh awaie the childrens bred, and giueth it to dogs. These are as drone bees, that liue vpon the spoile of the poore bees that labour and toile to get their liuing with the sweat of their faces. If such fellowes as these will not worke, but liue vpon begging, let them be punished and imprisoned till they be content to worke. The other sort of beggers are they that be old, aged, impotent, decrepite or lame, sicke, sore, or diseased: these I would wish should be looked vnto: and these are they that euerie Christian man is bound in conscience to releeue.

Theod. What order would you haue obserued in these respects?

Amphil. The former sort of sturdie valiant beggers, which are able to worke and will not, I would wish them to be compelled to worke, or else not to haue any releefe giuen them. And if they would not work, to punish them; if that will not serue, to hang them vp. But herein I would wish a prouiso, that being content to worke, they might haue maisters prouided them, with reasonable wages, for many would faine ²worke, and can get none; and than if they will not worke, to Tiburne with them. The other sort of beggers, which are either halt, lame, impotent, decrepite, blind, sicke, sore, infirme and diseased, or aged and the like, I woulde wish that they should be maintained, euerie one in his owne parish, at the costs and charges of the same. And if the parish be not able to maintain so manie, then that there should be collections & contributions made in other parishes to supplie their want, and so the former poore people

II. I. *I want an Almshouse in every Parish.* 43

to be maintained therevpon. For wante of which godlie order and conſtitution, there are infinite of the foreſaid perſons that die, ſome in ditches, ſome in holes, ſome in caues and dens, ſome in fields, ſome in one place, ſome in another, rather like dogs than chriſtian people. For notwithſtanding that they be neuer ſo impotent, blind, lame, ſick, old, or aged, yet are they forced to walke the countries from place to place to ſeeke their releeſe at euery mans doore, except they wil ſterue or famiſh at home, ſuch vnmercifulnes is in *Dnalgne*. Yea, in ſuch troups doe they flocke, and in ſuch ſwarmes doe they flow, that you can lightlie go no way, but you ſhall ſee numbers of them at euerie doore, in euerie lane, and in euerie poore caue; and as though this were not extremity inough [1] they driue them from citie to citie, from pariſh to pariſh, from towne to towne, from hundred to hundred, from ſhire to ſhire, and from country to country, like flocks of ſheepe. Here they dare not tarrie for this Iuſtice, nor there for that Iuſtice, here for this man, nor there for that man, without a licence or a paſport, wheras a man woulde thinke their old age, their hoare haires, their blindneſſe, lameneſſe, and other infirmities, ſhoulde bee paſports good inough for them to go abrod withal, if they cannot get releeſe at home. But if the former order, that euery pariſh ſhould maintaine their poore, were taken, then ſhould they neither need to go abroad, nor otherwiſe want their daily releeſe.

Theod. Are there no hoſpitals, ſpittles, lazar houſes, almes houſes, nor the like, for the releeſe of theſe poore people?

Amphil. Yes there are ſome ſuch in cities, townes, and ſome other places, wherein manie poore are releeued, but not the hundred part of thoſe that want. For the ſupplie wherof would God there might be in euerie pariſh an almes houſe erected, that the poore (ſuch as are poore indeede) might be maintained, helped and relieued. For vntill the true poore indeed be better prouided for, let them neuer thinke to pleaſe God. Is it not great pity when a man can paſſe [2] no waie almoſt neither citie nor country, but ſhall haue both halt, blind, lame, old, aged, ſicke, ſore, & diſeaſed, hanging vpon his ſleue, and crauing of releefe? Whereas, if the former order were eſtabliſhed, then ſhould none at al need to go abroad, but al ſhuld haue ſufficient at home. The reformed churches beyond ſeas, and euen the French, Duch, & Italian churches in *Dnalgne* are worthie of great com-

Sidenotes:
Now, many die in the fields like dogs.
They get no relief except by wandering about and begging.
You see poor aged and ſick Beggars at every door; and they're driven from town to town like flocks of sheep.
[1 Sig. G 1, back]
Not a hundredth part can be relieved in our Hospitals.
We want an Almshouse in every Parish,
[2 Sig. G 2]
and then the poor 'ud get enough at home.

44 II. 1. *Our Husbandmen are skilful, but rack-rented.*

The Reformd Churches abroad and the forin ones here, set us a good example in this.

mendations herin, & fhal rife vp at the day of iudgment to our condemnation except we repent & amend our vnmercifulneffe towards the poore. Thefe good churches, folowing the counfel of the almighty who biddeth that there be no begger amongft vs, fuffer neuer a one of their countrymen, nor yet any other dweling in their parifh, to beg or afke almes without his parifh, nor yet in his parifh neither; but by mutual contributions and collections maintaine them, & minifter to their neceffities in all things, Which thing G O D grant the churches of *Dnalgne* may once begin to practife amongft themfelues, that God may be glorified, and the poore members of Chrift Iefus releeued and maintained.

Our Husbandmen, or Farmers, are as skilld as any in the world.

Theod. Be there hufbandmen there & fuch others as manure and till the ground, for the further increafe of fruits, to the maintenance of the commonwealth?

[¹ Sig. G 2, back]

¹*Amphil.* There are of fuch indeed good ftore, and as excellent men in that kinde of exercife, as any be vpon the earth. They know exactly, I warrant you, the times and feafons of the yeere, when euerie kinde of graine is to be fowed, and what ground is beft for euerie kinde of corne. They are not ignorant alfo, howe to culture & dreffe the fame; and if it be barren, what kind of dung is beft to fatten the fame againe. They know the nature, the propertie, and qualitie of euerie foile, and what corne it will bring. They know alfo when the ground is to be tilled, when not, how long it will bring foorth good corne, how long not, when it ought to reft, when not, with all things elfe incident to the fame.

Theod. I thinke they haue good farmes and tenements, that are able to furnifh their ground in this fort, for otherwife they were not able to keepe their oxen, their horfes, their feruants, and other neceffaries, belonging thereto: haue they not fo?

But many have very poor farms,

Amphil. No truely haue they not. For fome haue fuch fatte farmes, and tenements, as either will bring forth no corne at all (in a manner) or if it doe, verie little, and that not without great coft beftowed vpon it. Otherfome haue houfes with no lande belonging to ²them at all, and yet notwithftanding fhall pay a good round fome for the fame alfo. And no marueile, for landlords and gentlemen take all the lands and lyuelode wherevpon there poore tenants fhoulde liue, into their owne hands, and fuffer not the poore hufband-

and others only houses with no land,
[² Sig. G 3]

II. I. Rack-rents. These Hellish Ingraters. 45

men to haue fo much ground as will finde them corne for the maintenance of their poore families, nor which is more, fcarcely to keepe one cow, horfe, or fheepe vpon, for their continuall releefe. Or if they haue any, they fhall pay tenne times fo much as it is worth, to their vtter vndooing for euer. But if landlords would confider that the earth is the Lords, and all that is therein, and that it is theirs, but onely in title, intereft and propertie (hauing their fouereigntie, or chieftie thereof) and the poores in vfe and poffeffion, and if they would remember that the poore ought to liue vpon the earth as well as they, than would they not vfe fuch tirannie, fuch exactions, fuch pooling, and pilling, and the like, as they doe without all compaffion. *or hardly enough to keep a cow on.*

Landlords are so grasping.

Theod. There being fuch ftore of hufbandmen, and the fame fo expert in their agriculture as your words import they be, it muft needes follow, that there is great plentie of corne, and all kinde of other graine, and the fame verie good cheape : is it not fo? *We've lots of Corn,*

[1] *Amphil.* There is great ftore of corne, and all kind of graine, no nation vnder the funne like vnto it; but as I told you before, thorowe the infatiable greedines of a few couetous cormorants, who for their owne priuate commoditie, tranfport ouer feas whole mountaines of corne, it is made fometimes very fcarfe. Other-wife there would be gret ftore at al times. And whereas you fay it is good cheape, it is nothing leffe[2], as euerie daies fucceffe prooueth true. [1 Sig. G 3, back]

but the export of it often makes it scarce.

Theod. How can that be, that there being fuch ftore of corne, yet fhould be deare alfo. *Its dearness comes from*

Amphil. I will tell you. It commeth to paffe three manner of waies. Firft, for that landlords racke their rents fo extreemely, and aduance their fines fo vnreafonably, that the poore man is forced to fell euerie thing deere, otherwife he fhould not be able to pay his landlord his due, whereas if he had his fearme good cheape, he might afforde to fell good cheape. The fecond caufe is (as I haue faid), for that the fame is carried and conueighed ouer Seas. The third caufe is, thorow a forte of ingrators, or foreftallers, who intercept euerie thing before it come at the market, or elfe being come to the market, and hauing mo[3]ney at will, buy vp either all, or the moft part, and carieng it into their celles, and garners at home, keepe it till time of the yeere that corne is fcarfe, and fo confequentlie deere. *1. Rack-rents,*

2. Export over seas,

3. Ingraters or Forestallers buying it up, [3 Sig. G 4] and keeping it till it gets scarce and dear.

[2] It's any thing but that. It's dear.

II. 1. Ingraters' Dodges. Farmers' tricks.

And when there is want of it, then they sell it deere, and when there is plentye, then they make it deerer by buying it vppe in whole heapes as they doe. Thus you see, by this meanes, these hellishe ingratours, and forestallers make corne and all thinges else deere, all times of the yeere. Nowe iudge you what a horrible abuse is this, for one man to buy vppe all things, and that not for anie neede or want in himselfe, but to sell it againe, deerer then they bought it, thereby to inriche himselfe with the impouerishing of many a thousande.

Theod. Is there not punishment for this horrible abuse, for me thinke great inconueniences doe followe it?

Amphil. There be great penalties, and forfaitures ordained, as well for the repressinge of this, as of any other outragious abuse; but they playe with this as with all other good lawes, they inuente quirckes and quiddities, shiftes, and put offes ynough [1] to blinde the eies of the magistrates, and to deliuer themselues (trimly, trimly) from the danger and penaltie of the lawe. For they will say that they buy but for the necessarie prouision of their owne families, and not to sell againe. And then when they doe sell it againe, they will beare you in hande it was of their owne tillage. Or if this way will not serue the turne, then procure they another man to buy it with their owne mony vnder his owne name, and so to sell it againe when hee seeth tyme; but who hath the commoditie, iudge you. But if all these waies faile, then buie they it couertly, and sell it againe as couertly; and thus they buy and sell their owne soules for corruptible monie, which in the last day shall beare witnesse against them, and consume them: yea, as Saint Iames saith: The monie which they haue vniustlie got with the polling and pilling of the poore, shall rise vp in iudgement against them, and the rust thereof shall eate and deuoure their flesh as it were a canker. But let these iollie felowes (as subtil and as politike as they would seeme to be) take heed vnto themselues, and beware: for though they can blinde mens eies, and deceiue their iudgements, yet let them be sure that they can not deceiue the iudgement of the Lord, but he [2]that made the eies shall surely see, and he who knoweth the secrets of all harts, shall one day declare the same to their perpetuall confusion, except they repent.

Theod. What be these husbandmen? honest, plaine dealing and

Sidenotes:
- These hellish Ingraters make everything dear.
- We have laws against Forestallers, but they invent put-offs to dodge the Law. [1 Sig. G 4, back]
- They buy only for their families; they grow all their corn;
- they get a man to buy for em, &c.
- But these jolly fellows
- can't take-in God. He'll expose em. [2 Sig. G 5]
- Husbandmen,

simple persons, and such as in whom there is no abuse; or else fraudulent, deceitfull and craftie persons?

Amphil. They are for the most part verie simple and plaine men in outward appeerance, yea, such as if you sawe them, and heard them talke, you would thinke they had no gall, or that there were nothing in them in the world. But if you looke into their dailie exercises, practises, and deeds, you shall find them as craftie and subtill in their kind, as the deuill is in his, if it be possible. For the simplest of them all, if he make a bargaine with another, he wil be sure to make it so as he himselfe may gaine by it. And it is well, too, if the other though neuer so wise, circumspect, or prouident, be not vtterly decciued (or to speake in plainer termes, cosoned at their hands), such subtiltie, such policie, and such craftie conueiance, they practise vnder the garment of simplicitie. Yea truly, it is growne to be almost their profession to deceiue, defraud, and beguile their brethren, insomuch as they count him a wise man, a worldly [1] felow, and such a one as will liue in the world, that can not deceiue, and beguile men in bargaining. This is their [2] *Columbina simplicitas*, (Nay rather, *Vulpina, et serpentina astutia*) which Christ would haue al his children to practise in all things, all daies of their life. But so farre from this christian simplicitie are many, that their whole life (almost) is nothing else, than a continuall practise of fraud, and deceit, as for example: You shall haue some that, sending corne to the market to be sould, they will put good corne in the top or mouth of the bag, to seeme faire to the eie, and in the bottome of the sacke, very good also (that when it is powred forth of the same, it may yet seeme exceeding good still,) but in the middest shall be neuer a good corne, but such as is mustie, sprouted, and naught. Whereof can be made neither good bread nor drinke, for mans bodie. I haue knowne otherome, that hauing a barren cow, and being desirous to put hir away, haue taken a calfe from another melch cowe, and so folde the former barren cowe with hir adulterate calfe, for a melche cowe, whereas shee was nothing lesse.[3] With infinite the lyke sleights, which for breuities sake I omit.

Theod. I perceiue then it is good for a man to be warie, that deales with these simple [4] fooles?

tho they look so simple,

are as crafty as the Devil himself.

It's almost their business to cheat.

[1 Sig. G 5, back]

Nearly their whole life is a fraud.

They'll put musty corn in the middle of a sack.

They'll sell a barren cow with another cow's calf as if it were hers.

[4 Sig. G 6]

[2] *Orig.* there.   [3] Anything but that. See p. 45; p. 54, l. 2.

48   II. 1. *Sellers to be honest & tell Faults in Goods.*

<small>The Fox may go to school to con.</small>

Amphil. It were good fo indeede, elfe he may chaunce to cough himfelfe a dawe for his labour. For I tell you, the foxe, for all his crafte, may go to fchoole to thefe felowes, to learne the rudiments of deceit and craft. Such fkilfull Doctors are they herein. If they fell you a cow, an oxe, a horfe, or a mare, they will fet the price on him,

<small>They tell lies about the animals they want to sell.</small>

I warrant you, and with-all will proteft and take on woonderfullie, that hee is but this olde, and that olde, this yoongue, and that yoongue. And which is woorft of all, though they knowe a hundred faultes by them, yet will they not reueale anye vnto him that buyeth the fame, which is a playne, and a mainfeft deceite before the LORDE, and one daye fhall be anfwered for, I dare be their warrante.

<small>Every seller ought to tell the buyer the faults of the things he sells.</small>

Theod. Would you haue euerie man to declare to the buyers the faultes and imperfections, which they knowe to be in thofe thinges they fell? then fhould he fell but a little.

Amphil. Euery true chriftian ought to do fo, or elfe, befides that he doth not to others, as he would wifh to be done to (for this is the chaine wherwith euery chriftian is bound to another,) he alfo breketh

<small>[¹ Sig. G 6, back]</small>

the cords of charity, & committeth ¹moft horrible cofonage, and wilful prefumptuous deceit before God, which is a fault punifhable in the iuftice of God, with eternall death, in the lake that burneth with

<small>We should do to others as we wish they'd do to us.</small>

fire and brymeftone for euer. And feing we ought to doe to others as we would wifh to be done vnto vs, let the deceiuer afke of himfelfe when he goeth about to deceiue, thefe queftions: Would I be coofoned? Would I be vndone and fpoiled? Would I count him an honeft man, or a good chriftian, that would fupplant me in bargaining? Oh no. No more ought I to doe to others, that which I would not fhould be done to my felfe. Befides this, confider that the apoftle faith, The Lord is the reuenger of all fuch as deceiue their brethren in bargaining. If they would fall into this or the like confideration, I doubt not, but fraude, deceit, lieng, diffimulation, coofonage, and guile, would be abandoned and put to flight in fhorte time; which God grant.

<small>But we can't live without husbandmen;</small>

Theod. Well, notwithftanding, I cannot fee how we could liue without hufbandmen anie maner of waie, could we?

Amphil. No truly. Neither king, prince, earle, duke, lord, knight, efquire, high nor low, rich nor poore, nor yet any potentate,

<small>[² Sig. G 7]</small>

power or principalitie vpon the earth (how great a mo²narch foeuer)

II. 1. *Chandlers' tricks, and their bad Candles.*

could liue or continue without the vſe of huſbandrie and huſband-men. And therefore they are not only to be beloued of vs, but alſo to be preferred and to be made much of amongſt vs, without whoſe induſtrie and labour no man could liue long vpon the face of the earth. For this cauſe we read the vſe of huſbandry to be commended vnto vs in ſundry places of holy ſcripture ; and which is more, the kingdome of heauen many times to be compared and aſſimiled to the huſbandman for diuers purpoſes and reſpects. And when Adam our firſt parent was expulſed paradiſe, he was by God himſelfe inioined to manure, to dreſſe and till the ground ; whereby we may ſee both the antiquitie, auncientie, and excellencie of huſbandrie, euen from the verie beginning of all things. And therefore doubtles is it to be had in reuerence and eſtimation of all men. But hereof inough.

their labour is needful for our life.

Adam was bidden by God to till the ground.

Theod. Be there any Chandlers there as in other places ?

Chandlers

Amphil. Yea, that there are inow, I warrant you, and more than deale inſtly in euerie reſpect.

Theod. What do they ſell for the moſt part ?

Amphil. Almoſt all things, as namelie butter, cheeſe, fagots, pots, pannes, candles, and a [1] thouſand other trinkets beſides.

ſell cheeſe, pots, pans, and other trinkets.
[¹ Sig. G 7, back

Theod. What be the abuſes which they commit, I pray you ?

Amphil. Abuſes, quoth you ? They dare not commit anie, I trowe. But ſeeing you would ſo faine knowe, I will giue you an inkling of them. Firſt they buy that butter, cheeſe, and other things, which is naught, bicauſe they may haue it for a little monie, and then ſell it for verie good : this, manie a poore prentiſe and other can tell to be true. Or if they buy that which is good, then they either ſell it wonderfull deere, or elſe keepe it till it be paſt the beſt, and yet vtter it for as much and more than it coſt them. Beſides this, that they keepe their butter & cheeſe till it be muſtie and mould, yea, till it ſmell that no man can eate it, they haue alſo their falſe waights & counterfet meaſures to deceiue the poore people withall. And notwithſtanding that they buy ſometimes 2. or 3. fagots for a penie, yet wil they not ſel one, be it neuer ſo litle, vnder a penie, gaining aboue the one halfe in the other. And as for the ſtuffe whereof they make their candles, I am aſhamed to ſpeake of it. For whereas they ſhould make them of good liquor and ſweet, they make them of all kind of kitchen ſtuffe, & other ſtinking baggage, ſo that they ſhal waſte &

They buy bad goods cheap, and ſell em dear.

They have falſe weights and meaſures.

They make their can'les of ſtinking baggage,

consume [1] away like vnto ware against the fire, and yet shall neuer burne cleere, nor giue good light, but run ouer, and about the candle-sticke too shamefully. And as for the wikes within them, they are of hurds, rope ends, & such other good stuffe. Besides all this, they haue sleights to make the liquor of the candles alwaies to remaine soft, to the end it may waste & consume the faster, with legions of the like diuises, God be mercifull vnto vs!

Theod. What say you of the barbers and trimmers of men? are they so neate, and so fine fellowes as they are said to be?

Amphil. There are no finer fellowes vnder the sunne, nor experter in their noble science of barbing than they be. And therefore in the fulnes of their ouerflowing knowledge (oh ingenious heads, and worthie to be dignified with the diademe of follie and vain curiositie) they haue inuented such strange fashions and monstrous maners of cuttings, trimmings, shauings and washings, that you would wonder to see. They haue one maner of cut called the French cut, another the Spanish cut, one the Dutch cut, another the Italian, one the newe cut, another the old, one of the brauado fashion, another of the meane fashion. One a gentlemans cut, another the common cut, one [2] cut of the court, an other of the country, with infinite the like vanities, which I ouerpasse. They haue also other kinds of cuts innumerable; and therefore when you come to be trimed, they will aske you whether you will be cut to looke terrible to your enimie, or amiable to your freend, grime & sterne in countenance, or pleasant & demure (for they haue diuers kinds of cuts for all these purposes, or else they lie.) Then, when they haue done al their feats, it is a world to consider, how their mowchatowes must be preserued and laid out, from one cheke to another, yea, almost from one eare to another, and turned vp like two hornes towards the forehead. Besides that, when they come to the cutting of the haire, what snipping & snapping of the cycers is there, what tricking & toying, and al to tawe out mony, you may be sure. And when they come to washing, oh how gingerly they behaue themselues therein. For then shall your mouth be bossed with the lather, or some that riseth of the balles (for they haue their sweete balles wherewith-all they vse to washe); your eyes closed must be anointed therewith also. Then snap go the fingers, ful brauely, god wot. Thus this tragedy ended, [3] comes in

---

[1] Sig. G 8]

and their wicks of rope-ends.

Barbers:

There are no finer fellows under the sun!

Our Barbers have all kinds of cuts of beards.

[2] Sig. G 8, back]

They ask you whether you'll be trimd to look fierce or pleasant.

Your Moustachios are twisted up like horns; the scissors go snip snap,

your face is washt with sweet balls;

snap go the fingers;
[3] Sig. H 1]

II. 1. *Barbers. Beastliness of long Hair.*

warme clothes, to wipe and dry him withall; next, the eares muſt be picked, and cloſed togither againe artificially forſooth. The haire of the noſtrils cut away, and euery thing done in order comely to behold. The laſt action in this tragedie is the paiment of monie. And leaſt theſe cunning barbers might ſeeme vnconſcionable in aſking much for their paines, they are of ſuch a ſhamefaſt modeſtie, as they will aſke nothing at all, but ſtanding to the curteſie and liberalitie of the giuer, they will receiue all that comes, how much ſoeuer it be, not giuing anie againe, I warrant you: for take a barber with that fault, and ſtrike off his head. No, no, ſuch fellowes are *Raræ aues in terris, nigriſque ſimilimi cygnis,* Rare birds vpon the earth, and as geaſon as blacke ſwans. You ſhall haue alſo your orient perfumes for your noſe, your fragrant waters for your face, wherewith you ſhall bee all to beſprinkled: your muſicke againe, and pleaſant harmonie, ſhall ſound in your eares, and all to tickle the ſame with vaine delight. And in the end your cloke ſhall be bruſhed, and 'God be with you Gentleman!'

Theod. All theſe curious conceits, in my iudgement are rather done for to allure and prouoke the minds of men to be bountifull and [1] liberall towards them, than for any good elſe, which they bring either to the bodie or health of man?

Amphil. True it is that you ſay, and therefore you muſt needes think they are maiſters of their ſcience that can inuent al theſe knacks to get money withall. But yet I muſt needs ſay (theſe niſities ſet apart), barbers are verie neceſſarie, for otherwiſe men ſhould grow verie ougglisom and deformed, and their haire would in proceſſe of time ouergrowe their faces, rather like monſters, than comlie ſober chriſtians. And if it be ſaid that any man may cut off the haire one of another, I anſwer, they may ſo, but yet not in ſuch comelie and decent maner as theſe barbers exerciſed therein can doe, and beſides, they knowe that a decorum in euerie thing is to be obſerued. And therefore I cannot but maruell at the beaſtlineſſe of ſome ruffians (for they are no ſober chriſtians) that will haue their haire to growe ouer their faces like monſters, and ſauage people, nay rather like mad men than otherwiſe, hanging downe ouer their ſhoulders, as womens haire doth: which indeed is an ornament to them, being giuen them as a ſigne of ſubiection, but in man it is a ſhame and reproch, as

warm cloths are brought, your nostril-hair cut,

and then you're to pay 'What you please, Sir.'

You have fragrant waters, and music;

your cloak brushed, and good-bye!

[1] Sig. H 1, back.

Barbers are necessary. Without em men ud look like monsters.

I wonder at the beastliness of some ruffians letting their hair grow so long.

52 II. 1. *Surgeons and Physicians look only to money.*

[¹ Sig. H 2]

the Apoſtle prooueth. And thus much of barbers and their ¹ſcience.

Theod. Haue you ſurgeans, and phyſicians there, as in other places, and are they ſkilfull and expert in their myſterie; and not onelie ſkilfull, but alſo conſcionable in their dealings, as well toward the poore as toward the rich?

Surgeons and *Physicians*

Amphil. There are both ſurgeans and phyſicians, good ſtore. And as they be manie, ſo are they verie vnconſcionable in their dooinges, for, as for both the one and the other, ſo farre from godlineſſe and good conſcience in all things are they, as if a poore man that hath

'll only work for money.

not monie to giue them at their pleaſure, ſtande in need of their helpe, they will either not come at him, or if they doe, they will ſo handle him, as it were better for him to be hanged, than to ſuſtaine

Doctors 'll do nothing for a poor man without money.

the paines that they will put him to. But for the moſt part, neither of them both will come at him, but rather contemne him, and reiect him as a thing of naught, yea, as much will they doe for the diuell himſelfe, as for a poore man, if hee haue not money. And againe, as long as moneye runneth, they will applye gentle and eaſie potions, medicines, and ſalues, bearing their patient in hand, that he ſhall

[² Sig. H 2, back]

recouer without ²all doubt, with what diſeaſe, maladie, or ſore ſoeuer he be infected, wheras in truth they can do nothing leſſe. But

As soon as that fails, they give you the nastiest stuff they can.

Deficiente pecunia, Monie wanting, they applie bitter potions, nipping medicines, gnawing corroſiues, and pinching plaiſtures to greeue their patient withal, therby to ſtraine out what liquor of life (that is, what monie or goods) they are able to giue. And thus they abuſe their gifts, to the diſhonor of God, the hurt of their felow brethren, and their owne damnation, except they repent.

Theod. Are ſurgeans and phiſitians then neceſſarie in a common wealth, as you ſeeme to inferre?

Amphil. Salomon ſaith the Phiſition (by the which worde he vnderſtandeth both the phiſition and the ſurgean, bicauſe the one is cooſin germaine to the other) is to be honored for neceſſitie. And if for neceſſitie, then muſt it needes follow, that the ſame is moſt neceſſarie in a common wealth. But as the good, learned, and

We've many ill-taught doctors.

diſcreet phiſitions and ſurgeans, are neceſſarie, and may doe much good, ſo the vnlearned, and naughtie (as the world is to full of them) may and doe much hurt dailie, as experience teacheth.

II. 1. *Every Ignoramus is allowd to practise Physic.* 53

Theod. You say truth. But are all indifferently suffered to practise the same noble misteries of phisicke and surgerie, without any choyse or exception at all? [¹ Sig. H 3]

Amphil. There is to great libertie permitted herein. For now a daies euerie man, tagge, and ragge, of what insufficiencie soeuer, is suffered to exercise the misterie of phisick, and surgerie, and to minister both the one, and the other, to the diseased, and infirmed persons; but to their woe, you may be sure. Yea, you shall haue some that know not a letter of the booke (so farre are they from being learned, or skilful in the toongs, as they ought to be, that shoulde practise these misteries) both men and women, yoong and old, that, presuming vpon experience forsooth (for that is their greatest skill) will arrogate great knowledge to themselues, and more than the learnedst doctor vpon the earth will doe. And yet notwithstanding, can doe in manner nothing at all. But if they chance at any time to doe any good (as *forte luscus capiat leporem* somtime by chance a blind man may catch a hare) it is by meere chance, and not by any knowledge of theirs. And yet shall this exploit of theirs be founded foorth with a trumpet, which indeede may hardly be blowne vp with an oten pipe, for any praise it deserueth. This bringeth the laudable sciences of phisick and surgerie, into hatred, obloquy, & contempt, ²maketh it of no estimation in the world, and vtterly discrediteth it amon[g]st men. For when as any sick, infirmed, or diseased, either miscarieth vnder the hands of his phisition or surgean, or else when the medicine or salue worketh not his effect, then fall they to accuse the science it selfe, and to reproch it altogither, whereas in truth the whole blame consisteth in the ignorance of the practicioner himselfe. Great pitie it is therefore, that there is such libertie in permitting euery one that lust, to prophane and to abuse these venerable sciences of phisicke and surgerie as they doe. For euery man, though he know not the first principles, grounds or rudiments of his science, y͞e lineaments, dimensions, or compositions of mans body, the poores, arteries, temperament, or constitution, no, nor yet so much as the naturall complexion, qualitie, or disposition of the same, will yet notwithstanding take vpon him the habite, the title, y͞e name, and profession, of a phisition or surgean. This we see verified in a sort of vagarants, who run stragling (I wil not saie roging) ouer the countries,

Any man, tag and rag, can practise both physic and surgery.

If any person makes a cure, he puffs it everywhere.

[² Sig. H 3, back]
If any doctor loses a patient, then the Science is abus'd.

Any Ignorant can set up as a Surgeon or Physician. Vagrant Quacks make a lot of money.

II. 1. Doctors ought to be examind and licenst.

and beare men in hand of gret knowledg, when as there is nothing leſſe in them. By which kind of theft, (for this cooſoning ſhift is no better) they rake in great ſomes of mony, which when they haue got, they leaue their [1] cures in the duſt, I warrant you, and betake them to their heeles as to their beſt refuge. And thus be the noble ſciences of phiſicke and ſurgerie vtterly reproched, the world deluded, and manie a good man and woman brought to their endes, before their time.

[1 Sig. H 4]

Theod. If phiſicke be good, would you not haue euery man to practiſe it that will, without reſtraint?

Amphil. Phiſicke is good, and yet would I not haue euerie ignorant doult that knoweth not the vſe nor benefit thereof, to practiſe the ſame. For that maketh it to take ſo little effect, and ſo ſmally to be eſteemed of, as it is now a daies; (for reformation wherof) I would wiſh that euery ignorant doult, & eſpecially women, that haue as much knowledg in phiſick or ſurgery as hath Iackeanapes, being but ſmatterers in the ſame noble ſciences (nor yet al that), ſhould be reſtrained from the publike vſe therof, yet not from priuate exerciſe thereof either for their owne ſinguler benefit, or any other of their freends (prouided that they do it *gratis*) not making an occupation of it, but rather for deſire to helpe, then for lucre of gaine. Than woulde I wyſhe that the others who ſhoulde exerciſe the vſe of Phiſicke and Surgerie ſhoulde firſt bee Graduates in [2] either of the vniuerſities; and being graduates, yet not to be admitted therefore, but firſt to be tried and examined, as well for their knowledge, diſcretion, and ſufficiencie in their art, profeſſion and calling, as alſo for their godlines, chriſtian zeale, pure religion, compaſſion, and loue to their brethren; and being found ſufficient for the foreſaid reſpects, to be admitted and licenſed, vnder hand and ſeale authentike, by thoſe that be of authoritie. And if he abuſe himſelfe or his facultie, then out with him, let him be *Officiperda*, Iacke out of office, make him a *Quondam*, and let him go to plow and cart, rather than to robbe the poore (as manie of them doe) yea, to murther and kil them without reprehenſion. And as I would wiſh none but godlie, learned, and ſuch as feare God, to be admitted to the exerciſe and practiſe hereof, ſo I would wiſh, that either they might be allowed anual ſtipends, for their better ſuccouring of the poore diſeaſed, or elſe

I'd let no stupid Dolt or Woman practiſe medicine or surgery except *gratis*.

I'd have all doctors Graduates, [2 Sig. H 4, back] examind for character as well as learning,

and then licenst to practiſe; and if they did wrong, out with em!

I'd pay em

1. Doctors' and Apothecaries' tricks. Astrologers.

might be conftrained to take leffe of their poor patients than they doe. For now they ruffle it out in filckes and veluets, with their men attending vpon them, whereas many a poore man (GOD wot) fmarteth for it. Yea, fo vnreafonable, and fo vnconfcionable are they, as fome of them will not fet one foot out of his owne doores, without [1] twentie fhillings, fortie fhillings, three pound, twentie nobles, ten pound, twentie pound, and fome more, fome leffe. And hauing this importable fee, If they minifter anything to the partie difeafed, than befides, muft they haue twenty fhillings, for that that ftands them not in twentie pins; fortie fhillings, twentie nobles, for that that coft them not twentie pence, & fo foreward. This is a great wickednes, God be mercifull vnto vs, and fuch as the Lord will one day reuenge, if they preuent not his iudgements by fpeedy repentance. Befids thefe abufes, there are otherfome, that if they owe euill will to any, man or woman being ficke, or if they hope for any preferment by their deaths, wil not make any confcience of it, to giue them fuch medicines, fuch potions, and drinkes, as will foone make a hand of them; and this fhall be done inuifible in a clowde, Vnder the pretence of phificke, forfooth; and if he die, why it was not the medicine that killed him (no it were *Blafphemia in fanctos ruminare*, blafphemie to thinke it of thefe holie fathers) but it was death, that cruell tyger, that fpareth none. And to fuch corruption are they grown, that for mony I am perfuaded they can make away with any whom they haue acceffe vnto. Therefore I aduife euery man to be carefull to whom [2] he committeth the cure of his bodie. They are likewife in league with the apothecaries, in whome there are great abufes alfo, as well in compounding and mixing of their elements & fimples togither, as alfo in felling chalke for cheefe, one thing for another, & the like, fo as it is hard to get anything of them that is right pure and good of it felfe, but druggie baggage, and fuch counterfait ftuffe as is ftarke naught. But of them inough.

Let vs fpeake a worde or two of a certeine kinde of curious people, and vaineglorious, called aftronomers, and aftrologers, the corruptions and abufes of whom are inexplicable. This done, we will make a final ende at this time of fpeaking any further conferning the abufes, corruptions, and imperfections, of the temporaltie, till occafion of more matter hereafter fhall be offered.

II. 1. *Absurdity of Astronomy and Astrology.*

Theod. These names of astronomers, astrologers, prognosticators, and the like, are so vnquoth and strange to my eares, that I knowe not what to make of them. Wherefore I pray you shewe me as neere as you can, the meaning of them, and what kinde of marchants the professors thereof be?

Amphil. The astronomers, astrologers, prognosticators (and all others of the same societie, and brotherhoode, by what name or title soe¹uer they be called) are a certeine kinde of curious phantasticall and vaineglorious fellowes, who *secreta dei temere remantes,* Searching the secrets of God rashlie, which he would haue kept close from vs, and onely knowne to himselfe, take vpon them, & that vpon these grounds (forsooth), namely, the obseruation of times & seasons, the aspects & coniunctions of the signes and planets, with their occurrents, to presage, to diuine, and prognosticate, what shall come or happen afterwards, as though they sate in Gods lap, knew his secrets, & had the world and the dispofement thereof in their own hands. It is an olde saieng, and verie true, *Quæ supra nos, nihil ad nos,* Those things that are aboue our reach, conferne vs not, and therefore we ought not to enter into the bowels & secrets of the Lord—(for as the wise man saith, *Qui scrutatur absondita dei, obruetur gloria eius,* hee that seacheth out the hidden things of GOD, shall bee ouerwhelmed with the glorye of the same,—but to content our selues with so much as hee hath reuealed vnto us in his sacred worde, committing the euent, the successe, and dispofement of all things else to his sacrede Maiestie, the GOD of all glorie. For to them that goe about, and labour so buselye by speculations, by astronomie, ²astrologie, and the like curious arts to iudge of things to come, and thinke they can tell all things by the same (but *Dum parturiunt montes nascetur ridiculus mus,* whilst the mountains doe trauell, a seely mouse will be brought forth) Christ our sauiour saith, *non est vestrum nosse tempora, & momenta temporum, quæ ipse pater in sua ipsius constituit potestate,* It is not for you to knowe the times and seasons, which the Lord God hath reserued to himselfe. And how much our sauiour Christ disliketh this vaine curiositie, of astronomicall & astrologicall speculations, we may gather by that vehement reprehension or commination in the 16. of Matthew, thundred out against the people of the Iewes, who were, as it seemeth, too much addicted

Marginalia:
and *Prognosticators* are fantasticall fellows. [¹ Sig. H 6]
They affect to foretell things by the stars,
and go poking about into God's secrets
[² Sig. H 6, back]
Christ

to the fame. Where he fharply rebuketh them, and calleth them diffembling hypocrites, in that they obferued and marked with fuch ferious attention and diligence, the elemental fignes & tokens in the firmament, being in the meane time, ignorant of greater things, namely of the fignes and tokens of the fonne of G O D Chrift Jefus, the true Meffias, and fauiour of the world.

rebukes em, and calls em hypocrites.

Theod. Vppon what grounds, certeinties, rules, and principles doth this curious fcience confift?

[1] *Amphil.* It ftandeth vpon nothing elfe, but meere coniectures, fuppofals, likelihoods, gheffes, probabilities, obferuations of times and feafons, coniunctions of fignes, ftarres, and planets, with their afpects, and occurrents, and the like, & not vpon anie certeine ground, knowledge, or truth, either of the word of God, or of natural reafon. But to argue the vntruth and the vncerteintie of this foolifh curious fcience, we need not to go farre for examples and arguments. For the contrariety that euer hath beene in all ages amongft the verie doctors and maifters themfelues, but moft fpecially of late, doth approoue the fame to be moft fantafticall, curious, vaine, vncerten and meere prophane. For there being a maruellous ftrange coniunction (as they faid) of two fuperiour planets, So manie as writ of the fame, neither iumped togither in one truth, nor yet agreed togither, either of the day, houre, or moneth, when it fhould be: but in al things fhewed themfelues like themfelues, that is, plaine contradictorie one to another. Infomuch as they writ in defence of their errors, and confutation of the contrarie, one againft another, fhamefully to behold. By which more than prefumptuous audacitie, and rafh boldneffe of thefe, they brought the world into a woonderfull perplexi[2]tie and ceafe, expecting either a woonderfull alteration of ftates and kingdomes (as thefe foolifh ftarre tooters promifed) or elfe a finall confummation and ouerthrowe of all things. Or if not fo, yet the ftrangeft things fhould happen, that euer were heard or feene fince the beginning of the world. Wheras, God be thanked, at the verie houre and moment when (as fome of them fet downe) thefe woonders and portents fhould haue happened, there was no alteration nor change of any thing feene or heard of, the element being as faire, as bright, as calme, and as pleafant, and euerie thing as filent, and in as perfect order and forme, as euer they were fince the beginning of the world.

[1] Sig. H 7]
Their science is founded only on guesses and star-gazing.

On April 28, 1583 (see Holinshed, 1587, iii. 1356), or some other day that they couldn't agree on,

[2] Sig. H 7, back]
the foolish star-tooters foretold fearful events,

and yet everything passed off quietly as usual.

58 II. 1. *Infinite fooleries, these Astrologers pretend to.*

By all which appeereth the vanitie and vncerteintie of their curious science. I woonder where these fellowes sate, whether vppon the earth, or in the firmament of heauen, when they saw these coniunctions. Or with what eies they could see that, that no man else could see. But peraduenture they haue *Argus* eies, and can see all things, euen those things that be not. I maruell whether they haue dwelt in the region of the aire, and who told them the names, the scituation, the houses, aspects, and locall places of the signes and planets, of the sunne, moone, and starres, with the number [1] thereof also, which indeed are innumerable. I woonder what spirite tolde them which planets were higher than other, and which lower than other, which be good and which be euill, which be moist and which be drie, which bee colde, and which be hote, which be gentle and affable, and which bee cruell and terrible, which giue good fortune, and which giue euill, which be good to take iourneies in hand, or to attempt any great thing, and which bee naught, which bee good for a man to take a wife in, that she may be amiable and gentle, and which be contrarie, which be dangerous to take diseases in, or to fall sicke, and which bee not, with infinite the like fooleries, which I ouerpasse. Now from whence they haue learned these things I cannot tell, but certeine I am, that out of the booke of G O D, they neuer fetched them, the same being in euerie point contrarie vnto them, and reproouing, yea, condemning to hell, their vaine curious searching of Gods secrets, and the successe of things by such fallible and vncerteine accidents.

Theod. Me thinke this is the next way to withdrawe men from G O D the Creator, to depende and hang vpon creatures, is it not?

[2]*Amphil.* It is the onely waie: For who, hearing that the creatures, as the sun, the moone, the starres, the signes & planets doe giue both good things and euill, blessing and cursing, good successe, and euill successe, yea, life and death, at their pleasure (as these brainesick fooles hold they doe) and that they rule, gouerne, and dispose al things whatsoeuer, yea, both the bodies and soules of man (for so some shame not to say) who, hearing this, I say, would not fall from God, and worship the creatures that giue such blessings vnto man? What can be a neerer way to withdrawe the people, not onelie from God, but also to hale them to idolatrie, and wholy to depend vpon creatures as the heathen do to their eternall damnation for euer.

[¹ Sig. H 8]

Where did these astrologing fellows learn all their fooleries? Not in the book of God, I know.

[² Sig. H 8, back]

For if the Planets give good and evil, and rule men,

men 'll turn from God, and worship the stars.

II. 1. *God, and not the Stars, rules Men & their Fates.* 59

But, say they, though we giue authoritie, great power, great rule and gouernement to the creatures, yet we giue vnto God the cheefest stroke and the cheefest rule in all things, all other creatures being but the instrumentall, or secundarie causes, or (that I may speake plainlie) as it were his deputies, substitutes, or instrumentes whereby he ruleth and worketh all things. Is this any thing else, than to saie with certeine heretikes, that though God made all things, yet he ruleth them not, nor hath no care ouer them, but hath committed the rule [1]and gouernement of them to his creatures. Then which, what blasphemie can be greater? is not this a flatte deniall of the prouidence of God, which scripture so much setteth forth and commendeth vnto vs? Shall we thinke that God made all things, and now as one wearie of his worke, committeth the gouernemente of them to other creatures? Saith not our Sauiour Christ, *Pater et ego operamur*, my father worketh, and I worke? Meaning thereby, that as he wrought in creating all things, so he worketh still in ruling them by his power, gouerneing them by his wisdome, and preseruing them by hys prouidence, and will do to the end of the world. But when they haue proued that he hath committed the rule and gouernement of his creatures, to his creatures, then I will saye as they say. In the meane time I say & holde, that it derogateth greatly from the glorie and maiestie of God, to saye or affirme that creatures haue the gouernement of all things committed vnto them. For if there should be many kings, princes and rulers in any one realme or country, must not the dominion and rule of the chief prince or regent be lesser, than if he ruled and gouerned alone? Woe were vs, if wee were at the rule and gouernement of creatures; but blessed be our God, who, as he knoweth our [2]frailtie (hauing therefore compassion of our infirmities) so he ruleth and gouerneth all things, whether in heauen, earth, hell, or else wherfoeuer, according to the good pleasure of his will. In the 1. and 2. chapters of Genesis, besides infinit the like places in holie scriptures, we read that the sun, the moone, the stars, with all creatures else, were created & made for the vse and commoditie of man, being made subiect to him, and he constitute lord ouer them; & yet notwithstanding, are they becom now his lords, and he their subiect, vassal bondslaue? This is preposterous geare, when Gods ordinance is turned topsie turuie, vpside downe. It is time these phantasticall

Side notes:
- To pretend that Planets are God's deputies, is blasphemous nonsense too.
- [1 Sig. I. 1.]
- God works and rules still, as he did at the Creation.
- [2 Sig. I. 1. back]
- God made the stars for the use of man. Who made them his lords?

II. 1. *The 12 Signs governing Men's Limbs.*

These fantastical fellowes turn God into a Jack out of office.

fellowes were looked to in time, that wil go about to difthronize the mightie God Jehoua of his regall throne of maieftie and glorie, makin gan *Officiperda* of him, a iacke out of office, & to pul him (as it were) *E cœlis*, Out of the heauens, downe to the earth, giuing him no power nor authoritie at all.

Theod. Haue the fignes and planets then no power nor authoritie at all vpon things on the earth?

Amphil. Yes, they haue their power, their operation, force, ftrength and effect in thofe things whereto G O D hath created them, as namely in the growing, increafing, cherifhing, foftering, renewing, comforting [¹ Sig. I. 2.] & reuiuing of ¹ all natural things, And alfo they haue their influence & operation in mans bodie, for letting of bloud, receiuing of purgations & the like. But to fay they worke thefe effects of their own proper force & ftrength, or that they rule or difpofe the fpirits & foules of man, is vtterly falfe, & at no hand true. And yet notwithftanding, fo *The busy-headed astronomers assign every kind of man to a particular Sign,* far infatuat are thefe bufie heded aftronomers, & curious ferching aftrologers, that they attribute euery part of mans body to one particular figne & planet, affirming that part of the bodie to be ruled by that figne, or planet. And therefore to Aries they haue affigned the gouernement of the head & face. To Tau[rus] the necke and throte. To Gem[ini] the fhoulders, the armes & the hands. To Leo the hart and back. To Can[cer] the breft, ftomake and lungs. To Lib[ra] the raines and loines. To Vir[go] the guts & bellie. To Scor[pio] the priuie parts & bladder. To Sag[ittarius] the thighes. To Capr[icornus] the knees. To Aqu[arius] the legs. To Pifc[es] the feet. And thus haue they, & doe, beare the world in hand that the whole bodie of man both *Interne & externe*, within & without, *and every month too.* is ruled and gouerned by the xii. fignes, by ftarres, and planets, & not by God only. For the confirmation of which fained vntruth, they pretend the xii. moneths in the yere to be ruled & gouerned by the xii. fignes in the element, and the feuen daies in the weeke *The 7 Days they put to the 7 Planets.* to be ruled by the feuen planets ² alfo. Befides this, they haue their [² Sig. I. 2. back] particular houres, times and feafons, wherein they chiefly worke their effects, and haue greateft ftrength. So that by their reafons, no moneth in the yere, nor day in the weeke, no, nor houre in the day nor night, but it is ruled and gouerned by the influence and conftel-

II. 1. *If the Stars giue Life & Death, they're Gods.* 61

lation of the ftarres and planets, and nothing is effected or brought to paffe, but what they will, and intend.

Theod. Are the fignes and planets, liuing creatures and reafonable, or infenfible creatures, and things without life? <small>But these Signs and Planets</small>

Amphil. They are no liuing or reafonable creatures, it is without all controuerfie, but meerely infenfible, and without life. And being without life and reafon, how is it poffible that they fhould bring life or death (as thefe fellowes hold) ficknefse or health, profperitie or aduerfitie, heate or cold, faire weather or foule, beautie or deformitie, long life or fhort, or any thing elfe? And if they be not able to giue thefe things, how much leffe able are they then, to gouerne, rule, and difpofe all thinge[s] in heauen, earth, the aire, or elfe wherfoeuer, to ouerthrowe monarchies, kingdoms, nations, countries, and people, and finally to work althings after their owne defire and will? Will they [1]haue dumbe and vnreafonable creatures to rule the reafonable? If that were true, why fhould God be praifed either for his mercie, or feared for his iuftice and iudgement, and not rather the planets, fignes, and ftarres, which worke all in all in all creatures? If bleffing come by the influence of ftarres and planets, then let men praife them, and not God, for the fame. And if curfes proceed from the ftarres, let them be feared for them. Briefly, if life and death, and all things elfe, come by the force of the elementall creatures, and celeftiall bodies, then let them be honoured with divine worfhip. If thefe effects iffued from creatures, then why fhould the homicide, the murtherer, adulterer, or wicked perfon be punifhed, wheras he might fay, it was not I, it was *Planetarum iniuria*, The force of the planets that compelled me to finne*? Or why fhould the godlie man be praifed for dooing well, whereas he is inforced thereto, by the ftarres and planets? *In Summa*, why fhould not planets and ftarres be adored and worfhipped as gods, if they coulde worke thefe effects? They that attribute thus much to the ftarres, not onelie rob the maieftie of God of his honour, but alfo ftrenhthen the hands of the heathen, pagans, infidels, and idol-atrous people, to perfeuere in their curfed ido[2]latrie ftill. Nay, do they not rather fhake hands with them, that as they worfhip the

<small>are without life and reason.</small>

<small>How then can they rule the World and Men?</small>

<small>[1 Sig. I. 3.]</small>

<small>If blessings and curses come from the Stars,</small>

<small>they should be worshipt as Gods.</small>

<small>But this robs God of his honour.</small>

<small>[2 Sig. I. 3, back]</small>

---

* Cp. Edmund in *Lear*, I. ii. 134-5: "Drunkards, liars, and adulterers, by an enforced obedience of planetary influence."

62 II. 1. *Absurdity of man's Fate depending on Stars.*

sunne, the moone, the ſtarres, fire, water, and other creatures, for their God, ſo doe theſe worſhip the ſame, though not for their chiefe Gods, yet for their ſecond gods, whereby they commit moſt filthie idolatrie, and are giltie of moſt hainous tranſgreſſion. Indeede, I confeſſe they haue effects and operations, but yet are they not the efficient cauſes of any thing either good or bad. Otherwiſe than thus, that it pleaſeth the maieſtie of God to worke by them, as by his inſtruments, whatſoeuer is his good wyll and pleaſure, and not after any other ſort.

Theod. I haue heard of ſome of theſe aſtronomers that would take vpon them to tell a mans fortune, onely by their conſtellation: forſooth, is it poſſible, ſuppoſe you?

Amphil. No, at no hand. For if it were ſo, that all things were, and man himſelfe, gouerned and ruled by the ſtars alone (as who is ſo forſaken of God to beleeue it?) And that they knew the minds, the purpoſes, the intents, the inclination, the diſpoſition & qualities of euery ſtarre, then might it be (peraduenture) true, that they might tell the fortune, and deſteny of any man. But otherwiſe they can tel as much as a horſe. I would faine learne of theſe ſtarre [1] gaiſers, who teach that man is drawne to good or euill by the conſtellations, and influence of ſtars, whether all the people that were euer borne ſince the beginning of the world, or ſhal be borne to the ende of the ſame, were al borne vnder one planet or ſtar? For they had all one fortune, all ſinned in *Adam*, & all were in the iuſtice of God condemned to euerlaſting fire. I would know alſo whether all the Sodomits and Gomorreans being conſumed with fire & brimſtone from heauen were borne all vnder one ſtarre & planet? For they had all one deſtinie, and all one end. Whether all the whole world in the daies of *Noah*, was borne vnder one and the ſame ſtar, or planet, for they had all one deſtenie, being ouerwhelmed with an vniuerſall deluge. Whether the whole hoſt of *Core, Dathan,* and *Abiram*, were borne all vnder one ſtar or planet, who had al one iudgment, one deſtinie, and one kind of death. Whether all the hoſt of *Pharao* were borne vnder one and the ſame ſtarre and planet, who all ſuſtained one kinde of death, and had all one deſtinie. Whether *Eſau*, and *Iacob* were not borne both in a moment, and both at one birth, and yet had they contrarie natures, qualities, diſ-

---

Marginal notes:

I confeſſe that Stars have effect; but yet they're not Efficient Causes.

Let these stargazers show me, if they can,

[1 Sig. I. 4.]

that all the ſinners in Sodom and Gomorrah, who had one fate, were born under one star;

why Esau and Jacob, who were born under one star, had different ends;

II. I. *The living God alone rules men.* 63

positions and ends. Finally I would learne of them, whither none that euer liued since the ¹first beginning of the worlde, nor any that shall be borne to the end of the same, hath not, or may not be borne in the same houre, and vnder the same planet & constellation, that Christ Iesus was borne in. If they say there haue not beene any borne in the same houre that Christ Iesus was borne in, common reason, and daily experience would disprooue them, for there is not one minute of an houre wherein there are not infinite children borne into the world. And if they say that there are that haue beene borne in the same houre, and vnder the same starre and planet, than must it needes follow (if man should necessarily be ruled, gouerned, disposed & affected according to the naturall disposition, and inclination of the planets & stars) that he that hath bin, is, or shall be, borne in the same howre, and vnder the same planet or star that Iesus Christ was borne vnder, should bee as good & as perfect in euery respect, as Christ Iesus himselfe; and so should we haue had manie chrifts before this time. But God blesse all his children from once thinking of any such impietie, and blasphemie. By all which reasons and arguments it apeareth manifestly that man is nothing lesse, than ruled, gouerned or destined, after the inclination, or influence of stars or planets, but onely by the liuing God, who doeth ²whatsoeuer pleaseth him in heauen & in earth. This being so, twise vnhappy be those parents that thinke any moneth, day or houre, infortunate for their children to be borne in, or that some be more fortunate and happie than otherfome. And thrise cursed be those wicked deuils, that taught them those lessons. What? Doe they thinke that the Lorde is asleepe those houres; or being wake, hath no power to rule? Hath he not made all things pure and good? Then cannot the good creatures of God make vs euil, or incline vs to sinne. But it is the malice of the deuill, the corruption of our nature, and the wickednes of our owne harts, that draweth vs to euill, and so to shamefull destinies, and imfamous ends, and not the starres, or planets. Whereof if we were truely perswaded, we wold leaue of, when we come to any shamefull end, to saie: "Oh, I was borne to it, it was my destonie," and I cannot tell what: whereas in truth we were borne to no such ends. But rather to glorifie our heauenly father by integritie of life & godlines of conuersation, whilst we liue vpon the face of the earth. Certein

[¹ Sig. I. 4. back]

why the children born when Christ was, were not like him.

Man is not swayd by Stars, but by the living God.
[² Sig. I 5]

It's the Devil and our own wickedness, and not planets, that make us sin. (Cf. Edmund in *Lear* I. ii.)

64 II. 1. *Folly of the Zodiacal Signs influencing men.*

Tho God sees that some men will come to a bad end, he doesn't fore-ordain them to it. [¹ Sig. I 5, back]

it is, that God by his prouidence, & prescience, doth foresee that such a man through his wickednes shall come to such an ende, yet did not the Lord foreordeine, or foreappoint him to the same, ¹but rather dehorteth him from comitting that wickednes, which may purchase such an end. Wherefore to conclude. Seing it is sinne that bringeth man and woman to shamefull ends, and neither fate, destonie, birth-star, signe or planet, constellation, nor anything else whatsoeuer, let euerie one endeuour himselfe to serue his GOD truelie, in singlenesse and purenesse of heart, and himselfe to liue well and vprightlie,

Serve God, and

Walking in the lawes, and commaundements of the Lord; and I warrant him for euer comming to anie euill end or destinie. That

He'll preserve you.

God whom he hath serued, will keepe him as he kept *Sidrach*, *Misaac*, and *Abednago*, from the rage of the fire, *Susanna* from the stake, *Daniel* from yᵉ chawes of the greedie lions, & manie others that serued him in feare.

Theod. I haue hea[r]d some that woulde take vpon them to tell a man whither he shoulde be poore or rich, a seruant or a lord, a theefe or a true man, cruell or gentle, and what kinde of trades he should haue prosperous successe in: how shoulde they doe this?

Amphil. I will tell you how they pretende to doe it. There are

Some say that the 12 Signs of the Zodiac and the 7 Planets and their Aspects fix men's natures and fates. [² Sig. I 6]

(as they saye) certeine signes in the element (but yet I maruell what *Apollo* tolde them so, when they were there, and sawe them, or how they knew the shape ²and proportion of them) as Aries, Taurus, Gemini, Cancer, Leo, Virgo, Libra, Scorpio, Sagittarius, Capricornus, and Pisces, with their planets, and aspects, as Sol, Luna, Mars, Mercurie, Iupiter, Venus, and Saturne. Now say they, he that is borne vnder Aries, (which is a signe in the *Nusquam region*, Like to a ramme, or sheepe vpon earth) shall be a riche man. and too too wealthie. And whie so? Marke their droonken reason. Forsooth

But what a drunken reason they give for it!

because the rame is a fruitfull beast vpon earth, and yeldeth to his master two or three fleeces a yeere. Againe, he that is borne vnder Taurus (which is a signe (say these liers) in the element like vnto a bull, vpon earth); now sir, he that is borne vnder him, shall be pore,

Because a Bull is a yoke-beast here, therefore a man borne under him shall be a bond-slave!

& a bondslaue all his daies. And why so? Mary, say they, bicause the bull on earth is a beast vsed to the yoke, and to much slauerie & drudgery. He that is borne vnder Leo (which is a signe quoth these iuglers like to a lion) shal be strong, couragious, & feared of

II. 1. *Folly of the Zodiacal Signs influencing men.*

al men, & fhal be lord & ruler ouer many, And why fo? Bicaufe the lion is a ftrong & mightie beaft, & is lord & king ouer all other beafts. He that is borne vnder Scorpio, fhal be a murtherer, a robber, a theefe, and a wicked perfon. Why fo? Forfooth bicaufe the Scorpion is a serpent full of poyfon & malice vpon earth. [1]He [[1] Sig. I 6, back] that is borne vnder Gemini fhall be rich, and haue manie children, bicaufe Gemini is a figne of two twinnes. He that is borne vnder Virgo fhall be beloued of women, fhall be amiable, faire, gentle, and I cannot tell what, bicaufe maids are fo affected. He that is borne vnder Cancer, fhall be crabbed and angrie, bicaufe the crab fifh is fo inclined. He that is borne vnder Libra, fhall be fortunate in merchan-dize, in waights and meafures, bicaufe Libra is a figne of a paire of ballance. He that is borne vnder Sagittarius, fhal be a good fhooter, bicaufe Sagittarius is a figne like to a fhooter. He that is borne vnder *He that's borne under Capricorn* Capricornus fhall be a flouenly, ill fauoured, and vncleane fellowe, *shall be un-cleanly, because* bicaufe the gote is a beaft filthie, ftinking and vncleane. He that is *the goat's a stink-* borne vnder Aquarius and Pifces fhall be fortunate by water, bicaufe *ing beast!* watermen haunt the waters, and fifhes fwim in the fame. Thefe be cupftantiall reafons and well feafoned arguments, and as ftrong to prooue their purpofe, as a caftell of paper to refift the enimie. Thus you may fee they haue no other reafons, than to heape one lie vpon another. As firft that thefe figues and planets in the heauens are like to earthly creatures, then that their natures, and qualities are knowne by the natures and qualities of [2]earthly creatures. Iefu God, what cun- [[2] Sig. I 7] ning felowes are thefe, that can knowe the nature of heauenly bodies, and celeftiall creatures, by thefe terreftriall bodies and earthly crea-tures? Thefe are profound fellowes indeed, and by all likelihood, *These Astrologer fellows must* haue dwelt long in the clouds, that are fo perfect in euery thing there, *have livd long in the clouds to* and can iudge of future accidents with fuch fingular dexteritie. By *know so much about heavenly* this time I thinke they are afhamed of their profeffion, therefore I *bodies.* need to fay no more of them, till further occafion be offered, befeech-ing the Lorde God to giue them grace to fearch for the truth of the worde of God, letting all fuch curious fearchings of Gods fecrets alone to God, who onely knoweth all fecrets whatfoeuer.

Theod. If you condemne aftronomie, and aftrologie altogither, as *Prognosticators* you feeme to doe, then it followeth that you condemne prognofti- *and Almanac-makers I con-* cators, and fuch as make almanacks for euerie yeere: doe you fo? *demn too.*

II. 1. *Against Prognosticators & Almanac-makers.*

Amphil. I neither condemne aftronomie nor aftrologie, nor yet the makers of prognoftications, or almanacks for the yeere. But I condemne the abufe in them both, and wifh they were reduced to the fame perfection that they ought, and to be vfed to the fame endes and purpofes which they were ordeined for. [1]The funne, the moone, the ftarres, and the celeftiall bodies whatfoeuer, created by the Lord not onelie to fructifie and increafe the earth by their influence, but alfo to fhine and giue light to man in this life, and to diuide the light from darknefe, the day from the night, winter from fommer, and to diftinguifh one feafon and time from another. Now how much may make or conduce to the knowledge hereof, fo much I doubt not is verie tollerable, and may be vfed. But when we go about to enter into Gods fecrets, and to diuine of things to come, by coniectures, and geffes, then make we the fame wicked and vnlawfull. Therefore prognofticators are herein much to be blamed, for that they take vpon them to forefhew what things fhall be plentie, and what fcarfe, what deere, what good cheape. When fhal be faire weather, when foule, and the like, whereas indeede the knowledge of thefe things are hid in the fecrets of GOD, and are beyond their reach, therefore ought they not to meddle with them. But if they would keepe them within their compaffe, as namely to fhew the times and feafons of the yere, feftiuals, vigils, to diftinguifh winter from fommer, fpring from harueft, the change of the moone, the fall of euerie day, the ecclipfes, epacts, dominical letter, golden num[2]ber, circle of the funne, leape yeere, and other the like neceffarie points, then were their profeffion laudable, and greatly for the commoditie of the commonwealth. And thus much with their patience be it fpoken briefly hereof.

Here ende the abufes of the
Temporalitie.

Marginalia:
- [1 Sig. I 7, back]
- when they pretend to pry into God's secrets,
- and foretell what 'll be plentiful and what scarce.
- Let Almanac-makers keep to their proper business,
- [2 Sig. I 8]
- and then they'll be useful folk.

THE CORRVPTIONS

AND ABUSES OF THE

SPIRITVALITIE.

Theodorus.

Auing now spoken sufficiently of the corruptions and abuses of the temporalitie, if I might be so bold, I would request you somewhat to say concerning the corruptions and abuses of the spiritualitie, or (as some call it) of the ecclesiasticall hierarchie. For I am fully persuaded, that the one being so corrupt, the other can hardly bee without blemish.

<small>As to the corruptions of the Ecclesiastical Hierarchy,</small>

[1] *Amphil.* I am verie loth to enter into that fielde, the view whereof offereth such store of matter to intreat of, as if I shoulde enter the same, I shoulde rather not knowe where to end, then where to begin. Besides, you knowe the olde prouerbe, *Non bonum est ludere cum sanctis*, It is not good to meddle with these holie ones, for feare of thunderbolts, to insue. But for that, he is not onely a false prophet, and a traitor to the truth, that teacheth false doctrine, but as well he that knoweth the truth, and either for feare of death, or desire of life, wil not expresse the same to the worlde. And for that, not onely the author of any euill or mischiefe is giltie of offence before God, But also he that might by [2] discouerie thereof preuent the same, and yet either will not, or for feare of death dares not. And for that as the olde prouerbe saith, *Qui tacet, confentire videtur*, he that concealeth the truth, seemeth to consent to errors, for these and the like causes, I will laye downe vnto you some such corruptions and abuses, as seeme to be inormous, and staude in neede of reformation, omitting in the meane time to speake perticulary of all (for that they be innumerable) vntill I see how these fewe will be brouked of them.

<small>[1 Sig. I 8, back]</small>

<small>let the meddler with them look out for thunderbolts.</small>

<small>But I'll tell you some of our worst Abuses in the Church.</small>

<small>[2] *Orig.* vy</small>

II. 2. *All Churches are markt off into Parishes.*

[¹ Sig. K. 1.]

For it is a point of good phyficke, you knowe, to fee how the former ¹meate receiued into the ftomacke, will be digefted, and concocted, before we receiue anye more into the fame.

Theod. You fay very well. Giue me leaue then (by your patience) to afke you fuch queftions as I thinke conuenient for my further inftruction, that by your good meanes, I knowing the truth, may praife God in you, and alfo haue iuft occafion to giue you thanks for the fame.

Amphil. Afke what you thinke good, in Gods name, and I will doe the beft I can, to refolue you in anything that you fhall demand.

All our churches and congregations

Theod. Then this fhall be my firft demand. Be the churches, congregations, & affemblies there, diftincted into particulars, as into parifhes and precincts, one exempt from another, or are they difperfed here and there abroad, without any order, exemption, or limitation of place at all?

are divided into parifhes,

Amphil. Euerie particular church, congregation, affemblie, or conuenticle, is diuided one from another, and diftincted into parifhes and precincts, which feuerall precincts and parifhes are fo circumgired and limited about with bounds and marks, as euerie one is knowne of what parifh he is, and vnder whofe charge he liueth. So that

[² Sig. K. 1. back]
so that every flock knows its pastor.

euerie fhepheard knoweth ²his flocke, euerie paftor his fheepe. And againe, euerie flocke knoweth his fhepheard, and euerie fheepe his paftor, verie orderlie and well, in my fimple iudgement.

Theod. Doe you allow then of this partition of churches, and of one particular congregation from another?

Amphil. Yea trulie. It is not amiffe, but a verie good order, for thereby euerie paftor doth knowe his owne flock, euery fhepheard his owne fheepe, which without this diuifion could not be. Befides that,

In early days,.

we read that euen in the apoftles daies (who writ to particular churches themfelues, as to the Rom. Corint. Thes. Phil. &c.) in the daies of Chrift, & in the times of the prophets before Chrift, churches,

assemblies were always separate.

affemblies, and congregations were euer diftincted one from another, & diuided into feuerall flocks, companies, and charges. So that although they had not the name of this word 'parifh' amongft them, yet had the thing ment thereby, in effect.

Theod. Then it followeth by your reafon, that there are infinite churches in *Dnalgne*; and I haue learned out of the book of God

II. 2. Of Churches, The Church, and their Rulers. 69

that there is but one true church, and faithful spouse of Christ vpon the earth. How reconcile you these two places?

Amphil. Verie well. For although there be [1]infinite particular churches, congregations, and assemblies in the world, yet doe they all make but one true church of God, which being diuided in time and place, is notwithstanding one church before God, being members of the mystical body of Christ Iesus, & felow members one of another, so as they can neuer be diuided, neither from themselues, nor from their head, Christ.

[1] Sig. K. 2.] But these separate churches all make up One true Church,

Theod. Who doe you constitute the head of the vniuersall church of Christ vppon earth? Christ Iesus, the pope, or the prince?

Amphil. Christ Iesus, whose the bodie is, must needs be, & is the onely true head of the vniuersall church. Then next vnder him euerie christian prince in his kingdom. And as for the pope, he is head ouer the malignant church, the church of the deuil, and not of Christ Iesus. No, he is so far from being head ouer the vniuersal church of Christ, that he is no true member of the same, but rather the childe of perdition, the first borne of satan, a diuell incarnate, and that man of sin (euen Antichrist himselfe) that must be destroied with the breath of Gods mouth.

whose Head is Christ: under Him each King in his kingdom;

[The Pope's the head of the Devil's Church

Theod. By whom be these particular churches and congregations gouerned & ruled?

Amphil. By bishops, pastors, and other inferiour officers.

and under them Bishops, Pastors, &c.,

Theod. Do you shut out the prince then from gouerning the church?

[2]*Amphil.* No, God forbid. For take awaye *Brachium seculare*, The lawfull power, and gouernement of the temporal magistrate from the regiment of the church, and ouerthrow the church altogither. And yet notwithstanding the necessitie hereof, the dooting anabaptists and brainesicke papists haue most deuilishly denied the same. The anabaptists denie (most absurdly) the authoritie of the magistrate altogither. The papists seing themselues conuinced by the manifest worde of GOD, denye not their authority absolutely; but that their authority extendeth to the gouernement of the church, forsooth they vtterly denie, hereby exempting themselues, and plucking away their neckes from vnder the yooke of christian obedience due vnto

[2] Sig. K. 2. back] and temporal Magistrates.

The Anabaptists deny the temporal power altogether; the Papists deny it extending to Church Government.

magistrates[1], contrarie to the expresse word of our sauiour Christ, and his apostles, who saith *Omnis anima subdita sit potestatibus supereminentibus!* Let euery soule be subiect to the higher powers, for there is no power but of God. And therefore they are to be obeyed as the ministers of God of all whatsoeuer.

Theod. Well than I gather thus much, that euery king, prince, or potentate, is supreame head next vnder God, ouer the church of GOD dispersed through his kingdomes, and domini[2]ons: is not this true?

Amphil. Verie true. And therefore that antichrist of Rome, hath plaide the traitor a long while, both to Christ Iesus and all christian kings, in arrogating and vsurping to be supreame head ouer all the world. Whereas indeed he, being a greasie priest, & smered prelate, hath no more authority than other oiled shauelings haue, nor so much neither, and yet that authoritie is but ouer the malignant church of antichrist, and not of Christ Iesus. I beseech the Lord therefore to breake of that power, to grind in peces that stumbling blocke of offence, and to wipe off the heads of that monstrous hidra, so as neuer any mo may growe thereof againe.

Theod. Seeing you say that euerie prince is supreame head ouer the church of God within his dominions, what authoritie therfore assign you to the prince to execute in the church.

Amphil. It is the office and dutie of a prince, not onely to see elected, sent forth, & called, good, able, & sufficient pastours, for the instruction of the church, but also to see that good orders, constitutions & rites be established, and duely performed, that the worde be preached, the sacraments truely ministred, excommunication, discipline and ecclesiasticall censures orderly [3]executed to the honor of God, and benefit of his church. But if it be said that these thinges are to bee executed of the ecclesiasticall persons onely, I answere, true it is; but if the ecclesiasticall magistrate be negligent, secure, slouthfull, and carelesse about the execution hereof (as who seeth not some be) than ought the prince to shew his authoritie in commanding and inioining them to doe their office. Besides this, it is the office of the prince to see all kind of sinne, as well in the church men themselues, as in all others of the church, seuerely punished.

[1] *Orig.* migistrates.

II. 2. *Of the King, Papal Antichrist, and Bishops.* 71

And though I grant the prince to haue the soueraigntie and primacie ouer the church of GOD, within his dominions, yet my meaning is not, that it is lawfull for the prince to preach the word, to minister the sacramentes, or to execute the sentence of excommunication, and other ecclesiasticall discipline and censures of the church, but (as before) to see them done, of them to whom it apperteineth. For saith the apostle, *nemo sumat sibi honorem, nisi qui legittime vocatus fuerit, vt fuit Aaron.* And againe, *vnusquisque in ea vocatione, qua vocatus est, maneat apud deum?* But in times past the papists bare the worlde in hande, that no temporall power whatsoeuer coulde, nor ought not, to [1]meddle wyth the clergie, and therefore made they vassals of most christian Princes. Yea, that pernicious antichrist of Rome, in those daies of ignorance hath not beene ashamed to make Kings, Queenes, Emperours, Dukes, Lords, and all other, how honorable or noble soeuer, his lackeis, his pages, his horsekeepers, and compelled them to hold his stirups, to leade his horse, and to prostrate themselues before him, whilest he trod vpon their neckes. But God be praised, this great antichrist is discouered to all the world, and his shame so laid open, as euery childe iustlie laugheth him to scorne.

and the Church's orders carried out.

[1 Sig. K. 4.]

The Antichrist of Rome formerly had kings as lackeys,

but his shame is laid open now.

Theod. You said before, that the churches there were gouerned by bishops, and pastors: how by them?

Amphil. The bishops are graue, ancient, and fatherlie men, of great grauitie, learning, and iudgement (for the most part) constituted by the Prince ouer a whole country or prouince, which they call their dioces. These graue fathers hauing authoritie aboue all other of the ministerie, in their dioces, do substitute vnder them in euerie particular church a minister, or ministers according to the necessitie of the same. And thus doeth euery bishoppe in hys owne dioces thorow out the [2]whole realme. So that no church, how small soeuer, but it hath the truth of Gods word, and of his sacraments, truly deliuered vnto it.

The Bishops are grave and learned men, set over Dioceses.

[2 Sig. K 4. back]

Theod. Are those preaching prelates, that the bishops do place in euerie congregation, or else reading ministers?

Amphil. It were to be wished that all were preaching prelates, and not reading ministers only, if it could be brought to passe, but though all be not preachers, yet the most part be, God be praised therefore.

All our ministers don't preach, some read only.

Theod. Be any, readers onlie, and not preachers: that is a great abuse. For I am persuaded that he that cannot preach, ought not to supplie a place in the church of God to read onlie: how say you?

Amphil. It is no good reason to say, bicause all ought to be preachers, that therefore readers are not necessarie. But indeed I am of this iudgement with you, that whoso can but read onelie, and neither is able to interpret, preach, expound, nor explane the scriptures, nor yet to refell and conuince the aduersarie, nor to deliuer the true sense and meaning of the scriptures, ought not to occupie a place in the church of God, as the pastor thereof. For God commandeth that the pastors be learned, saieng: *Labia sacerdotum custodiant veritatem, and edijcant populi verbum dei ex ore eorum*, Let the lips of the priests preserue knowledge, and let the people learne the truth out of their mouthes. And therefore those that haue not this dexteritie in handling the worde of God, they are not sent of God, neither are they Christs vicegerents or pastors to instruct his flocke. To such, the Lord saith: They rule, but not by me; they run, but I sent them not; they crie, thus saith the Lord, whereas hee neuer spake it. These are those idoll shepheards, and dumbe dogs, of whom speaketh the prophet, that are not able to barke against sinne. And therefore I beseech the Lord to remooue them, and place able and sufficient pastors ouer his church, that G O D may be glorified, and the church edified in the truth.

Theod. Bare reading, I must needs say, is bare feeding: but what then? Better it is to haue bare feeding than none at all.

Amphil. Verie true. And therefore are not they more scrupulous than they ought, more curious than needes, and more precise than wise, that bicause they cannot haue preaching in euerie church, doe therefore contemne reading as not necessarie? This is as though a man should despise meane fare, bicause he cannot come by better, whereas I thinke it is [2]better to haue meane fare than none at all, or as though a man, bicause he cannot come by the carnell at the first, will therefore cast awaie both the nut and the carnell. It were good (as saith the apostle) that all could prophesie, that is, that all could preach and expound the truth, but bicause that al haue not the gift, is therefore reading naught? And therefore a sort of nouatians lately sprong vp, haue greatly faulted herein, in that they hold that no reading ministers only ought to be permitted in the church of God, as though

II. 2. *The best men don't get Preferment.* 73

(as I say) becaufe a man can not haue daintie fare, therefore it is good to haue none at all. But to be plaine, as I will not defende a dumbe reading ministerie only, fo I will not condemne it for necessities fake, when otherwife euery place cannot be sufficiently furnifhed at the firft with good and sufficient men as it ought. *[marginal: Keep your Reading Ministers till you can get Preaching ones.]*

Theod. But it is thought that there are inow able men in the vniuerfities and elfewhere to furnifh euery particular church with a preaching minister?

Amphil. Truely I thinke there are fo, if they were fought for & preferred: but alas thofe that are learned indeed, they are not fought for nor promoted, but the vnlearned for the moft part, fomtimes by frendfhip, fomtime by mony [1] (for they pay wel for their orders, I heare fay) and fomtimes by gifts, (I dare not fay bribes) are intruded. This maketh many a good fcholar to languifh, and difcourageth not a fewe from goyng to their bookes. Whereby learning greatlie decaieth, and barbarifme, I feare me, will ouerflow the realme, if fpeedie remedie be not had herein. *[marginal: We've enough learned men, but, alas they don't get Preferment.] [1 Sig. K 6]*

Theod. As farre as I can gather by your fpeeches, there is both a reading and a preaching ministerie: whether doe you prefer before the other?

Amphil. I preferre the preaching ministerie before a reading ministerie only: and yet the reading ministerie, if the other can not be had, is not therefore euill, or not neceffarie.

Theod. But tell me this. If there might a preaching ministerie be gotten, ought not the reading ministerie to giue place to the fame?

Amphil. Yea, doubtleffe. And therefore the bifhops ought to feeke for the learned fort, and as it were to fue and make inftance to them, and finding them worthy, as well for their life as doctrine, to call them lawfully according to the prefcript of Gods word, & fo to fende them forth into the Lords harueft. And where the forefaide dumbe ministerie is, to difplace the fame, and place the other. By this meanes [2] the word of God fhould flourifh, ignorance (mauger the head of fatan) be abandoned, the church edified, and manie a one incouraged to go to their bookes, whereas now they practife nothing leffe, and all by reafon that by their learning they haue no promotion nor preferment at all. *[marginal: Bishops ought to seek out learned Ministers.] [2 Sig. K 6, back]*

Theod. Do these preaching ministers preach onely in their owne cures, flockes and charges, or else indifferently abroad else where?

Amphil. They preach for the most part in their owne charges and cures whereouer the holie Ghost hath made them ouerseers, and for which they shall render a dreadfull account at the day of iudgement, if they doe not their dutie diligently, as God hath commanded. But though they preach most commonly in their owne cures, yet doe they sometimes helpe their felowe brethren to breake the bread of life to their charges also. Wherein me thinke they do not amisse. For if a watch man appointed by a whole citie, or towne to giue warning when the enimie commeth, seeing an other citye or towne to be in danger, giueth sufficient warning to his owne citie, and goeth and warneth the other citie also, and so by this meanes deliuereth them both, I say, that in so doing, hee doth well, and according to charitie. And yet [1]notwithstanding, diuers new phangled felows sprong vp of late, as the Brownists, and there adherents, haue spoken verie blasphemouslie hereof, teaching in their railing pamphletes, that those who are lecturers or preach els wher than in their owne cures are accursed before god. Than the which, what can be more absurdlie, or vntruely spoken? For if they grant (as they cannot deny) that the word of God is good, then cannot the declaration of that which is good in one place, be hurtfull in another. And read we not that the apostles themselues went from place to place, preaching the word to euerie congregation? Christ Iesus did the same, & also taught vs, that he came not to preach to one citie onely, but to many?

Theod. Doe the reading ministers onely continue and read altogither in their owne charges, or not?

Amphil. The reading ministers, after they be hired of the parishes (for they are mercenaries) they read commonly in their owne charges, and cures, and except (which is a horrible abuse) that they haue two or three cures to serue, all vpon one day, and peraduenture two or three myles distant, one from another. Which maketh them to gallop it ouer as fast as they can, and to chop it vp with all possible expediti[2]on, though none vnderstand them, and as fewe be edified by them.

Theod. Be these reading ministers well prouided for, so as they want nothing, or not?

II. 2. Bad Pay and Pluralism of Reading Ministers. 75

Amphil. No truly. For if the other preaching ministers be not well prouided for (as in truth they be not) then how can the other be well maintained? And therfore they haue, som of them ten pound a yeere (which is the most), some eight pound, some fixe pound, some fiue pound, some foure pound, some fortie shillings; yea, and table themselues also of the same. And sometimes failing of this too, they runne roging like vagarents vp & downe the countries like maisterlesse men, to seeke their maintenance. Whereby some fall to one mischiefe, some to another, to the great slander of the Gospell of Iesus Christ, and scandall of the godlie. And yet part of these reading misters be too well prouided for, for some of them haue two or three, yea foure or fiue benefices apeece, being resident but at one of them at once, and peraduenture at neuer a one, but roist it out elsewhere, purchasing a dispensation for their discontinuance, and then may no man say: *Domine, cur ita facis?* Sir, why doe you so? For hee hath [1]plenarie power and authoritie granted him so to doe.

<small>Reading Ministers' pay runs from £10 to £2 a year, and keep themselues.</small>

<small>Some have 3 or 4 benefices apiece,</small>

<small>[1 Sig. K 8]</small>

Theod. That is an horrible abuse, that one man should haue two or three, or halfe a dozen benefices apeece as some haue: may anie man haue so manie liuings at one time, by the lawe of God, and good conscience?

Amphil. As it is not lawfull for anie man to haue or enioie two wiues at once, so is it not lawfull for any man, how excellent soeuer, to haue mo benefices, mo flockes, cures or charges in his handes, than one at once. Nay, I am fullie persuaded that it is more tollerable (and yet it is a damnable thing) for a man to haue two wiues or mo, than for a man to have two benefices at once, or mo. For by possibilitie a man might discharge the dutie of a good husband to two or three wiues (yet to haue mo than one is the breach of Gods commandements), but no man, though he were as learned as Saint Paule, or the apostles themselues to whome were given supernaturall and extraordinarie giftes and graces, is able sufficientlie to discharge his dutie in the instruction of one church, or congregation, much lesse of three or foure, or halfe a dozen, as some haue. And as one father cannot bee manie fathers, one pastor [2]manie pastours, nor one man diuerse men, so one sheepeheard or pastour cannot, nor ought not, to haue diuers charges, and flocks at once. Is it possible for any shepheard though he were neuer so cunning a man, to keepe two or

<small>which is worse than having 2 or 3 wives.</small>

<small>[2 Sig. K 8, back]</small>

<small>One Pastor cannot take charge of</small>

II. 2. Evils of Pluralism and Non-Residence.

three flocks or mo at once, and to feed them wel and in due season, dooing the dutie of a good shepheard in euerie respect, they being distant from him, ten, twentie, fortie, sixtie, an hundred, two hundred, or three hundred miles? Much lesse is there any man able to discharge the dutie of a good pastor ouer so manie flocks, churches, and congregations so farre distant in place, wheras the simplest flocke that is, requireth a whole, and perfect man, & not a peece of a man. Therfore I aduise al benefice mongers, *that* haue mo charges then one, to take heede to themselues, and to leaue them in time, for the blood of al those within their cures, or charges, that die ghostlie for want of the truth of Gods word preached vnto them, shall be powred vpon their[1] heads, at the day of iudgement, and be required at their hands.

Theod. If they haue so many benefices a peece, and some so farre distant from another, then it is not possible that they can be resident vpon them all at once. But the matter is in dispute, whether they may not as well be ab[2]sent, or present: what is your iudgment of that?

Amphil. To doubt whether the pastor ought to be resident with his flocke, is to doubt whether the soule should be in the bodie, the eie in the head, or the watchman in his tower. For this I am fully persuaded of, that as the soule is the life of the bodie, and the eie the light of the same, so the word of God preached is the life, and light, as well to the bodie as to the soule of man. And as necessarie as the one is to the bodie, so (and much more) necessarie is the other both to soule and bodie. Now certein it is, these things cannot be applied without the presence of the preacher or pastor; and therefore is his absence from his flocke a dangerous and a perilous thing, and as it were a taking away of their life and light from them, which commeth by the preaching of Gods word vnto them.

Theod. But they say, though they be not present by themselues, yet be they present by their substitutes and deputies: is not that a sufficient discharge for them before God?

Amphil. I grant they are present by their deputies and substitutes, but if a man shoulde looke into a great sort of them, he should finde them such as are fitter to feed hogs, than christian soules. For as for

---

[1] *Orig.* their their.

II. 2. *Ministers' ignorant tippling hired Deputies.*

some of them, are they [1]not such as can scarcely read true english? And for their zeale to Gods worde and true religion, are they not such as can scarce tell what it meaneth? The truth of Gods word they cannot easily preach nor expound. The aduersarie they cannot refell: barke against sinne they dare not, bicause their liues are licentious. They will read you their seruice faire and cleanly (as the doting papists did their blasphemous masses out of their portesses), and when they haue done, they will to all kinde of wanton pastimes and delights, with come that come will, and that vpon sabboth day, festiuall day, or other; no day is amisse to them. And all the weeke after, yea all the yeere (if I said all the yeeres of their life, I lied not) they will not sticke to keepe companie at the alehouse from morning till night, tipling and swilling till the signe be in Capricornus. Insomuch as if you would know where the best cup of drinke is, go to these malt woormes, and I warrant you you shall not misse of your purpose. By these mercenaries their deputies, and the like, I grant they are present in all their flocks, but so as it were better or as good they were absent, for any good they doe, but rather hurt by their euill example of life. The residence of these their deputies is no discharge for them [2]before the tribunall seate of God: for notwithstanding the same, let them be sure to answere for the bloud of euerie one of their sheepe, that miscarrieth through their default, or their deputies. Their deputies shall not excuse them at the day of iudgement, I dare be their warrant. Therefore I wish them to take heed to it betime, least afterward it be too late.

Theod. But I heare say, that what is wanting either in their deputies, or in themselues for not being daily resident, they supply either by preaching their quarter sermons themselues, or else (if they be not able) by procuring of others to do it for them. Is not that well?

Amphil. It is as though a man euery quarter of a yeere once, shuld take his plow, & go draw a furrow in a field, & yet notwithstanding should looke for increase of the same: were not he a foolish husbandman that wold do thus? And euen so he is no lesse vnwise, that plowing but one furow, that is, preaching but one poore sermon in a quarter of a yeere (& perchance but one in a whole yeere, nay in 7. yeeres) will notwithstanding loke for gret increse of the same. Now the cause why this ground bringeth not forth fruit is, for that it

[1 Sig. L. 1. back]

Tho they can read the Service, yet after it,

and on week-days, they'll swill all day at the Alehouse.

[2 Sig. L. 2.]

Pluralists may preach once a quarter, but that's no more good

than if a man plowd one furrow every quarter.

II. 2. *The shameful neglect of Preaching.*

[¹ Sig. L. 2. back]
Our churches don't bring forth fruit because they're not tilld with preaching.

is not plowed, furowed, & tilled al togither as it ought to be. So the caufe wherefore the pore churches doe not bring forth fruit ¹is, for that they are not furrowed, manured, and tilled, as they ought, and bicaufe the word of God is not preached vnto them, and as it were braied, punned, interpreted, and expounded, *that* it, finking down into the good ground of their harts, might bring forth fruit to eternal life. If the ftrongeft mans body that liueth vpon the earth fhould be nourifhed with nothing for a whole quarter of a yeeres fpace, but onely with two or three drops of aqua vite, aqua angelica, or the like, euery day, and at euery quarters end fhould be fed with all manner of dainties, I am perfwaded that his bodie notwithftanding would foone be weake inough. Nay, do you thinke it were poffible to liue one quarter of a yeere? Euen fo falleth out in this cafe. For although our foules (which liue by the word of God, as our bodies doe by meate) be daily fedde with hearring the word read as it were with aqua vite, or fweet necter, and at euerie quarters ende, haue a moft excellent & fumptuous banquet to pray vpon, yet may they macerate and pyne away notwithftanding, for lacke of the continuance of the fame.

God's Word fhould be preacht night and day without ceafing.

And therfore the worde of God is to be preached night and day, in time, and out of time, in feafon and out of feafon, and that without ceafing, or intermiffion. And if that faieng of the prophet be ²true (as without all controuerfie it is moft true) that he is accurfed, *Qui fecerit opus domini negligenter,* That doth the worke of the Lord negligently, or fraudulently, then muft it needs be, that thofe who hauing cure of foules, and doe feldome, or neuer preach, are within the compaffe of this curfe. Let them take heede to it.

[² Sig. L. 3.]

Woe to Minifters who won't preach it!

The apoftle Paule faid of himfelfe, *Vœ mihi nifi euangelizauero,* Woe be to me if I preach not the gofpel; and doe they thinke that the fame wo is not proper to them if they prech not? Haue they a greater priuiledge than the bleffed apoftle faint Paule had? No, no, thefe vaine excufes will not ferue them; therfore, as they tender the faluation of their owne foules, and many others, I wifh them to take heede, and to fhew themfelues painefull laborers in the Lords harueft.

Tho there's a law againft Pluralism,

Theod. As far as I remember, by the lawes of *Dnalgne* there is a reftraint, that none fhall haue no more benefices at once than one: how is it then, that they can holde fo manie a peece, without danger of the law?

II. 2. Dodges to avoid the Law against Pluralities.

Amphil. They make the lawes (as it were) shipmens hoosen, or as a nose of waxe, turning and wresting them at their pleasure, to anie thing they lust. But bicause they will auoide the lawes, they purchase a dispensation, a li¹cence, a commission, a pluralitie, a qualification, and I cannot tell what else, by vertue whereof they may hold totquots so manie, how manie soeuer, and that with as good a conscience as *Iudas* receiued the mony for the which he sold Christ Iesus the Sauiour of the world. Or if this way will not serue, then get they to be chaplines to honorable & noble personages, by prerogatiue whereof they may holde I cannot tell how manie benefices, yea, as manie as they can get. But I maruell whether they thinke that these licenses shall go for good paiment at the daie of iudgement. I thinke not. For sure I am that no licence of man can dispense with vs, to doe that thing which is against Gods worde (as these totquots is) and therfore vnlawful. They may blind the foolish world with pretended dispensations, and qualifications, but the Lorde will bring them to account for it in his good time: GOD grant they may looke to it! *(it's avoided by buying a dispensation. [¹ Sig. L. 3. back] getting a chaplaincy to a Nobleman, &c. But God 'll be down on these folk.)*

Theod. In whome doth the patronage, right, and gifture of these ecclesiasticall promotions and benefices consist? in the churches themselues, or in whom else?

Amphil. Indeede you saie well. For who shoulde haue the patronage, the right, the interest, and gifture of the benefices, but the ²churches themselues, whose the benefices are by right, and to whome, *Proprio iure,* They doe apperteine? For doe not the benefices consist either in tithes, or contributions, or both? Nowe, who giueth both the one and the other? Doe not the Churches? Then by good reason ought they to haue the gifture and bestowing of them, and the right and interest thereof ought to remaine in the power of the church, and not in anie other priuate man whatsoeuer. *(The Patronage of Benefices ought to be in the Churches' hands. [² Sig. L. 4.])*

Theod. Why? Then I perceiue you would not haue anie priuate or singuler man of what degree soeuer, to haue the patronage, the right, or gifture of anie ecclesiasticall liuing, but the churches themselues: is not that your meaning? *(Every parish Church ought to have the patronage of its own Living.)*

Amphil. Yes truely, that is my meaning, and so I am of opinion it ought to be.

Theod. Why so, I beseech you?

II. 2. Every Congregation should own its Patronage.

[It wouldn't abuse it as private Patrons do.]

Amphil. Bicause one man may easily be corrupted, and drawne to bestowe hys benefice eyther for fauour, affection, or monie, vppon such as bee vnworthie; the whole Church will not so. Againe, the whole liuing is nothing else but pure almes, or deuocion, or both, the Gentelman or other that pretendeth the gifture thereof, [1] giueth not the whole liuing himselfe, *ergo* hee ought not to haue in his owne power, the only gifture of the same. Thirdly, the whole church will not giue the same for simonie; one priuate man may be induced to doe it. Fourthlie, the church will keepe no part of the liuing backe from the pastor, if he doe his dutie, nor imploie it to ther owne vse; the singularitie of one man may easilie be abused: nay, the most patrones keepe the fattest morsels to themselues, and giue scarcely the crums to their pastors. But if the benefice be woorth two hundred pound, they will scarcely giue their pastor foure score. If it be woorth an hundred pound, they will hardly giue fortie pound. If woorth forty pound, it is well if they giue ten pound, imploieng the better halfe to their owne priuate gaine. Now if this be not sacrilege, and a robbing of the poore churches of their substance, as also defrauding of the Lords minister of his dutie and right, then I knowe not what sacrilege, and fraude meaneth. Yea there are some, that hauing ground in another parish than where they dwell, against the time that their sheepe, kine, and other cattell should bring foorth increase, will driue them thither, so that the fruit falling in the other parish, he shall not need to pay tithes for the same to his owne pastor [2] where he dwelleth. And against the time that the other pastor of that parish where his cattell fell, shall demand his tithes thereof, they will haue fetched home their cattell, so that by these sinister kinde of meanes, they will neither pay in the one parish, nor in the other. But if the one commence sute against him, he answereth, they fell not in his parish: if the other doe the same, he pleadeth that he is not of his parish, nor oweth him ought. But indeed they wil pay for their ground in the other parish a little herbage (as they call it), a thing of nothing, to stop his mouth withall. So that hereby the poore pastors are deteined from their right, and almost beggered in most places that I haue come in.

Theod. How came temporall men by the right of their patronages, and how fell they into their clowches, can you tell?

Marginalia:
- [¹ Sig. L. 4 back]
- Private Patrons often cheat their Pastors of half their income.
- And they move their cattle and sheep so as to avoid paying tithes on em.
- [² Sig. L 5]

II. 2. *How Laymen got their Church Patronage.*

Amphil. I will tell you, as farre as euer I could coniecture, how they fel into their hands. In the beginning, when Antichrift the pope exercifed his vfurped authoritie, and challenged the title of fupreme head ouer the vniuerfall church of Chrift vpon the face of the earth, to whomfoeuer would either erect churches, temples, and oratories (as the then world was giuen to blinde fuperftition, as to inftaurate ab[1]beies, prieries, nunries, with other fumptuous edefices, and houfes of religion, thinking the fame a worke meritorious, and to gilte, croffes, images, and the like fooleries) or elfe giue ground for the fame to be built vpon, his vnholie holines did giue the patronage and pretenfed right of the fame church, and benefice belonging to the fame. Otherfome thinke (to whome I willinglie fubfcribe) that the Churches (confifting of fimple and ignorant men for the moft part) abufing the fame benefices, and beftowing them vpon vnmeete perfons, the princes haue taken them out of their handes, and giuen the right patronage and poffeffion of the fame to the temporalitie, to the ende they might beftowe them better. But as they were taken from the churches for fome caufes, fo ought they to be remooued and giuen againe to the Churches for greater caufes. For nowe are they bought and foulde for fimonie, euen as an oxe or a cow is bought and fold for mony.

Theod. Are there no lawes for the reftrainte of fimonie, being fo horrible and deteftable vice in the church of God?

Amphil. Yes, that there are. As he that is patrone taking monie for his benefice, to loofe the patronage of the fame, and the [2]ecclefiafticall perfon, that giueth it, to loofe the fame benefice, the monie giuen or promifed to be giuen, and to remaine incapable of anie other ecclefiafticall promotion afterwarde for euer. But doe you thinke they are fooles? Haue they no fhift to defeate the lawe? Yes, I warrant you. For though they giue two hundred, or three hundred pound for a benefice, yet it fhall be done fo cloofely, as no dogges fhall barke at it. But bicaufe at the time of their initiation, inftitution, induction and admiffion, they are fworne whether they came by it by fimonie or no, whether they gaue anie monie for it or no, therefore, to auoide the guilte of periurie, they, the paftors themfelues, will not giue anie monie, but their friendes fhall doe it for them; and than may they fweare (with as good a confcience as euer Iudas betraied Chrift) that they gaue not a penny, but came

Laymen get their Church Patronage by the Pope having given it to all men who'd build churches or give ground for em;
[1 Sig. L 5, back]

and by the King having taken th. patronage from congregations, and given it to individuals.

We have laws against Simony,
[2 Sig. L 6]

but they're easily evaded.

Simony is avoided by paftors getting friends to pay money for them.

82 II. 2. *Abuses of Private Patronage of Livings.*

Or they buy a worthless thing for £100.

by it freely, as of gifte. Or if this waie fayle them, than muſt they giue the patrones a hundred pounde, or two hundred pounds vpon ſome bargayne, that is not woorth a hundred pence, and then maye they ſweare, if neede be, that they came by the benefice frankelye, and freelye, and that they gaue the money vppon ſuch and ſuch a bargaine, [1] without ſome of theſe practiſes, or without ſuch a diſh of apples as Maſter Latimer talketh of, with thirty angels in euery apple, thogh he be neuer ſo learned a man, I warrant him he gets nothing. But if he can get a graffe of this tree loden with ſuch golden apples, it will ſerue him better then all Saint Paules learning. For theſe and the like abuſes infinite, if the patronages were taken away from them that now enioy them, nay, that make hauocke of them, and either to reſt in the right of the Prince (as they ought) or elſe in the right of the churches, who will not be corrupted, it were a great deale better than nowe they bee. For now the poore paſtours are ſo handled at the hands of their patrones, that they neyther haue mony to buy them bookes withall, nor, which is leſſe, not to maintaine themſelues vppon, though but meanelye, but are manye times conſtrained either to wander abroad to ſeeke their liuings, or els to take vp their Inne in an alehouſe, or in ſome od corner or other, to the great diſcredite of the goſpell of Chriſt, and offence of the godlie. This argueth flatly that we loue not Chriſt Ieſus, who make ſo little of his meſſengers, and ambaſſadors. He that deſpiſeth you, deſpiſeth me, and he that receaueth and maketh much of you, he receiueth [2] me, and maketh much of me, ſaith Chriſt. The heathen gentils, and pagans, prouide better for their idolatrous prieſts, then we doe for the true preachers of the goſpell, and diſcloſers of the ſecrets of God. For when the Egyptians were ſore pooled of Pharao, the prieſts, by his commandement, were excepted, and permitted to haue all neceſſarie maintenance whatſoeuer. But we are of another mind, for we thinke whatſoeuer we get of them is won, it is our own good, whereas in truth, what we withdrawe from them (prouided that they be diligent preachers of the goſpell) we withdraw it from God, and ferrie it to the deuil. But hereof more ſhal be ſpoken (Chriſt willing) hereafter, when we come to this queſtion, whether it be lawful for preachers and miniſters of the Goſpell, to receiue wages and ſtipends for preaching of the worde.

[1] Sig. I. 6, back]

Private Patronages ſhould be aboliſht.

Poor Pastors haven't money to buy books.

[2] Sig. L 7]

Pagans take better care of their Priests.

II. 2. *The Minister's Right to his Tithes.*

Theod. By what law may a minifter of the Gofpell make claime to tithes, and other profits, emoluments, duties, and commodities, belonging to him, by yᵉ law of God, or of man? Minifters can claim Tithes

Amphil. God, in the law of Mofes, gaue fpeciall commandement that tithes, and other oblations, commodities and profits fhould be giuen to the priefts, to the end that they might attend vpon the diuine feruice of God and not ¹bufie themfelues in worldly affaires, which ordinance or fanction being meere ceremonial, is now fully abrogate by Chrift (for in him the truth, al ceremonies, fhadowes, types & figures ceafed, & toke their end) And therfore cannot a preacher of the Gofpel claime his tithes by the lawe of Mofes, but by the pofitiue lawes of Chriftian princes which are to be obeied in all things (not directly againft true godlineffe) vpon paine of damnation. [¹ Sig. L 7, back]
by the positive law of Christian kings,

Theod. Are tithes then due to be paid by the pofitiue lawe of man, and not by the law of God?

Amphil. Yea truly, by the pofitiue lawe of man: which godlie conftitution is now no leffe to be obeied vnder the Gofpel (being commanded by a chriftian prince) than the diuine inftitution was to be obeied vnder the law. And although tithes bee due by the pofitiue lawes of man, yet are the fame grounded vpon the word of God, as commanded as well by God as by man. And therefore he that breaketh this ordinance (being an excellent policie) violateth the commandements of God, and breketh the conftitution of his liege prince to his damnation, except he repent. grounded on the word of God.

Theod. Muft euerie one pay his tithes truely to euery paftor, whether he be ought or ²naught, learned or vnlearned, without any exception; or may he deteine it with good confcience from him that is an vnfit and vnable minifter? [² Sig. L 8]

Amphil. If he be a good paftor, and diligent in his calling, and withal able to difcharge the dutie of a faithful fhepheard ouer his flock, then ought he to haue al tithes paid him whatfoeuer with the better; and if any fhould withhold the left mite from him, he finneth againft the maieftie of God moft greeuoufly. And although he be a wicked man and not able to difcharge his dutie, though but in fmall meafure, yet ought euerie man to pay him his due faithfully and truly. For in denieng him his dutie, they might feeme to withftande authoritie, which they ought not to doe. In the meane time giuing Even tho a Minister's a wicked man, his tithes should be paid him, themselues to praier, and suing to them that haue the authoritie for his displacing, and placing of another that is more able in some measure to discharge the dutie of a faithfull pastor. Notwithstanding I know some are of opinion that if any man giue either tithes, or anie dutie else, to their pastor being an vnfit and an vnable person, he is partaker with him of his sinne, he communicateth with other mens offences, [¹ Sig. L 8, back] and he maintaineth him in his idlenesse, sloth, ignorance, ¹ and securitie, and therefore offendeth greeuously. But I am of opinion that euerye man ought to pay their dutie (for else he might seeme, as I said, to resist the power) & if he be not able to discharge his dutie, to pray for his remoouing, and to make instance to them that are in authoritie appointed for the redresse of such inormities, for his displacing, and so not to attempt anything without good and lawfull authoritie grounded vpon the word for the same.

Theod. May a pastor that hath a charge and a flocke assigned him to watch ouer (hauing a maintainable liuing allowed him of his flock) preach in other places for monie?

Amphil. Hee may sometimes, obtaining licence for some reasonable cause of his owne flocke, preach the word of God abroad in other places, but then he ought to doe it *gratis*, contenting himselfe with the liuing allowed him at home of his owne parish. Notwithstanding, if the other churches where he shall have preached, will voluntarily impart any thing to the supplie of his necessities, in respect of his painstaking, he may thankfully receiue the same, but he may not compell, nor constraine them to giue it him whether they will or not, against their wils, as manie impudently doe.

[² Sig. M. 1.]

Theod. Then I perceiue if it be not law²full for a pastor that hath a flocke, and a stipend appointed him, to receiue monie vppon constraint of strangers for preaching the worde abroad in other places, then is it not lawfull for him to take monie in his cure for preaching funerall sermons, marriage sermons, christening sermons, and the like, as many do. What say you to this?

Amphil. There are manie woorthie of great blame in this respect. For though they receiue fortie pound, a hundred pound, or two hundred pound a yeere, of some one parish, yet will they hardly preach once a moneth, nay happily not once in a quarter of a yeere, and sometimes not once a twelue moneth, for the same. And if a

Marginalia:
- but his parishioners should try to get him remoued.
- An endowd Minister may not
- force men to pay him for preaching in other places.
- Ministers may not take fees for sermons

II. 2. *Preachers not to take fees for Funeral Sermons.* 85

man requeſt them to preach at a burial, a wedding, or a chriſtening, they will not doe it vnder an angell, or a noble at the leaſt. And therefore the papiſts and aduerſaries to the Goſpel call our Goſpel, 'a polling Goſpel,' our ſermons 'roiall ſermons, angell ſermons, and noble ſermons.' You call, ſay they, our bleſſed maſſe 'a polling maſſe;' but, ſay they, your preachings are more polling. For we ſay they would haue ſold a maſſe for a grote; you will not ſell a ſermon vnder a roiall, or a noble. And thus theſe fellowes are a ſlander to the Goſpel, and robbers of their fellowe brethren. If I ſhould hire a [1]man for fortie pound, an hundred pound, or more, or leſſe, to teach my children nurture or knowledge, if he for the execution therof ſhould aſke me more for the ſame than we agreed for, were not this man a naughtie, exacting, and fraudulent felowe? Nay, if I compound with him to teach them in the beſt maner he is able for ſo much, and he doth it not, and yet receiue my monie, haue not I good lawe againſt him? If he ſhould ſay vnto me, I will not doe it except you giue me more, were not this a very vnreaſonable man? For, hauing his monie that was couenant, is hee not bound both by lawe and conſcience to teach them to the vttermoſt of his power? Or if he ſhall not doe it, and yet take my monie, is not he a theefe and robber? Is this true in a priuate man, & not in an eccleſiaſticall perſon? Is he not hired to that end & purpoſe to preach the word of God to his flocke? And hath hee not wages for the ſame? Shall he now denie to preach the ſame word except he haue more monie? Or is he not bound in conſcience to preach the ſame night and day without ceaſing? And if he doe not, is he not a deceiuer, a theefe, & a robber? The paſtor therefore, hauing taken vpon him the cure & charge of his flocke, and hauing his ſtipend appointed for the ſame, is bound to preach the worde of [2]God to all his flocke indifferently whether it be at buriall, wedding, chriſtening (yea then eſpecially) or at any other time whenſoeue, without taking or requiring of any more monie, than the ſtipend he was hired for. For if he take any more, it is plaine theft before God, and one day ſhall be anſwered for: let them be ſure of it.

Theod. You condemne not funerall ſermons then, ſo that they be good, doe you?

Amphil. No, God forbid. Why ſhould not godlie ſermons be as

at Burials, Weddings, &c.

Those that do are a slander to the Gospel.

[1 Sig. M. 1. back]

They get their salary, and yet won't preach without more pay.

[2 Sig. M. 2.]

[marginal note: I think godly Sermons at Funerals are very needful, and do great good.*]*

wholſome (and as neceſſarie) at the burials of chriſtians, when wee haue ſuch liuely ſpectacles before our eies, of our mortality, miſerie, and end, as they be at all other times? Yea truely at that preſent I thinke godlie ſermons verie neceſſarie to put the people in remembrance of their mortalitie, of their great miſerie, and frailtie, of their fatall end, of the immortalitie of the ſoule, of the generall reſurrection at the laſt day, and of the ioie, felicitie, and beatitude of the life to come, with the like godlie inſtructions, that they may the better prepare themſelues to the ſame when God ſhall call them hence to himſelfe. And although of late ſome phantaſticall ſpirites haue

[¹Sig. M. 2. back] taught that the vſe of them is naught, in that they [1] ſtand in place of popiſh diriges, and I cannot tell what, yet cannot I be eaſilie drawne to aſſent vnto them, for that I ſee them in that reſpect a great deale more curious than godlie wiſe.

Theod. Is it lawfull, thinke you, for miniſters, and preachers of the Goſpell, to receiue ſtipends, and wages for their preaching?

[marginal note: Ministers ought to have Stipends, so as to be free from worldly business, and keep their families.*]*

Amphil. Why not? Otherwiſe how ſhould they bee able to keepe themſelues free from worldly occupations, and trauels of this life (as they ought) to applie their ſtudies for the diſcharge of their duties, to maintaine themſelues, their family, and houſhold; or how ſhuld they keepe hoſpitalitie for the releefe of the poore? all which they are bound to doe both by Gods lawe, and good conſcience. Therefore take away liuings and wages from the preachers, and ouerthrowe preaching altogither, the ordinarie meane to ſaluation in Chriſt. This cauſed the apoſtle to enter diſputation of this point, where he prooueth by inuincible arguments, that a preacher or miniſter of the Goſpell of Chriſt Ieſus, may (*Salua conſcientia,* With a good conſcience) receiue wages and ſtipends for his peines ſuſteined in the affaires of the Goſpell, and that for the cauſes abouesaid. Therefore ſaith this apoſtle:

[² Sig. M. 3.] *Boui* [2] *trituranti non ligabis os,* Thou ſhalt not muffle the mouth of the oxe that treadeth foorth the corne. Whereby is ment, that he that laboreth and taketh paines in any good exerciſe, ought not to be denied of his meed for his paines. Againe he ſaith: *Dignus eſt operarius mercede ſua,* The workman is woorthie of his reward. And ſtill inſiſting in the ſame argument, hee ſaith: *Qui euangelium prædicant, ex euangelio viuant,* They that preach the Goſpell, let them liue vpon the Goſpell. And yet further proſecuting the ſame more at

[marginal note: St. Paul says that Ministers who preach the Gospel should live by it.*]*

large, he faith: *Quis militat*, etc. 'Who goeth on warfare at any time of his owne charges? Who planteth a vineyard, and eateth not of the fruit? Who feedeth a flocke, and eateth not of the milke of the flock?' By al which reafons and arguments it appeareth, that he who preacheth the Gofpell ought to liue of the Gofpell. But as euerie paftor that hath a peculiar flocke affigned him, may, with the teftimonie of a good confcience, receiue wages and maintenance of his flocke, for his paines taken amongft them: fo may he not, nor ought not, to take wages or falarie of any other flocke adioining, if fo be it, that either vpon requeft, or his owne voluntarie good will, he preach the word of God amongft them. To them that are thus prouided for, Chrift our [1] fauiour faith: *Gratis accepiftis, gratis date*, Freely you haue receiued, freely giue againe. But if any haue not a fpeciall flocke or charge affigned him, then may he with good confcience receiue the beneuolencie, the friendly contributions and rewards, of the churches to whom he hath preached. And this is probable, both by the word of God, and the examples of the apoftles themfelues.

But benefift Ministers may not take extra pay.

[1 Sig. M.3.back]

Theod. What fay you of preachers, and lecturers, that haue no peculiar flockes, nor charges appointed them; are they neceffarie, and may they receiue wages, with a good confcience, of the flockes and charges where they preach the word of God?

Amphil. Firft you afke me whether preachers and lecturers that haue no peculiar flocks nor charges of their owne to attend vpon, be neceffarie. Whereto I anfwere. That confidering the ftate & condition of the church at this day, they are moft neceffarie. But if it were fo, that euerie church and congregation had his preacher (as euery one ought to preach, elfe is he not fent by the Lord) then were they not fo neceffarie; but confidering that moft churches are planted and fraught with fingle reading minifters, they are verie behouefull to helpe to fupplie the defect of the others, that [2] through the good induftrie as well of the one, as of the other, the churches of G O D may bee inftructed and nourifhed with the worde of G O D to eternall life. Then you afke mee whether thefe lecturers and preachers may receiue wages of the churches to whom they preach, with a good confcience, whereto I anfwere, that they may. But yet I am perfuaded, that it were much better for them to haue particular flocks of their owne, to the end that they, receiuing fufficient maintenance of them, might

Unbenefist preachers are now necessary,

as most Churches have only Readers.

[2 Sig. M. 4.]

Unbenefist clergy may take pay for Preaching.

88 II. 2. *Ministers to be content with poor Livings.*

(if they were at anie time difpofed to beftowe any fpirituall graces abroad) doe it *Gratis*, frankly and freely, without any charges to the poore churches of Iefus Chrift.

Theod. But what if the paftors liuing be not maintaineable nor fufficient for him to liue vpon, may hee not take wages of other flocks abroad?

But benefist ones may not, even if their Livings are very poor.

Amphil. I am perfuaded no. For if his liuing be too little, then ought the church to mend it; but if the church, either for want of zeale will not, or through extreame pouertie cannot, increafe his liuing, then ought the paftor to content himfelfe with that little which God hath fent him, following the example of the apoftle, who biddeth

[¹ Sig. M 4. back]

the children of G O D [1] to be content with their wages, bee it little or be it much: for if they haue meate, drinke, and cloth, it is inough, and as much as nature requireth. We brought nothing (faith he) into this world, neither fhall we carrie any thing out. Againe, thofe that will be rich, fall into diuers temptations, and fnares of the diuell, which drowne men in perdition and deftruction. Therefore if it be fufficient to yeelde him meate, drinke, cloth, and other neceffaries, he

They must be content with em,

is bound to content himfelfe with the fame. Which if he doe (for the zeale he beareth to his flocke), I doubt not but the L o r d will open the harts of his flock towards him, and both make them able

and wait till the Lord opens men's hearts to give them more.

and willing to fupport his neceffities. For if hee deliuer vnto them fpirituall things, doubtleffe the Lord will moue them to giue vnto him temporall things. And therfore ought he to perfeuere; and in his good time, without all peraduenture, the Lord will looke vpon him, as he hath promifed.

Theod. Doe you allow of that vagarant minifterie, which is in manie countries, but moft fpecially in *Dnalgne* fprong up of late, to the difcredite of the Gofpell of Iefus Chrift, and offence of the brethren?

[² leaf M 5]
The present Vagrant Ministers,

Amphil. Allow of it, quoth you? No, God forbid! But I rather deplore it with all my hart, [2] knowing that it is moft directly againft the word of God, the example of the primitiue age and all good reformed churches thorough the world. Is it not a pitifull cafe that two hundred, three hundred, fiue hundred, a thoufand, fiue thoufand, yea poffible ten thoufand, fhall be called into the minifterie, in one countrie, not a quarter of them knowing where to haue any liuing or

II. 2. *The abuse of Vagrant Ministers.* 89

charge? And what do they then? Runne ſtragling and rouing ouer countries, from towne to towne, from citie to citie, from ſhire to ſhire, and from one place to another, till they haue ſpent al that euer they haue, and then the moſt of them either become beggers, or elſe attempt wicked and vnlawfull meanes to liue by, to the great diſhonour of God, and ſlander of the word. <small>roaming all over the country, I condemn.</small>

Theod. Me thinke this is a great abuſe, that ſo manie, or any at all, ſhould be called into the miniſterie, not hauing flocks and charges prouided for them before.

Amphil. It is a great abuſe indeed. For if paſtor come of *Paſco*, to feed, if he be not a ſhepheard that hath no flock, and if he be not a feeder, that giueth no ſuſtinance, nor a father that hath no childe, then are they no ſhepheards, nor no watchmen ſent from the Lord, that haue neither flocks, nor charges to watch ouer. For [1] he that is made a ſhepheard (or a miniſter) that hath no particular flocke readie to receiue him, is ſo far from being a lawfull ſhepheard, by reaſon of his former admiſſion, that he is rather made a paſtor by the church that hireth him to be their watchman and guide, than of him that firſt called him into that function. And therefore woulde I wiſh that biſhops and others to whome it doth (*Ex officio*) apperteine to call, and admit paſtors, and teachers in the church of G O D, to bee verie carefull heerein, and not raſhly to lay their handes vpon any, before they haue had ſufficient triall, as well of their life and doctrine, as alſo of the flock and charge where they ſhal be reſident, that they go not like maiſterleſſe hounds, vp and downe the countries, to the ſlander of the Goſpell. <small>[1 leaf M 5, back]</small> <small>Bishops should stop these men running about like masterless dogs.</small>

Theod. Why? Then I perceiue you would haue none called into the miniſterie, before there be a place void for him: is not that your meaning? <small>No one should be ordaind till a place is ready for him.</small>

Amphil. That is my meaning indeed.

Theod. But are you able to prooue your aſſumption out of the word of God, or elſe I will giue but ſmal credit to you in ſuch matters of controuerſie as this is?

Amphil. I haue not, neither doe I meane to ſpeake anie thing vnto you touching theſe matters, but what I am able (I truſt) to [2] prooue by the worde of G O D. And yet I grant *Errare poſſum* (for *Hominis eſt labi, & decipi*, Man may bee deceiued and fall) but <small>Bible examples prove this. [2 leaf M 6]</small>

II. 2. *No one to be ordaind till he has a Cure.*

Hereticus esse nolo, Erre I may, but heretike I will not be. No, so soone as I shall be conuinced by the manifest worde of God, of any of my former positions or assertions, I will willingly subscribe to the truth. But being persuaded as I am, giue me leaue, I beseech you (vnder correction) to speake what I thinke. But now to the purpose. In the first chapter of the Actes of the apostles recorded by the Evangelist Saint *Luke*, wee read that *Matthias* succeeding *Iudas* the traitour in the administration of the apostleship, was not chosen nor elected (notwithstanding that the apostles by the reuelation of the Spirite of GOD, knew that he should fall from the same in the end) vntill the place was voide, and emptie. In the sixt chapter of the Actes of the apostles wee reade also of seuen deacons, which were chosen for the dailie ministring to the poore; but when, I pray you? Not before the church (destitute of their seruice) had need of them, nor before there [1] were places readie to receiue them, wherein they might exercise their function, and calling. Then if the apostles would not choose not so much as deacons, which is an office in the church of God farre inferiour to the office of the pastor, or preacher, before places were void and readie to receiue them, much lesse would they, or did they choose or call any pastor into the church of God, before the church stood in need of him, and before there be a place readie to receiue him. Besides that, we read not thorough the whole euangelicall historie, that euer the apostles called any to be pastors and preachers of the word, before such time as there were places void for them. Common reason, me thinke, and daily experience, should teach us this truth sufficiently, if we were not wilfully blinded, that when any church or congregation is destitute of a pastor, it were better to place there one able person, than to make two or three hundred or mo vnable fellowes, and they, for want of liuing, to runne stragling the countries ouer, without any liuing or maintenance at all, being glad of any thing. For as the old saieng is: Hungrie dogs eate sluttish puddings.

Theod. What order would you have obserued in this?

[2] *Amphil.* Me thinke this were a verie good order: That euerie church or congregation being destitute of a pastor, should present to the bishops, and others to whom it dooth apperteine, one or two, three or foure able persons, or mo, or lesse, as they conueniently can,

II. 2. *How Ministers should be appointed to Churches.* 91

whofe liues and conuerfations they haue had fufficient triall of, whofe foundneffe in religion, integritie of life, and godly zeale to the truth they are not ignorant of. Then the bifhops and others to whom it doth apperteine, to examine and trie them thoroughly for their fufficiencie in learning, foundneffe in doctrine, and dexteritie in teaching, and finding them furnifhed with fufficient gifts for fuch an honorable calling, to admit them, to lay their hands vppon them, and to fend them foorth (the chiefeft of them) to that congregation or church fo deftitute. *and he should ordain the best for that Church.* Which order, if it were ftrictly obferued and kept (as it ought to be) then fhould not fo manie run abroad in the countries to feeke liuings, then fhould not churches bee peftered with infufficient minifters. Then fhould not the bifhops be fo deceiued in manie as they be. And no maruell. For how fhould the bifhop choofe but be deceiued in him, whom he neuer fawe before, whofe conuerfation he knoweth not, whofe difpofition hee is ignorant of, and [1] whofe qualities and properties in generall, he fufpecteth not? [[1] leaf M 7, back] Whereas if this order were eftablifhed, that euerie church deftitute of a paftor fhould prefent certeine able men, whofe conuerfation and integritie of life in euerie refpect they perfectly knowe (for the whole church is not likely to erre in iudging of their conuerfations, who haue been either altogither, or for the moft part conuerfant among them) then (as I fay,) fhould not the bifhop be deceiued in any, nor yet any church fcandalized with the wicked liues of their paftors (or rather depaftors) as they be. For now it is though fufficient for the certeintie of his conuerfation, if he either haue letters dimifforie from one bifhop to another (whereas they little or nothing knowe the conuerfation of the man) or elfe letters commendatorie from any gentleman, or other, efpecially if they be of any reputation. *Now, a Bishop gets but small proof of a candidate's fitness.* If he can get thefe things, he is likely to fpeede, I warrant him. Which thing is fcarce well, in my iudgement. For you knowe one priuate man or two, or three, or foure may, peraduenture either write vpon affection, or elfe bee corrupted with bribes or gifts, whereas the whole church cannot, nor would not. Therefore is the other the furer way.

[2] *Theod.* How prooue you that the churches that are deftitute of a paftor, ought to prefent him whom they would haue admitted, to the bifhop, and not the bifhop to intrude vpon the church whom he will? [[2] leaf M 8] *Bishops ought not to intrude their nominees on churches,*

11. 2. Bishops ought not to appoint whom they like.

Amphil. In the first chapter of the Actes of the apostles before cited, we read, that after the defection of Iudas the traitour, the apostle *Peter* knowing it necessarie that one shoulde be chosen in his place, to giue testimonie and witnesse of the resurrection and ascension of Christ Iesus, commanded the church to present one or two, or mo, as they thought good, that hee with his fellowe brethren might confirme and allow them. And therevppon, saith the text, they chose two, to wit, *Matthias*, and *Ioseph*, surnamed *Bersabas*. And the church hauing presented them, they were elected, confirmed and allowed of the apostles and elders. Also in the foresaide sixt chapter of the Acts of the apostles, when the deacons (whose office was to make collections for the poore, and to see the same bestowed vpon them without fraud or deceit) were to be chosen, the text saith, that the apostles desired the church to choose foorth seuen men from amongst them, of honest report, & ful of the holie Ghost, which they might appoint to that businesse. [1]By all which reasons appereth, that the church ought to present him, or them, whom they would haue to be admitted, and not that the bishop ought to present, to allow, or to intrude him vpon the church at his pleasure, against the will thereof.

Theod. Why would you not haue pastors to be thrust vpon the churches, whether the churches will or not?

Amphil. Bicause it is manifest that no church will so willingly receiue, nor yet so louingly imbrace, him that is intruded vpon them against their wils, as they will doe him that they like of, choose, and allow of themselues. And if the churches beare not a singular loue, fauour, good will, and affection to their pastor, it is vnpossible that they should heare him, or learne of him with profit to their soules. And if they heare him not *Auide & sitienter* (as we say) Greedily and thirstily thereby to profit, then shal they perish euerlastingly, in that the word of God is the ordinarie meane appointed by the diuine maiestie. And therefore in conclusion, if there be not a mutual amitie, loue, and affection betwixt the pastor and his flocke, and if that the one loue not the other, as themselues, it is not to be looked for that either the one shall teach, or the other receiue, any thing to their soules [2]health, but rather the cleane contrarie.

Theod. I pray you what is your iudgement in this? What if a

Marginal notes:

for the Apostles

bade the Church present successors to Judas Iscariot.

They also bade the Church choose Deacons.

[[1] leaf M 8, back] So now each Church should choose its Pastor.

If it doesn't, it won't like him.

[[2] Sig. N. 1.]

II. 2. *When a Minister may turn Layman again.*

man be once lawfully called into the ministerie, may he euer vpon anie occasion whatsoeuer, leaue off the same function, and applie himselfe to secular affaires?

Amphil. There is a twofold calling. The one a diuine calling immediately from God, the other a humane calling immediately from and by man. Now he that hath the first diuine calling (his conscience suggesting the same vnto him, and the spirit of God certifieng his spirit of the certeintie thereof) being furnished with gifts and graces necessarie for such a high function and office (as God calleth none, but he indueth them first with gifts, and graces necessarie for their calling) and afterwards is lawfully called of man according to the prescript of Gods word, hauing a flocke appointed him wherevpon to attend, this man may not, nor ought not at any hand to giue ouer his calling, but to perseuere in the same to the end, for that he hath both the diuine and humane callings, being furnished with all gifts and graces necessarie (in some measure) for the discharge of his high function and calling. Yet notwithstanding, in time of extreame persecution, when Gods truth is persecuted, and his glorie defa[1]ced, if he haue not wherewithall to maintaine his estate otherwise, he may for the time giue himselfe to manuall occupations, and corporall exercises in the affaires of the worlde, as we see the apostles themselues did, who, after Christ Iesus was crucified, gaue themselues to their old occupations of fishing, making of nets, tents, pauilions, and the like. But vpon the other side, if a man haue not this diuine calling, his conscience bearing him witnesse thereof, nor yet the graces, gifts, and ornaments of the minde, fit for his calling (which, whosoeuer hath not, it is a manifest argument that the Lorde hath not sent him, for those that hee sendeth, hee furnisheth with all kinde of graces and giftes necessarie for their callings) this man, though he be called by humane calling neuer so precisely, yet he may, nay, hee ought, to leaue his function, as vnwoorthie to occupie a roome in the church of God, representing (as an idoll doth) that thing which hee is not. Besides, hee that is compelled and inforced either by friendes (as manie are), or by pouertie (as not a few bee), or for anie other respect else, to take that high function vpon him, without the testimonie of a good conscience, being not furnished with gifts, and graces fit for such a calling (which argueth di[2]rectly that God hath not called him)

[marginalia:] As to a Minister giving up his office, if he's calld by God's Spirit, and then by man, and is given a flock, he must continue a Minister to the end. [¹ Sig. N. 1. back] But if he's not calld by God, and hasn't fit gifts for his work, he should at once give up his office. Men forst by friends or poverty into the Ministry, and being unfit, [² Sig. N. 2.]

hee, I say, is so farre from being bounde neuer to leaue his function and calling, that hee ought not one minute of an houre to continue in the same, though he bee called by man a thousande times. Therefore he that is a minister, and hath charge of soules committed vnto him, let him if hee bee not furnished with such gifts as his high calling requireth, in the name of G O D make no doubt of it to giue ouer his function vnto others that are able for their giftes to discharge the same, in the meane time giuing himselfe to godlie exercises of life, as God may be glorified, his conscience disburthened, and the commonwealth profited.

Theod. But I haue heard of some that, considering the naughtinesse of their calling, and their owne insufficiencie to discharge the same, haue therefore left off their function, giuing themselues to secular exercises, and in the ende haue beene inforced to resume their former function vpon them againe, and that whether they would or not. How thinke you of this?

Amphil. I thinke truely that they who compelled them to take againe that function which they were not able to discharge, and [1] therefore left it, haue greeuously offended therein. This is as if I, knowing a simple ignorant foole presumptuously to haue taken vpon him a great and waightie charge, yea, such a charge as all the wisedome in the world is not able thoroughly to performe, and when he, in taking a view of his owne insufficiencie, shuld be mooued to leaue his charge to others better able to execute the same than hee, I should notwithstanding not onely counsell, but also compell him to resigne againe his former great charge, which I knowe he is neither woorthie, nor yet able, euer to accomplish. Thinke you not that he that compelleth him to take againe that office or calling which before he had leaft for his inabilitie, shall not answere for the same? yes truely, you may be sure of it. In conclusion, he that is sufficiently furnished with such gifts as are necessarie for his calling, & withal is found able to discharge in some sort his duty, ought not to leaue his function (for to such a on that so doth, Christ faith 'hee that laieth hande vppon the plough, and looketh backe, is not fit for the kingdome of God'). But againe, he that hath not these gifts, and graces sufficient for his calling, to the discharge of his dutie, ought not to occupie a place in the church of God, as the pastor thereof, much lesse ought he, [2] when

II. 2. *No unfit Pastor should be re-appointed.* 95

he hath (for his inabilitie) leaft the fame, to be conftrai[n]ed to refume againe his former function and calling, which he is not able to difcharge. But hereof inough.

Theod. Then I perceiue that any minifter or ecclefiafticall perfon that hath not gifts fufficient to difcharge his duty, may with good confcience leaue their functions, and giue themfelues to liue by their labors, as other temporall men doe: may they not? *[They'd better work for their bread.]*

Amphil. Yes, with a better confcience than to retaine them, being not able to difcharge them in any fmall meafure. For with what confcience can he receiue temporall things of his flocke, and is not able to giue them fpirituall? With what face can a fhepeheard receiue of his fheepe, the milke, the wooll, and fleece, and yet will not, or cannot giue to the fame either meate or drinke fufficiently? With what confcience can he receiue fortie pound, a hundred pound, or two hundred pound, a yeere, of his poore flocke, and is not able to breake to them the breade of life, in fuch forme and maner as he ought? Nay, how can he euer haue quiet confcience that knowing that the blood of all thofe that die ghoftlie for want of inftruction fhal be powred vpon his head at the day of iudgment, and be demanded at his handes, will yet not[1]withftanding reteane the fame charge and function to himfelfe ftill, not being able to difcharge the leaft iote of the fame? Therefore would I wifh euery man of what office, function, or calling foeuer he be, if he be not able to difcharge his dutie in the fame, to giue it ouer, and not for greedineffe of a little mucke or dung of the earth, (For monie is no better) to caft away their foules, which Iefus Chrift hath bought with his moft precious blood. *[How can a Pastor fairly take pay for what he can't give?]* *[¹ Sig. N. 3. back]* *[Let unfit men resign at once.]*

Theod. Is it lawfull for a paftor or minifter that hath a flocke to departe from the fame, In the time of plague, peftilence, or the like, for feare of infection?

Amphil. Is he a good fheepeheard that, when he feeth the wolues comming, will take him to his heeles and runne away? Or is he a fure freend that, when a man hath moft neede of his helpe, will then get him packing, not fhewing any freendfhip towardes him at all? I thinke not? And truly no more is he a good paftor, or minifter, (but rather a depaftor, and minifter) that in time of any plague, peftilence or ficknes whatfoeuer, will conuey himfelfe away *[A minister is no Pastor, but a Depastor, who 'll run away for fear of infection.]*

96 II. 2. *No good Pastor will run away in Plague time.*

from his flocke, for feare of infection, at the houre of death, when the poore people haue most need of comfort aboue all other times, then is he their pastor that shoulde feede [1] them, the furthest from them. When they stande vppon the edge, as it were, of saluation or damnation, then permits he the wolfe to haue the rule ouer them. Our Sauiour Christ saith *Bonus pastor animulam dat pro ouibus*, A good shepheard giueth his life for his sheepe, but these felowes are so far from giuing their liues for their sheepe, that they seeke to saue their owne liues with the destruction of their whole flocke. This is the loue that they beare vnto their flocke, this is the care they haue ouer their soules health, which Christ Iesus bought so deere with the price of his blood. Out vpon those shepheards that for feare of incurring of corporall death (which is to the Godly an entraunce into parpetuall glorie) will hazard manie a thousande to die a corporall and a spirituall death both, yea, a death of damnation both of body & soule for euer. Do they thinke that their blod shall not be asked at their handes at ye gret day of the Lord. Do they thinke *that* their flieng away from their flock, is a mean to preserue their liues ye longer vpon earth? Is not God able to strike them as well in the fields, as in the city, as well in the country as in the towne, in one place, as well as in another? Is not his power eueriewhere? Is not his messenger death in al places? Saith he not in the booke of Deuteron. that if we doe [2] not those things which he hath commanded vs in his sacred word, cursed shall wee bee at home, and cursed in the fields. And saith he not further, that the plague and pestilence, the botch, bile, blaine, or else what deadly infection soeuer, shall followe vs, and lay hold vpon vs, in what place soeuer we be, and shall neuer depart from vs, till it haue quite consumed vs from the face of the earth? And doe these fugitiues that ouerrun their flocks in time of infection, thinke that they shall escape the heauie wrath and vengeance of God for their tergiuersation and backsliding from their duties? Doe they thinke that God cannot saue them from corporal death but with the breach of their duties towards God? Is not the Lord as well able to defend them from any deadly infection, if it be his good pleasure, as he was to defend *Sidrach, Misaach,* and *Abednego* from the flaming fire? *Daniell* from the mouth of the lions, *Ionas* from the iawes of the mightie whale, with manie others that trusted

[1 Sig. N. 4.]

Such runawayes, to saue their bodies, will hazard a thousand soules.

[2 Sig. N. 4. back]

But God will follow and strike them.

Cannot God protect his seruants now from death?

II. 2. God can protect his own. Duty to the death.

in him? Doe they thinke that his arme is shortened, or his power weakened? Is he not able to deliuer his children, that in dooing of their duties depend vpon his prouidence? And to bee plaine with them, me think that in flieng away from their flockes, they shew themselues to thinke [1] that either God is not almightie, or else not mercifull, or neither. For if they beleeued that he were almightie, and that hee were able to saue them, then they would neuer run awaie from their flocke, but depending vpon his prouidence, beleeue that he is as well able to deliuer them in one place as in another, if it bee his good pleasure. And if they beleeued that he were mercifull, then would they rest vpon the same, not doubting, but as he is almightie, and omnipotent, and therefore can doe al things, so he is most mercifull, and therfore wil preserue al those that put their trust in him. If a temporall magistrate that exerciseth but a ciuil office in the commonwealth, shuld go away from his charge for feare of infection or plague, wheras his present abode might do more good than his absence, he greatly offendeth; how much more then offendeth he, that being a pastor or feeder of soules, flieth away from his charge, wheras his presence might doe a thousand times more good than his absence? And if it please the Lord to take them away to himselfe, are they not most happie? Enter they not into eternall glorie? And haue they not an end of all miseries and paines in this life, and the perfect fruition of perpetuall ioie in the heauens? Are they not blessed, if when the Lord shal call them, he find [2] them so well occupied as in feeding, & breaking the bread of life to, the pore members of Christ Iesus for whose sakes he shed his hart blood?

[1 leaf N 5]

He will preserve all those who trust in him.

And if he takes them to himself, happy are they.

[2 leaf N 5, back]

Theod. But they say, we ought not to tempt God, which thing they must needs doe if they shoulde tarrie when they see death before their face. And they say further, that it is written that we must keepe the whole from the sicke, and the sicke from the whole. Besids, saie they, *Natura dedit, potestatem tuendi vitam omni animanti,* Nature hath giuen power of defending of life to euerie liuing creture. Againe, euery thing fleeth from his contrarie, but death is contrarie to nature, for it came through the corruption of nature, therfore we flie from the same by the instinct of nature. These and the like fond reasons they alledge for their excuse in flieng from their flocks and charges: what say you to them?

Cowardly Pastors' excuses for fleeing from infection.

SHAKSPERE'S ENGLAND: STUBBES, II.   H

Amphil. I can saie little to them. But onelie this, that none of all these reasons doe priuiledge them to discontinue from their flockes and charges. And whereas they saie, that their staieng were a tempting of God, it is verie vntrue, it is rather a reuerent obedience to this tripled commandement, *Pasce oues meas, pasce oues meas, pasce oues meas,* Feede my sheepe, feede my sheepe, feede my sheepe. But indeede if it were so that a priuate man who hath no ¹kind of function nor office, neither ecclesiasticall nor temporall, seeing himselfe if he staie stil in great danger of death, & might auoid the danger by flieng, & so by the grace of God prolong his life, and yet will not, this man, if he tarrieth, tempteth the Lord, and is a murtherer of himselfe before God. And to such it is said, 'thou shalt keepe the whole from the sicke, & the sick from the whole.' This is the meaning & sence of these words, and not that they do priuiledge any man for not doing of his dutie. But notwithstanding all that can be said in confutacion of this great & extreeme contempt of their duties, I haue knowne and doe know some ministers (nay, wolues in sheepes clothing) in *Dnalgne* that in time of any plague, pestilence or infection, thogh there hath bin no gret danger at all, that haue bin so far from continuing amongst their flock, *that* if any one of them were sicke, although of neuer so common or vsuall disease, yet fearing to be infected with the contagion thereof, they haue absented themselues altogither, from visiting *the* sick according as they ought, & as dutie doth bind them. Yea, some of them (suppose you of mercenaries, & hirelings, but not of good pastors) are so nice, so fine & so fearefull of death forsoth, *that* in no case they cannot abide to visit the sicke, neither by day nor ²by night. But in my iudgement it is as incident to their office and dutie, to visite, to comfort, to instruct, and relieue the sicke, at the houre of death, as it is for them to preach the word of God to their flocke al the daies of their life. And peraduenture they may doe more good in one howre at the last gaspe, then they haue done all the daies of their life before. For he that in his life time hath had in small estimation the blessed worde of God, but following his owne humors in hope to liue long, hath lead a very wicked and impenitent life, nowe through the consideration and sight of death, which he seeth before his eies, togither with godly exhortations, admonitions, and consolations, out of the word of

II. 2. *Sinners converted on Deathbeds. Ministers elected.*

God, may eafilie be withdrawne from his former wicked life, and dieng in the faith of Iefus Chrift, with true repentance for his finnes to-fore committed, liue for euer in ioye both of body & foule, whereas, if exhortations had not bin, he might (happily) haue died irrepentant or vtterly defperate to his euerlafting deftruction for euer. Yea, it is commonly feene, that thofe who could neuer be wonne to Chrift Iefus, all the daies of their life before, yet at the laft howre they are foone recouered. Therefore ought not the paftors to neglecte their duties therein, but [1] warely and carefully to watche ouer their flocks night and day without ceafing, that when the great fhephard of the fheepe commeth, he may rewarde them with the immerceffible crowne of eternall glory. And thus much be it fpoken hereof.

may eafily be drawn to repent on their dying beds.

[1] leaf N 7]

Theod. In whome doth the election of the minifter or paftor confift? in the church onely, or in the bifhops?

The Election of Paftors.

Amphil. I tolde you before (as I remember) that the church might examine the life, the conuerfation, and difpofition of him, or them, whome they would haue to be their paftor, and finding the fame good, to prefent him, or them, to the bifhops or elders to whome it apperteineth, to examine for his fufficiencie in knowledge, and dexteritie in teaching and handling the word of God; and finding him a man furnifhed with gifts and graces neceffary for fuch a high vocation, to call him lawfullie according to the word of God, and fo to fende him foorth into the Lords harueft, as a faithfull laborer therein.

Their lives should be lookt into by the Church; then the men fhould be prefented to the Bifhop.

Theod. But fome are of opinion that the churches themfelues of their owne abfolute and plenarie power ought to choofe their paftor, and not bifhops.

Amphil. The churches haue no further [2] power in the election of their paftor, than as I haue told you, that is, to iudge of his conuerfation & integritie of life, referring the whole action befides to the bifhops and elders. For if the churches fhould elect their minifter or paftor of themfelues abfolutely, befides that it would breed confufion (for fome would choofe one, fome another, fome this, and fome that, neuer contenting themfelues with any) the church fhould doe that alfo, which were directly contrarie to the word of God. For certeine it is, the church hath no abfolute power by the word of God

[2] leaf N 7, back]

Churches should not elect their Minifters without the Bifhop's approval.

II. 2. *No sole right in a Church to appoint its Pastor.*

to elect their paſtor, to chooſe him, to cal him orderly in ſuch forme as is appointed in the word, obſeruing all kinde of rites, ceremonies, & orders belonging thereto. Neither was it euer ſeene that any church did euer practiſe the ſame. For in the dais of the apoſtles, did the churches any more than chooſe foorth certeine perſons of a tried conuerſation, & preſented them to the apoſtles? And did not the apoſtles then, (whom our biſhops now in this action do repreſent) lay their hands vpon them, approue them (after triall had of their ſufficiencie in knowledge) and ſent them foorth into the Lords vineyard? The churches laid not their hands vpon them, or as ſome call it, conſecrated them not, nor vſed not any other ceremoniall rite in the [1]election of them, as the apoſtles did. But as I grant that the church for ſom cauſe, and in ſom reſpects, is not to be excluded from a conſultatiue voyce (as before) or from being made priuie at al to the election of their paſtor, ſo I denie that the church may abſolutely of his owne plenarie power cal their paſtor, all ceremonies and rites thereto belonging obſerued, for that is to be done and executed of the biſhops & elders, and not of the churches conſiſting of lay men, and for the moſt part rude, and vnlearned.

Theod. What ſay you to a ſeigniorie or elderſhip? were it not good for the ſtate of the church at this day that yᵉ ſame were eſtabliſhed in euery congregation, as it was in the apoſtles daies.

Amphil. The ſeueral eſtates and conditions of the apoſtolicall churches, and of ours (al circumſtances duly conſidered) are diuers and much different one from another, and therefore, though a ſeigniorie or elderſhip then in euerie particular church were neceſſarie, yet now vnder chriſtian princes it is not ſo needfull. The churches then wanted chriſtian princes and magiſtrates to gouerne the ſame, and therefore had need of ſome others to rule in the church. But God be thanked, we haue moſt chriſtian kings, princes, and gouernors, to rule and gouerne the church, & therfore [2]we ſtand in leſſe need of the other. And yet notwithſtanding, I grant that a ſeigniorie in euery congregation were to be wiſhed, if it could be brought to paſſe, yet cannot I perceiue, but that it would rather bring confuſion, than reformation, conſidering the ſtate of the church at this day. For in the apoſtles times when ſeigniories were ordeined, we read not of any ſhires, dioces, or precincts, where biſhops and eccleſiaſticall magiſtrates

II. 2. *Elders not needed.*   *Churchwardens as Deacons.* 101

might exercife their authoritie and gouernement, as now they doe, and therefore, there being neither bifhops, ecclefiafticall nor ciuill magiftrates (as we haue now), it was neceffarie that the feigniories fhuld be ordeined. But now we, hauing al thefe things, ftand not in fuch neceffitie of them, as the churches in the apoftles daies did. Befides, the inftitution of elders was but meere ceremoniall, and temporall, and therefore not to continue alwaies, neither ought the neceffitie thereof to binde all churches. Neither doe I thinke that all churches are bound for euer to one forme of externall gouernement, but that euery church may alter, and change the fame, according to the time and prefent ftate therof, as they fhal fee the fame to make for the glorie of God, and the comon peace of the church. is not needed now.

Every Church may alter its forme of external government from time to time.

¹*Theod.* What fay you to deacons? Is their office neceffarie or not in the church of God at this day?   [¹ Sig. O. 1.]

Amphil. Their office (which was to make collections for the poore, to gather the beneuolences, and contributions of euerie one that were difpofed to giue, and to fee the fame beftowed vpon the poore and needie members of the church) is very neceffarie, and without doubt ought to be continued for euer. But yet is not the church tied to their names onely, but to their office. Which office is executed by honeft fubftantiall men (called Churchwardens or the like) chofen by the confent of the whole congregation to the fame end and purpofe, who daily gathering the friendlye beneuolencies of the churches, beftow, or fee the fame beftowed vpon the poore and indigent of the fame church, which was the greateft part of the deacons duties in the apoftles daies. So that albeit wee haue not the name, we yet hold their office in fubftance and effect. The office of *Deacon* is ftill very necessary.

Now it is filld by Churchwardens, who daily gather almes and give em to the poor.

Theod. What is your iudgement, ought there to be any bifhops in the churches of chriftians?

Amphil. To doubt whether there ought to be bifhops in the churches of chriftians, is to doubt of the truth it felfe. For is there not ²mention made of their names, dignities, functions, and callings, almoft in euery chapter of the new teftament, in all the epiftles of *Paule,* of *Peter,* of *Iohn,* of *Iude,* and of all the reft? Befides that, did not the apoftles themfelues conftitute and ordeine bifhops and elders; and doe they not woonderfully commende the excellencie of their calling, inferring that thofe that rule well, are worthye of double   [² Sig. O. 1. back]

The Apoftles ordaind Bifhops.

honour? Whereby appeereth that bifhops are not onlye needefull in the churches of chriftians, but alfo moft needfull, as without whome I can fcarcely fee how the ftate of the church could well bee maintained. And therefore thofe that contend that they are not neceffarie in a Chriftian Common wealth, fhewe them felues either wilfull, waiwarde, or maliciouflye blinde, and ftriuing to catch their owne fhadowes, they labour all in vaine, giuing manifeft demonftration of their more than extreame follie to all the world.

> *The state of the Church couldn't be kept up without em.*

Theod. Well. Let it bee granted (as it cannot bee denied) that they are mofte neceffarie, yet in this I would verie gladlye bee abfolued, whether they maye lawfully vendicate or challenge to themfelues fuperioritie, and primacie aboue their fellowe [1] brethren of the minifterie or no? for fome holde that there ought to be equalitie in the minifterie, and no fuperioritie at all: how fay you?

> [[1] Sig. O. 2.]

Amphil. They doe not vendicate or challenge anie fuperioritie or primacie to themfelues ouer their brethren in refpect of their common callings and functions (for therein the pooreft paftor or fhepheard that is, is coequall with them, they themfelues will not denie) but in refpect of dignitie, authoritie, and honour, which the prince and church doth beftowe vpon them. So that the fuperioritie that they haue ouer their brethren, refteth in dignitie, authoritie, and honour, which it hath pleafed the prince to dignifie them withall aboue their felowe brethren, and not in calling, function, or office, for therein they are all coequall togither. But if any curious heads fhould demand why the prince fhould aduance any of the cleargie to fuch high dignitie, authoritie, and primacie aboue his brethren, I anfwer as it is in the Gofpell: ' Is thine eie euill, bicaufe the prince is good?' May not the prince giue his gifts, his dignities, and promotions to whom he will? And if the prince of his roiall clemencie be minded to beftowe vpon his fubiect any dignity or promotion, is it chriftian obedience [2] [3] to refufe the fame? Nay, is it not extreeme ingratitude towards his prince? Befides, who feeth not, that if there fhould be no fuperioritie (I meane in dignitie, & authoritie only) the fame honorable office or calling would growe into contempt? For is it not an old faieng, and a true, *Familiaritas, fiue æqualitas parit contemptum,* Familiaritie, or coequallitie doth euer bring contempt. And

> *They don't claim superiority to other Paftors as to their calling, but only as to the dignity that the prince has given em.*

> [[3] Sig. O. 2. back]

> *There must be superiority in dignity.*

> *Familiarity breeds contempt.*

[2] *Orig.* abedience.

therefore take awaye authoritie and honor from the magiſtrates either temporall or ſpirituall, and ouerthrowe the ſame altogither. If authoritie ſhould not be dignified, as well with glorie and eternall pompe the better to grace the ſame, & to ſhew forth the maieſtie thereof, would it not ſoone grow to be diſpiſed, vilipended, and naught ſet by? And therefore the more to innoble and ſet foorth the excellencie of this honorable calling of a biſhop, hath the prince & the churches thought it good to beſtow ſuch authoritie, dignitie, and honor vpon them, and not for anie other cauſe whatſoeuer. And therefore, ſeeing it is the pleaſure of the prince to beſtowe ſuch dignitie, authoritie, and honor vpon them, me thinke, any ſober chriſtians ſhould eaſely tolerate the ſame. *Sober Chriſtians ſhould tolerate Biſhops.*

Theod. Yea, but they ſaie, that there ought to be no ſuperioritie in the miniſterie, [1] bringing in the example of the apoſtles themſelues, amongſt whom was no ſuperiority, inequalitie, or principallitie at all? [1 Sig. O. 3.]

Amphil. Indeede amongſt the apoſtles there was no ſuperioritie, I grant, neither in office, calling, authoritie, nor otherwiſe, but al were equall in ech reſpecte, one to another. But what than? The apoſtles were ſent to preach to the churches, and not to gouerne (and therefore they chooſe elders to rule the ſame) but our biſhops are as well to gouerne and to rule the churches in ſome reſpects, as to preach the worde. And therfore, though there were no ſuperioritie amongſt the apoſtles, yet maye there be amongſt our biſhops in reſpect of gouer[n]ment, dignitie and authoritie. And wheras they ſaie there ought to be no ſuperioritie in the miniſterie at all, I anſweare, no more there is in reſpect of euerie ones function, forme of calling, and office to preach the word and miniſter the ſacraments. But in reſpect of gouernement, authoritie, dignitie, and honor, there is ſuperioritie, and I am perſwaded ſo ought to be. In which opinion, vntill they haue diſprooued it, I meane, Chriſt willing, to perſiſte. *Biſhops haue to rule as well as preach.*

Theod. But they adde further, and ſay that it ſtrengtheneth the hands of the aduerſaries, [2] the papiſts. For, ſaie they, the papiſts may as well affirme that chriſtian emperours, kings and potentates, and euen the churches of God themſelues, haue giuen to the pope that authoritie, that dignitie, and honor which he hath or claimeth aboue his fellowe brethren, as well as the biſhop may ſay ſo. Beſides, it confirmeth the opinion of foueraigntie ouer all the churches in the [2 Sig. O. 3. back] *The Papiſt argument that the*

II. 2. Bishops and the Archdevil Pope contrasted.

Marginal notes:
- Pope has his power from Kings, &c., as Bishops do.
- But, 1. Papists say that
- the Pope gets his power from God. Not true.
- [¹ Sig. O. 4] The Pope didn't get his superiority from God,
- but from the Devil, whose Lieutenant-General he is.
- Prince may lawfully give Prerogative in his own land.
- [² Sig. 4. back]
- May a Bishop be called 'My Lord,' &c. ?

world. For, say they, may not the pope saie that he receiued plenarie power to be head ouer all the world, from christian kings, emperours, and potentates, as well as the bishops may say, we receiued this power to be superior to our brethren from christian kings and princes. Now whether these reasons be a like, I would gladly know.

Amphil. They be verie vnlike, and so vnlike as there is no equallitie, comparison, or semblance betwixt them. For, first of all, let them note, that the pope nor any of his complices and adherents doe not holde, nor pretende to holde, (no, they dare as well eate off their fingers as to say so, for then were there state in a wofull case) that their archdiuell, their god, the pope, I should say, doth receiue his power either of authoritie, superioritie, primacie, soueraigntie, or head ouer all the world, from any earthly creature, but immediately from God ¹himselfe. But whereas hee sayth that hee receiued his power of superioritie ouer all the worlde from no earthie creature, but from God himselfe, it is manifest that he receyued it neyther from God (for his vsurped power is contrarie to God, and to his worde in euerie respecte) nor from anie christian man, but from the Deuill himselfe, whose vicegerent or Liefetenant generall in his kingedome of impietie he shewes himselfe to be. Than let them note, that although hee pretended to holde his vsurped authoritie from man (as hee doth not,) yet is there no man howe mightie an Emperour, King, Prince, or Potentate soeuer, that is able *proprio iure* to giue him authoritie ouer all the worlde, without great and manifeste iniurye done to all other Princes, as to giue the soueraigntie, or chieftie of their Landes from them, to a straunger. But a Prince may lawfullye bestowe and geue to his subiectes anie prerogatiue, title, authoritie, office, function, gouernment, or superioritie of anie thing within his owne dominions and kingdomes, but no further he maye not. And therefore this reason of theirs holdeth not, that the Pope maye as well arrogate the one to himselfe, as the Byshops may the other to themselues.

²*Theod.* Seeing now it cannot be denied, but that bishops are most necessarie, and that they may also lawfully hold superioritie ouer their brethren (in respect of gouernement, regiment or authoritie) being giuen them of the prince, what say you then to this? Whether may a bishop be called by the name of an archbishop, metropolitane, primate, or by the name of 'my Lord bishop, my Lords grace, the

II. 2. Bishops may bear Titles given by Princes.

right honourable,' and the like, or not? For, me thinke, these titles and names are rather peculiar to the temporalitie than to them, & do sauour of vainglorie, and worldly pompe, rather than of any thing else. And which is more, me thinke they are against the expresse word of God. Wherefore I couet greatly to heare your iudgement thereof?

Amphil. These names and titles may seeme to fauour of vaine-glorie indeed, if they should arrogate to themselues *Iure diuino*, as they doe not. But if you wil consider by whom they were giuen them, and how they doe require them, you will not thinke it much amisse, nor farre discrepant from the sinceritie of the Gospell. First therefore note that they were giuen them by christian princes to dignifie, to innoble, to decore, and to set foorth the dignitie, the excellencie, and worthines of their cal¹lings. Secondly let them note that they require them as due vnto them by the donation and gifture of men, and not *Iure diuino*, and therefore being giuen them for the causes aforesaid by christian kings and princes, they may in that respect hold them still without any offence to the diuine goodnesse, or his faithfull spouse vpon the earth. But if they shuld claime them as due vnto them by the lawe of God, as they doe not, then should they offend. For our sauiour Christ, seeing his disciples and apostles ambiciously to affect the same vainglorious titles and names, set before them the example of the heathen kings, thereby the rather to withdrawe them from their vaine humour, saieng: *Reges gentium dominantur eis*, &c. The kings of the gentils beare rule ouer them, and those that exercise authoritie ouer them, be called gratious Lords, but *Vos autem non sic*, You shall not be so. In the which words he vtterly denieth them (and in them, all others to the worlds end, that in the same office and function of life shuld succeed them) the titles of Lords, graces, or the like. The apostle also biddeth them to beware that they challenge not those vaine titles to themselues by the lawe of God, when he saith (speaking to bishops and pastors) Be not Lords ouer your flocks, &c. By ²these and manie other the like places of holie writt, it is cleare that they cannot arrogate these names or titles to themselues by yᵉ word of God; neyther doe they, but (as I haue said) by the donation, the beneuolence, and gifture of christian Princes, for the reuerent estimation they bare and ought to beare to

[Side notes:]
Yes, tho' these titles look vainglorious. God doesn't give 'em, but the Prince does.

[¹ leaf O 5]

If Bishops claim these titles by God's law, they do wrong.

Christ 'ud have none of this.

[² Sig. O 5, back]

These titles of 'Bishop,' &c., are not given by God's Word, but only by Christian Princes, their high function and calling, in that they are his Liefetenants, his vicegerents in his Church, his meſſengers, his Ambaſſadors, the diſcloſers and proclaimers of his ſecretes, and his Aungels (for ſo are they called in the ſcriptures) & therfore, in reſpecte of the excellencie hereof, theſe names were giuen and attributed vnto them. And truely to ſpeake my ſimple iudgement, I ſee not but that theſe names doe dignifie their callinges, ſhewe forth the maieſtie thereof, and doe moue the Churches to haue the ſame high calling in more reuerence, & honor, than otherwiſe they would, if they were called by bare & naked names onelie. But notwithſtanding either this that hath beene ſaide, or anie thinge els that can be ſaid herein, there are ſome waiward ſpirits lately reuiued, who hold the ſame names to be meere Antichriſtian, blaſphemous and wicked, and ſuche as at anie hande a Miniſter of the Goſpell ought not to bee called by. But whereas they holde them to bee Antichri¹ſtian, I holde them to be Chriſtian names, and geuen by Chriſtian Princes to the innobling and garniſhing of their offices, functions, and callinges, which doubtleſſe is a glorie to God, denie it who will, or who can. And therefore in concluſion I ſay, that Byſhops, though not by the lawe of God, yet by the poſitiue law, donation, and gifture of Chriſtian Princes, maye lawfully aſſume the ſaide titles and names to them, for the cauſes before cited. And therefore theſe names and titles beeing meere indifferent, and not derogating from the glorie of God, but rather making for the ſame, they are not, of anye wiſe, ſober, or faythfull Chriſtian, neyther to bee inueighed againſt, nor yet to bee in anye reſpecte diſlyked beeing vſed as before. And thus much of the names and titles of Byſhops.

Theod. Maye Byſhops exerciſe temporall authoritie together with Eccleſiaſticall; and maye they bee Iuſtices of peace, Iuſtices of Quorum, Iuſtices of Aſſiſes, Ewer, Determiner, and the lyke; or maye they, as Capytall Iudges, geue definytiue ſentence of lyfe and death vpon malefactors and others, that by the iudiciall lawe of man haue deſerued to dye?

²*Amphil.* There is neither of the callings temporall, nor eccleſiaſticall, but it requireth a whole and perfect man, to execute the ſame. And if there were neuer founde any one man yet ſo perfect, as could throughly and abſolutelie performe his office in either of

---

Marginal notes:
- and they dignify their holders callings.
- They are not Anti-christian but Christian,
- [¹ Sig. O 6]
- and Bishops may lawfully assume them.
- [² Sig. O 6, back]
- A man can only fulfill one calling.

the callings temporall or ecclesiasticall, much lesse can there euer one man be found, that is able to discharg them both. It is hard therefore that these two callings should concurre in one man. This is as though a man hauing an importable burthen alreadie vpon his backe, should yet haue an other almost as burthenous vrged vppon him. And therefore as it were absurde to see a temporall magistrate mount into the pulpit, preach the worde, and minister the sacraments, so absurde it is to see an ecclesiasticall magistrate exercise the authoritie temporall, and to giue sentence condemnatorie of life, & death, vpon any criminous person, which properlie belongeth to the temporall power. Besids, it is a great discredite to the temporall magistrate, because it may be thought that they are not wise nor politique inough to execute their office, nor discharge their duties without the aide and assistance of the other. And which is more, it hindereth them from the discharge of their duties in their owne calling, for [1]it is written, no man can serue two masters but either he must betraie the one or the other. When the woman taken in adultery was apprehended, and brought vnto Christ, he refused to giue iudgement of hir; and yet it was a matter in effect ecclesiasticall, & appertained to an ecclesiasticall iudge. Then what ought they to do in matters meere ciuil? Againe, our sauior[2] Christ, when the yong man requested him to deuide the inheritance betwixt his brother, & him, refused the same, saieng, *Quis me constituit iudicem inter vos?* Who made me a iudge or a deuider betwixt you? Whereby appeareth how farre ecclesiasticall persons ought to bee from hauing to doe with temporal matters. But whereas they say the bishops of *Dnalgne* do exercise temporall authoritie, and doe it as iudges capitall, giuing sentence condemnatorie of life and death, it is verie vntrue otherwise than thus, to be present at the same, & to haue a consultatiue exhortatiue, or consentatiue voice onely. Which vse me thinkes is verie good and laudable in my iudgement. For whereas the temporal magistrates not vnderstanding in euerie point the deapth of Gods lawe, if they shoulde doe anie thing either against the same, or the lawe of a good conscience, they might informe them thereof, that [3]all things might bee done to the glorie of God, the comforte of the poore members of Christe Iesus, and the benefit of the common welth.

[² sauior do *Orig.*]

Side notes: No ecclesiasticall officer should exercise temporall authority, like condemning men to death. [¹ Sig. O 7] No man can serue 2 Masters. Christ refused to be a Judge. And English Bishops haue only a consultatiue voice in giuing temporal Judgments. [³ Sig. O 7, back]

II. 2. *The Ministers that flaunt in Satin Doublets.*

Theod. What fashion of apparell doe the pastors and Ministers weare vsually in their common affaires?

Amphil. The same fashion that others doe, for the most parte, but yet decente, and comlie, obseruing in euerie point a *decorum*. But as others weare their attire, some of this colour, some of that, some of this thinge, some of that, so they commonly weare all their apparell, at least the exteriour part, of blacke colour, which, as you know, is a good, graue, sad, and auncient colour. And yet notwithstanding herein some of them (I speake not of all) are muche to bee blamed, in that they cannot content themselues with common, and vsuall fashions, but they must chop and chaunge euerie day with the worlde. Yea, some of them are as fonde in excogitating, deuising, and inuenting of new fashions euerie day, & in wearing the same, as the veriest Royster of them all. And as they are faultie in this respect, so are they herein to be blamed, in that they cannot contente themselues with cloth, though neuer so excellent, but they must weare silkes, veluets, satans, damaskes, grograms, taffeties, and the like. I speake not agaynst [1] those that are in authoritie, for wearing of these thinges (for they both maie, and in some respectes ought to weare them for the dignifying of their offices and callings, which otherwise mighte growe into contempte), but against those that bee meane pastours and Ministers, that flaunt it out in their saten doblets, taffetie doblets, silke hosen, garded gownes, cloakes, and the like. Alas, how shoulde they rebuke pryde, and excesse in others, who are as faultye therein as the reste? Therefore sayde Cato veryè well, *Quae culpare soles, ea tu ne feceris ipse:* for, sayeth he, *Turpe est doctori, cum culpa redarguit ipsum.* Which is, those thinges which thou blamest in others, see that thou thy selfe bee not guiltye in the same, for it is a foule blemish and a great shame and discredit, what that euyll which thou reprouest in an other, is apparent in thy selfe. For in so doing, a man reprehendeth as well himselfe as others, is a hinderance to the course of the Gospell, and what he buildeth with one hand, he pulleth down with the other. Christ Iesus, the great pastor of the sheepe, was himself contented to go daily in one poore coat, beeing knit, or wouen all ouer without seeme, as the maner of ye Palistinians is to this day. This me think was but a simple cote [2] in the eie of the world, and yet Christ Iesus thought it pretious inough. Samuel was accustomed to

Pastors dress like other folk,

and generally in black.

But some are very fond of new Fashions,

and wear silks, &c.,
[1 Sig. O 8]

satin doublets, &c.

This is a foul blemish in them.

Christ wore but one poor coat,

[2 Sig. O 8, back]

walke in an old gowne girded to him with a thong. *Elias* and *Elizeus* in a mantell, Iohn the baptift in camels haire, with a girdle of a fkin about his loines. The apoftle Paule with a poore cloke, and the like; wherby appeareth, how farre a minifter of the Gofpell ought to be from pride, and worldly vanitie, obferuing the rules of chriftian fobrietie, as well in apparell, as in al things elfe, knowing that he is as a citie fet vppon an hill, and as a candle fet vppon a candlefticke to giue light, and fhine to al the whole church of God. Therfore faith Chrift: *Sic luceat lux veftra coram hominibus*, &c. Let your light fo fhine before men, that they, feeing your good works, may glorifie your father which is in heauen: which God grant we may all doe.

and Paul a poor cloak.

Let the Minifters be sober in dress.

Theod. Haue they no other kind of apparell different from the common fort of men?

Amphil. Yes, marie, haue they. They haue other attire more proper, and peculiar vnto them (in refpect of their functions and offices) as cap, tippet, furpleffe, and the like. Thefe they weare, not commonly, or altogither, but in efpecial when they are occupied in, or about, the execution of their offices and callings, to [1] this end and [2] purpofe, that there may be a difference betwixte them and the common forte of people, and that the one maie be diftincte from the other by this outward note or marke.

But, when officiating, they wear Cap, Tippet, Surplice, &c.

[1 Sig. P. 1.]

Theodo. Is it of neceffitie than required, that the Paftors and Minifters of the worde, fhoulde be diftincted from other people, by anie feuerall kind of attire?

Amphil. It is not required as of neceffitie, but thought meete and conuenient to be ufed for a decencie, and comlines, in the Church of God. But notwithftanding the chiefeft thyng wherby a paftor or minifter oght to be known from the common & vulgare forte of people is, the preaching of the word of God, the adminiftration of the facraments, the execution of ecclefiaftical difcipline, and other cenfures of the Church, and withall his integritie of lyfe, and foundneffe of conuerfation in euerie refpecte. Thefe are the true notes and markes wherby a Minifter of the Gofpell ought to bee knowen and diftincted from the other common forte of people. And yet though thefe bee the chiefeft notes whereby they are diftinct from others of the temporalitie and laitie, yet are they not the onelie notes,

But their chief distinction should be in Preaching and Holy Life.

[2 end end *Orig.*]

110 II. 2. *Ministers may well have a distinct dress.*

[¹ Sig. P. 1., back]
tho their outward mark is Cap, Surplice, &c.

or markes, for they are knowen and difcerned from others alfo, by exteriour habite, and attire, as namely by cappe, tippet, fur¹pleffe, and fuch like: That as the firft doth diftinguifh them from others, whileft they are exercifed about the fame, (for who is fo doltifhe, that feeing a man preache, minifter the facraments, & execute other eccleſiafticall cenfures of the church, that will not iudge him to bee a Minifter of the Gofpell) fo the other notes of apparell (the furpleffe except) may make a difference, and diftinguifhe them from others of the laitie abroad. To this end, that the reuerence which is due to a good paftor, or minifter of the Gofpell may be giuen vnto them. For as the Apoftle faith, thofe elders that rule well, are worthie of double honour.

As to thofe who object to a different dress for Paftors,

Theod. But I haue heard great difputation and reafoning *pro & contra*, to and fro, that the paftors and minifters of the Gofpell, ought not to be diffeuered from the common forte of people, by anie diftincte kinde of apparell, but rather by founding the Lordes voice on high, by miniftring the facramentes, and the like: what fay you to the fame?

and try to justify their opinion by the Bible,

Amphil. Indeede there are fome, I confeffe, that are of that opinion, and they bring in the example of Saule, enquiring of Samuell for the feers houfe, inferring that the Prophet was not diftinct from other common people in his attire, for than Saule fhould

[² Sig. P. 2.]

eafelie ²haue knowen him by the fame. And the example of the damofell that fpake to Peter, inferring that whereas the mayde fayde, *Thy fpeech bewrayeth thee,* if he had bene diftincte from others in attire, or outwarde apparell, fhee would than haue fayd, *Thy apparel fheweth thee to bee fuch a fellowe.* Thefe, with the like examples, they pretende to prooue that paftors and Minifters are not to bee difcerned and knowen from the lay people, by anye kinde of apparell. But as I will not faie that they are to bee knowen and difcerned from others by apparell or habite onelye, (but rather by the lifting vp

I can't agree with em.

of their voices like Trumpets, as faith the Prophet,) fo I wyll not denye the fame to bee no note or marke at all to knowe a Paftour or Minifter of the Gofpell by, from others of the temporaltie, and laitie. And

I think a different dress justifiable.

truelye for my parte, I fee no great inconuenience, if they bee by a certaine kinde of decente habite (commaunded by a Chriftian Prince) known and difcerned from others. Yet fome more curious than wife, before they would weare anie diſtinct kind of apparell from others, they haue rather choſen to render vp both liuinges, goods, families, and all, leauing their flockes to the mouth of the wolues.

Theod. Is it lawfull for a miniſter of the Goſpell to weare a ſurpleſſe, a tippet or forked cappe, and the like kind of attire? [1 Sig. P. 2. back *If Tippets, forkt Caps, &c.*,]

Amphil. As they are commaunded by the Pope, the great Antichriſt of the worlde, they ought not to weare them; but as they be commaunded, and inioyned by a Chriſtian Prince, they maie weare them without ſcruple of conſcience. But if they ſhould repoſe any religion, holineſſe or ſanctimonie in them, as the doting Papiſts doe, than doe they greeuouſlie offende; but wearing them as things meere indifferent (although it be controuerſiall whether they bee things indifferente or not), I ſee no cauſe why they maie not vſe them. [*are orderd by a Chriſtian Prince,* *I think Miniſters may wear them,*]

Theod. From whence came theſe garments, can you tell? from Rome, or from whence els?

Amphil. The moſt hold that they came firſt from Rome, the poiſon of all the world; & moſt likelie they did ſo; but ſome other ſearching the ſame more narrowlie, do hold *that* they came, not from Rome, but rather from Grecia, which from the beginning, for the moſt part, hath euer been contrarie to the Church of Rome. But from whence ſoeuer they came it ſkilleth not much, for beeing mere indifferent, they maie be worn or not worne without offence, according to the pleaſure of the Prince, as things which of themſelues bee not euill, nor cannot hurte, excepte they be abuſed. [*even tho they firſt came from Rome.* 2 Sig. P. 3.]

Theod. Notwithſtanding they holde this for a *maxime*, that in as much as they came firſt from the Papiſtes, and haue of them bene idolatrouſlie abuſed, that therefore they are not, nor ought not to bee, vſed of anie true paſtors, or Miniſters of the Goſpell. Is this their *aſſumption* true, or not?

Amphil. It is no good reaſon to ſay ſuch a thing came from the Papiſtes, *ergo* it is naught. For we read that the Deuils confeſſed Ieſus Chriſt to be the ſonne of God: doth it follow therefore that the ſame profeſſion is naughte, becauſe a wicked creature vttered the ſame? All thinges are therefore to bee examined, whether the abuſe conſiſt in the thinges themſelues, or in others that abuſe them. Which being found out, let the abuſes be remoued, and the thinges remaine ſtill. A wicked man maye ſpeake good wordes, doe good [*Uſe of a good thing by Papiſts, doeſn't make the good thing bad.* *If a good thing is abuſd,*]

II. 2. Clear away abuses from good things abused.

works before the world, (but becaufe they want the oile of faith to fouple them withall, they are not good workes before the Lord) and maie ordaine a good thing which maie ferue to good ends, and purpofes. And becaufe the fame hath afterward beene abufed, fhall the thing it felfe therefore be quite taken away? No, take away the abufe, let the thinge [1] remaine ftill, as it maye very well without anie offence, except to them, *quibus omnia dantur fcandalo*, to whom all thinges are offence. And further, if thefe preficians would haue all things remoued out of the Church which haue beene abufed to Idolatrie, than muft they pull downe Churches (for what hath bene abufed more to Idolatrie and fuperftition?) pulpits, belles, and what not. Than muft they take away the vfe of bread and wine, not onely from the church, but alfo from the vfe of man in this life, becaufe ye fame was abufed to moft fhamefull idolatrie in beeing dedicate to *Ceres*, and *Bacchus*, twoo ftinking Idols of the Gentiles. Than muft they take away not onely the Epiftles, and Gofpels, but alfo the whole volume of the holy fcriptures, becaufe the Papiftes abufed them to idolatrie. By all which reafons, with infinite the like, it manifeftly appeareth, that manie things which haue beene inftituted by Idolaters, or by them abufed to Idolatrie, may be applied to good vfes, and may ferue to good ends, ye abufes being taken away. Yet wold I not that any thing that hath been idolatroufly abufed by the papifts, fhould be reteined in the churches of Chriftians, if by any meanes they might be remoued, and better put in place.

Theod. Is the wearing of thefe garments [2] a thing meere indifferent, or not? for fome hold it is, fome hold it is not?

Amphil. It is a thing without all controuerfy mere indifferent; for, whatfoeuer gods word neither exprefly commandeth, neither directly forbiddeth, nor which bindeth not ye confcience of a chriftian man, is a thing mere indifferent to be vfed, or not to be vfed, as the prefent ftate of ye church, & time requireth. But it is certen that the wearing of this kind of attire is not exprefly commanded in the word of God, nor directly forbid by the fame, & therfore is mere indifferent, and may be vfed, or not vfed, without burthen of confcience, as ye prefent ftate of time fhall require. And therfore feeing they be things indifferent, I wold wifh euery wife chriftian to tollerate ye fame, being certen that he is neither better nor worfe, for wearing or not wearing of them.

Marginalia:
- take away the Abuſe, and let the Good Thing ſtay. [¹ Sig. P. 3. back]
- If everything that idolatrous Papiſts have uſd is to be done away with,
- the Bible and moſt other good things 'll have to go.
- [² Sig. P. 4.]
- Theſe Garments are a mere matter of Indifference: do as you like about em.
- Put up with Garments: a man's no better or worſe for em.

II. 2. *Princes to be obeyd as to Garments, &c.*

Theod. Being things, as you say, mere indifferent, may any man lawfully refuse y⁶ wearing of them againſt the commandement of his prince, whom, next vnder God, he ought to obey?

Amphil. Euery man is bound in conſcience before God to obey his prince in all things, yea in things directly contrary to true godlines hee is bound to ſhew his obedience (but not to commit y⁶ euil) namely to ſubmit himſelfe life, lands, liuings or els whatſoeuer he hath, to y⁶ wil of his ¹Princes, rather than to diſobeie. If this obedience than be due to Princes in matters contrarie to true godlineſſe, what obedience than is due to them in matters of ſmall waight, of ſmall importaunce, and meere triffles as theſe garments be, iudge you? He that diſobeieth the commaundement of his Prince, diſobeieth the commaundement of God; and therfore, would God all Eccleſiaſticall perſons that ſtande ſo muche vpon theſe ſmall pointes, that they breake the common vnitie, & band of charitie in the church of God, would nowe at the laſt quallifie themſelues, ſhewe obedience to Princes lawes, and fall to preaching of Chriſt Ieſus truelie, that his kingdome might dailie bee increaſed, their conſciences diſcharged, and the Church edefied, which Chriſte Ieſus hath bought with the ſhedding of his precious hart bloud.

[¹ Sig. P. 4. back]

And if your Prince orders them, of courſe obey him in ſuch a Trifle.

Theod. Maie a paſtor, or a Miniſter of the Goſpell, forſake his flocke, and refuſe his charge, for the wearing of a ſurpleſſe, a cappe, tippet, or the like, as manie haue done of late daies, who being inforced to weare theſe garmentes, haue giuen up their liuings, and forſaken all?

Amphil. Thoſe that for the wearing of theſe garments, being but the inuentions, the traditions, the rites, the ceremonies, the ordinances & conſtitutions of man, will leaue their flocks, ²and giue ouer their charges, not caring what become of the ſame, doe ſhew themſelues to be no true ſhepheards, but ſuch as Chriſt ſpeaketh of, that when they ſee the Wolfe comming, will flie away, leauing their flocke to the ſlaughter of the greedie wolfe. They giue euident demonſtration alſo, that they are not ſuch as the holie Ghoſt hath made ouerſeers ouer their flocke, but rather ſuch, as being poſſeſſed with the ſpirite of pride and ambition, haue intruded themſelues, to the deſtruction of their flocke. If they were ſuch good ſhepheards as they ought to be, and ſo louing to their flocke, they would rather giue their life for

Any Paſtor who leaves his Flock becauſe he won't wear a Surplice, &c., [² Sig. P 5]

shows that he's no good Shepherd.

114 II. 2. *Surplices may be worn if the Prince bids.*

their sheepe, if neede required, than to runne from them, leauing them to the bloodie teeth of the mercilesse wolues. Is hee a good shepheard that watcheth dailie vppon his flocke, or hee that runnes from them for euerie light trifle? I thinke we would count him a verie negligent shepheard. And shall wee thinke him a diligent, or a good pastor, and one that would giue his life for his sheepe, as a good pastor should doe, that for such trifles wil estrang himselfe from his flocke for euer? Therefore I beseech God to giue them grace to looke to their charges, and to let other trifles alone, being no part of our saluation or damnation.

> *How can he be a good Shepherd who should give his Life for his Sheep, when he'll leave em for trifles like Garments?*

> [¹ Sig. P 5, back]

Theod. But they saie they refuse the wea¹ring of these garments, becuase they are offensiue to the godlie, a scandall to the weake brethren, a hinderaunce to manie in comming to the Gospel, & an induration to the papists hardning their hearts, in hope that their trumperie will once come in again, to their singular comfort.

Amphil. It is an old saying, Better a bad excuse, than none at all. And truly it seemeth they are driuen to the wall, and sore graueled, that will flie to these simple shifts. But whatsoeuer they say or affirme, certain it is, that offensiue to the godly they cannot be, who haue already learned to distinguish betwixt the things abused, and the abuses themselues. And who know also how to vse things mere indifferent, to good ends and purposes. And therfore this question thus I shut vp in few words, that the wearing of these garmentes beeing commaunded by a Christian Prince, is not offensiue, or scandalous to anie good Christians; and to the other, it mattereth not what it be. For they are such as the Lorde hath cast off into a reprobate sence, and preiudicate opinion, abusing all things, euen the truth it selfe, to their owne destruction for euer, excepte they repent, which I praye God they maye doe, if it bee his blessed will.

> *If these Garments are orderd by a Christian Prince, no good Christian should be offended by em.*

> ² Sig. P 6]

²*Theod.* I pray you why doe they weare white in their surplesses, rather than any other colour? and why a forked cappe rather than a rounde one? for the Papistes (if they were the authors of these garmentes) haue their misteries, their figures, & their representations in all things. Wherfore I desire to know your iudgment herein.

> *The Papists say that White signifies Holiness;*

Amphil. You say the truth, for the Papistes haue their misteries in all thinges after their maner. Therfore thus they say, that white doth signify holines, innocency, & al kind of integrity, putting them in mind what they ought to be in this life, and reprefenteth vnto them the beatitude, the felicitie, and happines of the life to come. And thys they prooue *ab exemplis apparitionum*, from the example of apparitions and vifions, in that aungels, and celeftial creatures haue euer appeared in the fame colour of white. Therefore forfooth they muft weare white apparell. The cornered cappe, fay thefe mifterious fellows, doth fignifie, and reprefent the whole monarchy of the world, Eaft, Weft, North, & South, the gouernment whereof ftandeth vpon them, as the cappe doth vppon their heades. The gowne, faye they, doth fignifie the plenary power which they haue to doe all things. And therefore none but the Pope, or hee [1] with whome hee difpenceth, maie weare the fame euerie where, bicaufe none haue *plenariam potestatem*, plenarie power, in euerie place, but (Beelzebub) the Pope. Yet the Minifters, faith he, maie weare them in their Churches, & in their owne iurifdictions, becaufe therein they haue full power from him. Thus foolifhlie do they deceiue themfelues with vaine fhewes, fhadows, and imaginations, forged in the mint of their owne braines, to the deftruction of manie. But who is he, that becaufe thefe fottifhe Papiftes haue and doe greeuouflie abufe thefe thinges, will therefore haue them cleane remoued? If all things that haue beene abufed, fhould be remooued becaufe of the abufe, than fhould we haue nothing left to the fupply of our neceffities, neither meat, drinke, nor cloth for our bodies, neyther yet (which is more) ye word of God, the fpirituall food of our foules, nor any thing els almoft. For what thing is there in ye whole vniverfall world, that eyther by one Hereticke or other hath not beene abufed? Let vs therfore take the abufes away, and the things maie well remaine ftill. For may not we chriftians vfe thefe thinges which the wicked Papifts haue abufed, to good ends, vfes, and purpofes? I fee no reafon to the contrarie. And therefore in conclufion I befeech the Lorde that wee [2] may all agree togither in one truth, and not to deuide our felues one from another for trifles, making fchifmes, ruptures, breaches, and factions in the church of God, where we ought to nourifh peace, vnitie, concord, brotherly loue, amitie, and frendfhip, one amongft another. And feeing we do all agree togither, and iump in one truth, hauing al one God our father, one Lord Iefus Chrift our fauiour, one holy fpirit of adoption, one price of redemption, one faith, one

[marginal notes:]
the Cornerd Cap the Monarchy of the World,
and the Gown the Pope's plenary power:
[[1] Sig. P 6, back]
all this is gammon.
But because Papists have abufed these things,
as well as the Word of God,
aren't we to ufe em? Surely we are.
[[2] Sig. P 7]
Do let us Reformers all agree, and not make rows.
We've all one God and Saviour,

hope, one baptifme, and one and the fame inheritance in the kingdome of heauen, Let vs therefore agree togither in thefe externall fhadowes, ceremonies and rites. For is it not a fhame to agree about the marrow, and to ftriue about the bone? to contend about the karnell, & to vary about the fhell? to agree in the truth, and to brabble for the fhadow? Let vs confider that this contention of ours among our felues, doth hinder the courfe of the Gofpell from taking fuch deepe roote in the heartes of the hearers, as otherwife it would doe. And thus for this time, brother *Theodorus*, we will breake off our talke concerning this matter, vntill yt pleafe God that we may meete againe. Which if it pleafe God we doe, I promife you in another woorke to difcourfe of the fame more at large. In the mean time let vs giue our felues, [1] to fafting, and prayer, moft humbly befeeching his excellent maiefty to bleffe our noble Queen, and to keepe hir grace as the apple of his eie from all hir foes, to maintaine his word and gofpell amongft vs, to plant vnity and concord within our walles, to increafe our faith, to graunt vs true and vnfained repentaunce for our fins, and in the end eternall life in the kingdome of heauen, thorow ye precious death, paffion, bloodfhedding, and obedience of Chrifte Iefus our Lord, and onely fauiour, to whom, with the father and the holy ghoft, one true, and immortal God, be al honor, praife, power, empire, and dominion throughout all congregations for euermore. And thus, brother *Theodorus*, I bid you farewell in the Lord, till I do fee you againe.

  Theodo. And I you alfo good brother Amphilogus,
   befeeching the Lord that if we meete not
    vpon earth, we maye meete yet in the
     kingdome of heauen, there to reft
      in perfect felicitie
       for euer.

     Amphil. The Lord grant it
      for his mercies fake.
       Amen.

FINIS.

LONDON
Printed by Roger Ward for William Wright, and are to be solde at his shop ioyning to Saint Mildreds Church in the Poultry, being the middle shop in the row.
1583.

INDEX.

Abuses, how to treat, 111
Adam had to till the ground, 49
adjacent upon, 4, bordering on
adulterate calf, 47, one belonging to another cow
Adulteration of Wine, 25
all-to-besprinkled, 51/14
all-to-betorne, 37, torn in pieces
all-to-tickle, 51/15
Almanack-makers who affect to foretell, condemd, 66
Almshouse, one wanted in every parish, 43
ambidexters, hollowe-harted friends, 7
Amphilogus, 1. Phillip Stubbes
Anabaptists, their absurd doctrine, 69
Angel, 12, a lawyer's fee, 6s. 8d. An Angel was a third of a pound: 10s. when the £ was 30s.; and 6s. 8d. when it was 20s.: see W. Stafford's *Examination*, p. 101. (Prof. Leo in his most comical explanation (!) of "Vllorxa" in *Timon* as 'v£ or x angels,' made 5£ = 3£ 6s. 8d.)
Antichrist of Rome, that pernicious, the Pope, 71: see 'Archdiuell'
Apothecaries cheating, 55
Apparel, abuses in, 33
Apparel, of Pastors and Ministers, 108-9
Apparel of Ministers discust, 108—116
appropriate to, 27, appropriated to, held as private property by
aqua vite, aqua angelica, 78
Archdiuell, the Pope, 104
art magike, 5
artificially, *adv.* 35, skilfully, well
Astrologers, their contradictory and false predictions, 57

Astronomers' and Astrologers' abuses, 55-65
auncientie, 49, ancientness

Bailiffs, Law-, cheating, 16
Barbers: their way of trimming amusingly described, 50-1
barbing, *sb.* 50/11, trimming beards, cutting hair, &c.
Beards, the many different cuts of, 50: see *Harrison*, Pt. I, p. 169
bear in hand, 22, 52, 54, pretend, persuade
bear in hand, 46/20, vow, declare
'beastlinesse of some ruffians' who let their hair grow long, 51
Beggars: 2 sorts. 1. the Strong and Sturdy, 2. the Aged and Sick, 42
Belzebub and Cerberus, archdiuels of great ruffes, 35
Benefices, having 2 or more, is as bad as having 2 wives, 75
Bishops, 71; their duties, 73, 89, 91, 103; their Titles, 104-6; not to exercise temporal authority, 107
Bishops not to intrude their Nominees on Churches, 92
Bishops, justified from the Bible, 101-2; should be tolerated by sober Christians, 103; should preach, 103; 'My Lord,' 104-5; shouldn't exercise temporal authority, 107
bossed, 50, puft up, swollen out
brabble, *v. i.* 116, dispute, brawl
brainsick fools, astrologers, 58
Brokers, jolly fellows who tempt folk to thieve, 38, 39; are the seminaries of Wickedness, 40. '*Riuendaiublo*, a retailer, a huckester, a fripper, a regrater,

a broker. *Riuendaglie*, any fripperie or olde ware or old trash sold againe.' 1598. Florio.
Brokery, a dunghill trade newly sprung up, 39: see Forewords
Brownists, 'new phangled felows,' 74
busie-heded astronomers, 60
Butchers, and their Dodges to make bad meat look good, 26
by: knowe .. faultes *by* them, 48, *in* them, *about* them

Candles made of stinking stuff, 49
Capytall Iudges, 106, Chief Justices, trying causes of Life and Death
cater cosins, 24
Caveat emptor, say the cheating Drapers, 24
chance medley, 14
Chandlers, their cheating dodges, 49
chauerell consciences, 12, stretching kid-leather ones, lawyers have. '*Birsa*, the cheuerill skinne to make purses with.' 1598. J. Florio. *A Worlde of Wordes*.
chawes, 64, jaws
Christ the Head of the Church, 69
Christians may go to law with one another, 11
Church, each to have the right to appoint its own Pastor, 79
Churches, all separate, are part of the One true Church, 69
Churches, to get the Bishop's approval of the Minister they elect, 99; may alter their form of government, 101
Churchwardens, their business, 101
Cicero on property in land, 31
circumgired, 68, surrounded, bounded
Cloth cheatingly rackt by Drapers, 24
Clothiers' tricks in making Cloth, 24: see Forewords
cobs, rich, 27/4, rogues
Cocatrice fawning and weeping, 6
Colleges and Schools perverted, 19
Commons and Moors enclozed from the Poor, 27: see *Harrison*, &c.
communicate with, 84/6, share, take part in

confrater, *sb.* 24/16, cheating brethren
Congregation, how to appoint its Pastor, 90-1
Congregations, separate, in parishes, 68
conscionable, 5²/5, conscientious
consentative, consultative, 107
Conveyances and Leases of Land, terribly long and dear, 32
Corn, tricks in selling it, 47
Cornerd Cap of a Priest, signifies the Monarchy of the World, 115
cough himself a dawe, 48, be made a fool of
Council, Queen Elizabeth's, 8
Counsellor's fee, an Angel (6*s.* 8*d.*), 12
countenance, a man of, 26, of good appearance, well-off
Cow, a barren one sold with another cow's calf, 47
cupstantiall, 65, parody of substantial
Curriers and Tanners' tricks, 36
Cuts of Beards, many kinds of, 50

Dancing minions that minse it ful gingerlie, tripping like gotes, 33
dangerouser, 6
Dark shops to cheat buyers in, 24
Dearness of every thing, 33
decore, *v. t.* 105/13, adorn
Decorum is to be observed, 51, 108/4
Deer and Conies from Parks eating up poor folk's corn, 28
Depastor is a Pastor who runs away from his flock for fear of infection, 95
'Destiny': humbug of a man's making this an excuse, 63
Devilry, the Pope's, 5
Diogenes's laughter, 14
disaminate, 39, dissuade
discommodious, 40, disadvantageous
disposement, *sb.* 56, disposing, ordering
disthronize, *v. t.* 60/1, dethrone
distincted, 68, distinguisht, divided
Dnalgne, 1, England
Doctors (of Medicine) should graduate at a University, 54
Dooting Anabaptists and brainesicke Papists, 69

Drapers and Clothsellers' tricks, 34
Dress of Christ and the Prophets, 108-9
Dress of Pastors and Ministers, 108-9
'Druggie baggage' sold by Apothecaries, 55
Drugs, doctors' profit on, 55/8

Ears pickt at the Barber's, 51/1
Education in England, 19; its abuses, 19-20: see Notes
Eldership or Seigniory in the Church, 100
ELIZABETH, Queen: twenty-five years peace in her time, 5; the Pope's Conspiracy against her, 5; she describd and praizd, 7-8; may her dislikers die! 18-19; the duty of praying for her, 116
else what . . . soever, 12, whatever other
England the wickedest Country under the Sun, 2, 4; its great fertility, and its situation, 4; at peace for 25 years, 5; its division into shires, 9
Englishmen, 3 sorts of, English, Cornish and Welsh, 4; all contentious and fond of going to law, 10
erogate, a. 23, handed over
Excuse: 'Better a bad excuse than none at all,' 114
exercised, 50, practist, traind
External Rites, Reformers to agree and not quarrel about, 116
Eye to be your Cook, 34

Fagots of wood, a penny a piece, 49
faulted, pp. 72 (at foot), committed a fault, erd
Fees, outrageous, in the Law-Courts, 16
Fines to Landlords; hardship of on Tenants, 29, 31
Forkt Caps, &c. may be worn by Ministers, 111
Fortune-telling by the stars, nonsense, 62
Fox may go to school to a cattle-dealer, to learn tricks, 48
friended: 'the law is ended as a man is friended,' provided with rich friends, 10

fuller, sb. 24, cleaner of wool
Funeral Sermons, 85

Games and amusements, rich man's, 33
Garments — surplices, &c. — the wearing of them is a thing indifferent, 112
geason, 51, plentiful—'as geason as blacke swans,' that is, very scarce
gifture, 79, 105/15, gift-bestowing
God still rules the World and the Heavens, 59
Gods penie, 29, a nominal rent
Golden Age, the, 2
Goldsmiths, rich, but yet tricky, p. 25
goose, sue the, 31, 'shoe the goose', waste his labour on trifles
Grasiers, greedy for profit, 26; keeping large flocks of sheep, 28
gravelled, 114, puzzled

Hair-cutting in a Barber's shop, 50
hand, 'make a hand of', 55, make away with, kill
Herod struck dead, 3
Hierosoltinitanes, 3, heathen inhabiters of Jerusalem
Hospitality, little shown by the Rich, 41
Hungrie dogs eate sluttish puddings, 90
Husbandmen, simple as they look, are as crafty as the Devil himself, 47

Idumeans, the, 1
Ignorants allowd to practise Physic and Surgery, 53
immercessible, 99/12, not to be paid for with hire, invaluable
impeopled, 31, inhabited
importable, 55, not able to be borne, very heavy (fee); 107/4
inaugured, to be, 10
indifferently, 14, fairly, equally
induration, 114/14
Ingrators and Forestallers, 46, buyers-up of corn and provisions
ingrosse, 22, buy up and hold
initiation (to a benefice), 81
inn, 82, abode: 'take vp their Inne in an alehouse'

inow, *pl.* 73/6, enuf, a sufficient number of
insensible, 61, without sensation or life
instance, entreaty: make instance to, 84, urge
instaurate, *v.t.* 81/7
interne and externe, bodie of man, 60
Iron Age in Stubbes's time, 3

Jack out of office, 50/3; 54
Jester's proof that a King pardoning a Murderer, had kild 2 men, 15
Jesuits, the Devil's Agents, 6
Judges not to take Bribes, 16
jump in one truth, 115 (at foot)
Justice, deferring of, specially poor men's causes, 9

Keeper of the Seal, his fees, 16
King of each country, Head of its Church, 70

Landlords are big Thieves, 14
Landlords, grasping, rack their rents, make tenants pay fines, &c. 29
Landlords (lewdlords), injustice to their Tenants, 32; are the cause of high prices, 33
Latimer, his Sermon before Edw. VI on delay in doing Justice, 9; and his story of the 30 apples with 30 angels in em, 82: see Notes
laurel crown of triple folly, 10
Law, don't go to, 10
Lawyers, greedy, 10, 16; their extortionate fees, 14, 16
Leaden Age in Stubbes's time, 3
Learning and Trade: the latter pays best, 19
Leather, tricks in curing, 36: see Forewords
Letters dimissory, and commendatory, 91
Livings, giving up for the wearing of a Surplice, &c. is not a true Pastor's duty, 113

Magistrate, the temporal, 69
maintainable, 84, 88/4, fit or enuf to maintain a man
Maisterlesse hounds, 89
mansuetude, 8, tameness, mildness, gentleness

Merchants' heavy profits, 21; dodges to get them, 22
Ministers, unfit, to give up orders at once, 93-5; their Dress, Surplices, &c. 108-116
miscarrying, *sb.* 18
Money 'll buy **Pardon for Crimes**, in England, 13
mowchatowes, 50, moustachoes
My Lord Bishop, 104-5

Nebuchadnezzar made to eat grass, 3
'no change,' the Barbers' maxim, 5
Nodnol, 1, London

of: putting of, 9, off
oiled Shauelings, 70, monks
orient perfumes, 51
ougglisom, *a.* 51, ugly, hideous

Papists, bloodthirsty, 6
Papists' reproaches to fee-taking Protestant pastors, 85
Parish, every one should have a well-paid Schoolmaster, 21
Parish-schools badly off, 20
Parks: towns puld down for, 28
Pastors to have only one charge, 75; the poor salaries they get, 82; not to take fees for Sermons at Burials, &c. 84-5
Pastors' duties in time of Infection, 95-8; their Election, 99; their Dress, 108-9; Preaching and Holy Life their true Notes, 109; their duty about wearing Surplices, &c. 113
Patronage in the Church, 80-2
Patrons, private, how they cheat Pastors, 80
Pharaoh drownd, 3
Phœnix Queen, the, 2; Elizabeth, 8
Physic, any fool allowd to practise, 53
Physicians: **their** faults, 52; now 'they ruffle it out in silckes and veluets', 55; they make away with awkward patients, 55
Planets and Signs, influence of, **on** Man, 60
Planets foolish pretensions of knowledge about them, 58
Pluralism, evils of, **74-5**
pollages and pillages, 32/17

Polling and pilling of the poor, 46
Poor, the, badly treated by lawyers, 11, 12, the Law 14, Judges 16; marrow suckt out of their bones in the Law-Courts, 16
Poor: curse Merchants for exporting goods wanted here, 22; are injured by greedy Grasiers, 27; their Commons enclozed, 27; their hospitality to one another, 41; cruelty of the rich to them, 41-2
Poor, aged and sick to be kept by their own parish, 42; now many die like dogs in the fields, 43
Poor, ill treated by Doctors, 52; should have a Doctor paid for them, 54
Pope, the Son of the Devil, 5; the Head of the Devil's Church, 69; Antichrist, 71; the Devil's 'Liefetenant generall', 104
Preaching Ministers, 71, 74; may take Stipends, 86; their pay, 95
Precisians, 112, folk over scrupulous about trifles
Preferment in the Church, not got by merit, 73
prejudicate, *a.* 114
prepensedly, 14, by forethought
preposterous geare, 59 (at foot), awful nonsense
Pride is followd by Destruction, 3
Prince's duty to the Church of his land, 70
Prince's power to pardon crimes, 14
Princes to be obeyd by Subjects, 17, 113; even when bad, 18
Princes may order Ministers to wear a special dress, Surplice, &c. 111
Prisons, abominable state of, 12
Private Patronage, how it arose, 81
Prognosticators, humbugs, 56-65; are to be condemd, 66
promptuarie, *sb.* 7
Provosts of Colleges take bribes, 20
Psalmograph, 30, Psalm-writer, David
put-offs, 46/15, excuses
Putter, or Putting-Stick, to stiffen Ruffs with, 36

quarrellous, 10, quarrelsome

Quarter[ly] Sermons, 77
quirckes and quiddities, 46

rack rent, 29, rackt, straind up to the full value
Rate in aid for poor parishes, 42
Reading Ministers, 72
Reading, not preaching, Ministers, 71-2
Receivers or buyers of stolen goods, Brokers, 41
refell, *vb.* 77/5
Reformd Churches oversea: their prompt judging of Law-Causes, 9, and Crimes, 13; they take better care of their Poor than we do, 43-4
regiment, 8, ruling, control
remit, 13, excuse, set free
reprivation, 13, reprieve
Rich favourd against the Poor, 16
Rich men eat up poor ones, 27; their duty to tenants, 30; the evil way they spend their money, 33; little hospitality, and want of kindness to the poor, 41-2. See 'Poor'
Rise in rents, twentyfold, 30
roging, 75, roguing, 53 (at foot)
Rome the poison of all the world, 111
Ruffs, great, the Cartwheels of the Devil's Chariot, 35

Schoolmasters badly paid, 20; should be examind for character as well as learning, 20; shouldn't be chargd for a License to teach, 21
Seigniory in the Church, 100
Sellers, if Christians, should tell Buyers the faults of the animals they sell em, 48
Setting-Sticks for Ruffs, 36. '*Piantatoio,* a dible or gardners setting sticke.' 1598. Florio. *A Worlde of Wordes.*
Shakspere's ridicule of 'planetary influence' enforst beforehand, 61
Sheep: whole parishes given up to, 28
Sheriffs' cheating, 16
shipman's hose, 79/1 (will fit anything)

Shoemakers' tricks, 37: see Forewords
Shoes bad and dear, 36
Short measure given in wine, 25
Signs of the Zodiac: supposed influence of each on a part of man, 60
Silver Age, 2
Simony, how avoided, 81
skilleth, 111, matters, is of consequence
smeard Prelate, 70
snap go the fingers, 50 (at foot)
snipping and snapping of the cycers, 50
snort in palpable ignorance, 20
Sodomits and Gomorreans, their punishment, 3
Soles of shoes, tricks in making, 37
Spiritualty, the Abuses of, 67-116
standing, 41, putting up with (?)
Starching-houses to stiffen Ruffs, 35
Stubbes, Phillip, his Father on Shoes, 37: his Family, and his trustworthiness: see Forewords
Subjects' duty to Princes, 17, 18
Substitutes and deputies of Pastors, fitter to feed hogs than Christian sowles, 76
supposal, 57/10, supposition
Surgeons and Physicians 'll only work for pay, 52; their heavy fees, 55
Surplice, cap, tippet, &c. may be worn by Ministers, 109
Surplus goods only to be exported, 23

Tailors invent new fashions daily, 33; their cheating tricks, 34
take-on, 48/6, vow, declare, go on
Tanners' dishonest tricks, 36
Temporalty, the Abuses of the, 1-66
Tenants rackt by Landlords, 29
thick, *v.t.* 24, thicken
Thieves under colour of Law—Landlords and Lawyers,— 14
Tithes, landlords' dodges to avoid paying, 80
Tithes, the ground of them, 83
too too, *adv.* 64
Tradesmen, English, as good as any under the sun, 21
trinkets: 'pots, pannes, candles, and a thousand other trinkets', 49
Tyburn, thieves hung at, 39, 42

Unbenefist Preachers may take fees, 87
Universities and Free Schools; places sold in, 20: see Forewords

vagarent, *sb.* 75, vagrant
Vagrant Ministers, 88-9
Vintners adulterate Wines, p. 25

water: the stiller the water standeth, the more dangerous it is, 7
Wax, fees for, 16
wet: with a wet finger, 39
'What you please, Sir,' the Barber's charge, 51
whether, 73, which of the two
White, why the colour of Surplices, 114-115
Wicks of candles made of rope-ends, &c. 50
Will-do-all or Money, power of, 13
Wines in England, 25
Women not to practise Physic for gain, 54
Wool, cheating in the sale of, 28

Zodiac, Signs of the, and their suppozed influence on man, 60, 64

www.ingramcontent.com/pod-product-compliance
Lightning Source LLC
Chambersburg PA
CBHW030257170426
43202CB00009B/786